Presidential
Personality and
Performance

Presidential Personality and Performance

Alexander L. George and Juliette L. George

Foreword by Fred I. Greenstein

■ WestviewPress
A Division of HarperCollins*Publishers*

The authors thank Princeton University Press for permission to quote from various volumes of Arthur S. Link et al., eds., *The Papers of Woodrow Wilson,* and *Political Science Quarterly* for permission to reprint and quote from Weinstein, Edwin A., Anderson, James W., and Link, Arthur S., "Woodrow Wilson's Political Personality: A Reappraisal," Vol. 93, Winter 1978, and from George, Juliette L., Marmor, Michael F. and George, Alexander L., "*Woodrow Wilson and Colonel House:* A Reply to Weinstein, Anderson, and Link," Vol. 96, Winter 1981-82. We also thank *World Politics* for permission to reprint Alexander L. George's article, "Assessing Presidential Character" from their January, 1974 issue.

Published in 1998 in the United States of America by Westview Press, 5500 Central Avenue, Boulder, Colorado 80301-2877, and in the United Kingdom by Westview Press, 12 Hid's Copse Road, Cumnor Hill, Oxford OX2 9JJ

Library of Congress Cataloging-in-Publication Data
George, Alexander L.
  Presidential personality and performance / Alexander L. George and Juliette L. George ; with a foreword by Fred I. Greenstein.
    p. cm.
  Includes bibliographical references (p.   ) and index.
  ISBN 0-8133-2590-0 (hardcover). — ISBN 0-8133-2591-9
(paperback)
  1. Presidents—United States—History. 2. Presidents—United States—Psychology. 3. Personality and politics—United States—History. I. George, Juliette L. II. Title.
JK511.G46 1998
324.6'3'0973—dc21
                                                                97-32849
                                                                      CIP

The paper used in this publication meets the requirements of the American National Standard for Permanence of Paper for Printed Library Materials Z39.48-1984.

10   9   8   7   6   5   4   3   2   1

For Juliette Douglass, with love

Contents

Foreword

Fred I. Greenstein

IT IS COMMONLY SAID THAT the American political system is one of laws and institutions rather than individuals; but Harry Truman, not some abstract commander in chief, authorized the use of the atom bomb; Lyndon Johnson, not the impersonal forces of the Cold War, authorized the transformation of the American advisory mission in South Vietnam into a full-scale military intervention. For better or worse, the personalities of presidents are as integral a part of the American political system as the constitutionally mandated instruments of government and are equally in need of close and continuing attention.

As unexceptionable as the previous assertion may seem to the layperson, specialists in the study of American politics and other intellectuals tend to be skeptical of efforts to account for political developments of any consequence in terms of the individual characteristics of presidents and other policymakers. Historians are critical of "the presidential synthesis." Political scientists devote far more attention to institutions than to individuals. Intellectuals in general, especially those who are directly or indirectly influenced by Marxism and other doctrines of historical inevitability, are particularly dubious of claims that individuals can make a difference, or at any rate that the impact of individuals on events is susceptible to rigorous inquiry.

A number of assumptions appear to account for such skepticism about the importance of the personalities of presidents and other political actors. One is that analyses of individuals are inevitably messy and imprecise and therefore cannot provide valid insights into the causes of historical outcomes. A second is that attempts to explain events in terms of the attributes of the participants are in their nature misguided, because they fail to account for the institutions and contexts within which actors are embedded. A third is that the occurrence of particular individuals in particular roles at particular periods of time is fortuitous and therefore not of systematic interest.

All three premises are flawed. The argument that presidential personality is of no interest because it is difficult to study has no more merit than that of the drunkard who lost his keys in a dark alley and searched for them under a street lamp, declaring, "It's lighter here." If the connections between the personalities of political actors and their political behavior are obscure, that is all the more reason to seek to illuminate them. The notions that attention to individuals precludes attention to their contexts and that the randomness of the occurrence of personality characteristics makes them unworthy of study are equally fallacious, as can be seen by considering the following analogy. Suppose that the institutions and other channels of the political process were the circuitry of a complex computer and that presidents and other leaders were its control mechanism. Attention to the qualities of the controls would not preclude attention to the mechanism that triggered them. Quite the contrary. And it would be all the more urgent to know the performance characteristics of controls if their operating properties were random, with some capable of tripping at inappropriate times, causing the loss of valuable information, and others failing to trip, exposing the system to the danger of meltdown.

The impact of presidential psychology on American (and by extension global) politics can be extraordinary. For evidence of that, one need only think of the natural counterfactuals that are provided by the possible substitution of presidents with their vice presidents. Without attempting to resolve the many debates about whether the Cold War would have occurred if Franklin D. Roosevelt had lived, or whether the United States would have intervened in Vietnam in a Kennedy presidency, few would argue that those events would have taken the precise form they did if either chief executive had lived. Similarly, the entire course of the 1930s and 1940s almost certainly would have been drastically different if the assassin whose bullet narrowly missed FDR early in 1933 had found his mark and the distinctly pedestrian John Nance Garner had taken office. The 1950s probably would have been different if Dwight Eisenhower had died before the 1954 Dien Bien Phu crisis and Vice President Richard Nixon, who favored U.S. intervention, had been in the Oval Office. And the 1960s might have been dramatically different if Vice President Hubert Humphrey, who opposed U.S. military intervention in Vietnam, had taken over early in 1965.

For many years one of the best ways for those intrepid scholars who were determined to identify the human antecedents of political behavior to learn their craft was to hunt down the often fugitive writings of Alexander and Juliette George. No writer since Harold D. Lasswell has contributed more than Alexander L. George to the congeries of the often disparate and tenuously connected intellectual enterprises that make up the field of political psychology. From the vantage point of the 1990s, however, that contribution might well seem mainly to have been through his writings on the psychology of collective political behavior, which place special emphasis on cognitive aspects of political decisionmaking, deterrence, coercive diplomacy, and crisis management. The relevant references would be to a prodigious outpouring of work, the bulk of which appeared in print after the 1960s (e.g., George, 1972, 1980, 1983, 1991; George, Hall, and Simon, 1971; George and Smoke, 1974).

Yet even if none of Alexander George's post-1960s contributions to the understanding of system-level phenomena had been made, his and Juliette L. George's contributions to that hybrid discipline would still be seminal. But they would be viewed as having been in an area that to some would seem peripheral to his later scholarship—the psychology of individual political behavior, including not only its cognitive but also its affective and psychodynamic aspects.

This recognition would be forthcoming first and foremost for the Georges' landmark psychobiography—*Woodrow Wilson and Colonel House: A Personality Study* (1956)—but also for a series of shorter writings by one or both of the Georges on the logic of studying individual political psychology (George, 1968, 1969, 1971, 1974; George and George, 1973). *Woodrow Wilson and Colonel House* is a vivid, historically informative work that has been widely recognized for the exemplary rigor and closeness of its analysis, but many of the authors' principles of evidence and inference are, as it were, under the table. Choosing to write in a manner that would be accessible to a general audience and to historians skeptical of explicit references to psychoanalytic theory, George and George offered only occasional theoretical and methodological asides. Instead, much of what made their very favorably reviewed book successful was the force and intrinsic persuasiveness of the narrative.

Fortunately for other would-be biographers, the Georges did not leave it at that. Instead, in a series of short writings over the years one or both of them thoughtfully and closely analyzed the requirements of systematic, insightful study of individual political actors: empathy, deep understanding of dynamic psychology, careful distinction between hypotheses and tested empirical claims, close attention to contextual factors, and much else. Now these works and a number of new contributions have been brought together in a publishing event of the greatest magnitude—one that will not only be of enormous value to those who are already committed to the study of individual political actors but that also promises to bring new recruits to this important but neglected realm of inquiry.

No one who is concerned with the analysis of individual political actors (American presidents and others) can afford not to be steeped in the richly reflective essays in this volume. That said, it is my function to step aside and invite the reader to delve into the contributions that follow.

References

George, A. L. 1968. Power as a compensatory value for political leaders. *Journal of Social Issues* 24:29–50.

———. 1969. The operational code: A neglected approach to the study of political leaders and decisionmaking. *International Studies Quarterly* 13:190–222.

———. 1971. Some uses of dynamic psychology in political biography: Case materials on Woodrow Wilson. In F. I. Greenstein and M. Lerner, eds., *A source book for the study of personality and politics* (pp. 78–98). Chicago: Markham.

———. 1972. The case for multiple advocacy in foreign policymaking. *American Political Science Review* 66:751–785.

———. 1974. Assessing presidential character. *World Politics* 26:234–282.

———. 1979. Case studies and theory development: The method of structured, focused comparison. In P. G. Lauren, ed., *Diplomacy: New approaches in history, theory, and policy.* New York: Free Press.

———. 1980. *Presidential decisionmaking in foreign policy: The effective use of advice and information.* Boulder: Westview Press.

———. 1983. *Managing U.S.-Soviet rivalry: Problems of crisis prevention.* Boulder: Westview Press.

———. 1991. *Avoiding war: Problems of crisis prevention.* Boulder: Westview Press.

George, A. L. and J. L. George. 1956. *Woodrow Wilson and Colonel House: A personality study.* New York: John Day. (Reprinted by Dover, 1964.)

———. 1973. Psycho-McCarthyism. *Psychology Today* 7:94–98.

George, A. L., D. K. Hall, and W. Simon. 1971. *The limits of coercive diplomacy.* Boston: Little, Brown. (Rev. ed., Westview Press, 1993.)

George, A. L., and T. J. McKeown. 1985. Case studies and organizational decisionmaking. In *Advances in information processing in organizations* 2: 21–58.

George, A. L., and R. Smoke. 1974. *Deterrence in American foreign policy: Theory and practice.* New York: Columbia University Press.

Acknowledgments

WE EXPRESS OUR DEEP APPRECIATION to Professor Fred Greenstein of Princeton University who read the entire manuscript, offered many helpful suggestions, and wrote a foreword to the book that is itself an important contribution.

Two scholars, Dr. David Wigdor, Assistant Chief of the Manuscript Division, the Library of Congress, and Dr. Ben Primer, University Archivist, the Seeley G. Mudd Manuscript Library, Princeton University, have earned our permanent appreciation by their helpfulness on numerous occasions past and present—this time in connection with Chapter 4 of this book. Their helpfulness in making available information necessary to our work, however, in no way implies their endorsement of our interpretation of Woodrow Wilson, which is controversial.

Our thanks go to Rachelle Marshall for incisive editing of the manuscript, many useful suggestions for clarifying our meaning, and helpful administrative assistance. We also thank Eliska Ryznar for a thoughtful index.

Juliette George would like to express special appreciation to Joan Krasner, Chief, Access Services, Stanford University Libraries, for many courtesies over the years, and to Nancy Okimoto, Deputy Director, Institute for International Studies, Stanford University. Both acted to facilitate her research and were a source of sustaining encouragement.

Leigh VanHandel provided accurate word processing and Belinda Yeomans timely library assistance. Our warm thanks to them both.

Our manuscript profited from the expert attention of Leo Wiegman, Senior Editor, and several of his colleagues at Westview Press. John Guardiano, copy editor, and Scott Horst, Melanie Stafford, and Kristin Milavec of the editorial production department, each lent not only intelligence and technical skill to the processing of the manuscript but also a cheerful willingness to deal with the queries and requests of not one, but two authors. Cordial thanks from both of us.

Alexander L. George and
Juliette L. George

Introduction:
An Overview

THE CONTENTS OF THIS BOOK reflect our interest for over half a century in the question of the impact of personality on the political behavior of political leaders. Over the years, Juliette George's focus has been on Woodrow Wilson. In addition to our joint work on Wilson, Alexander George has addressed some of the broad methodological problems of conducting such studies, and he has written about how personality factors were interwoven into the decisionmaking processes of other presidents as well.*

This book consists of six chapters: **Chapter 1**, "The Psychoanalyst and the Biographer," deals with the relevance of psychoanalytic theory to the biographer's work. We recognize at the outset that it is not possible to psychoanalyze an historical figure. Yet psychoanalytic theory has much to offer biographers, and there are similarities of mental and emotional qualities that, ideally, both analytically informed biographers and psychoanalysts bring to their work. These are, first, the capacity to empathize with the person whose life is being studied, in order to form insightful hypotheses about that individual's life experience; second, the capacity to be detached, in order to subject those hypotheses to dispassionate evaluation; third, the capacity to recognize one's own emotional reactions (i.e., countertransference reactions) to the individual whose life is being scrutinized and to the issues that come to the fore, in order the better to avoid inadvertently confounding the *subject*'s realities with those of the biographer or the psychoanalyst.

---

*We apologize for referring to ourselves in the third person, a stylistic device we have reluctantly resorted to because we have not found a satisfactory way to refer to each of us without using each of our names. Henceforth in this introduction Alexander George will be AG and Juliette George will be JG whenever initials seem less awkward.

The primary author of this chapter is Juliette George. It was first published as the preface to the second edition of *Woodrow Wilson and Colonel House*.[1]

In **Chapter 2**, "Some Uses of Dynamic Psychology in Political Biography: Case Materials on Woodrow Wilson," Alexander George addresses a central problem of interpretation faced by biographers seeking to understand the decisionmaking processes of political leaders, namely: To what extent is the leader's response to a particular set of circumstances reasonable, given its situational context and, conversely, to what extent is the response dictated by the idiosyncratic requirements of that leader's personality rather than by the requirements of the situation?

At present, no reliable method for dealing with this general problem is available. Drawing upon our study of Wilson, however, AG attempts to demonstrate that at least in this one case, the imponderables can be reduced and the personality component can be identified and traced in a systematic fashion. In doing so, he utilizes several psychodynamic hypotheses that permit the strong suggestion that Wilson was rationalizing when, first, as president of Princeton University, he insisted that he was bound by principle and conscience to resist yielding in his battle with Dean Andrew Fleming West, and second, as president of the United States, he insisted that commitment to principle and obedience to conscience precluded compromise with Senator Henry Cabot Lodge in order to secure U.S. entry into the League of Nations. In both instances this stubbornness led to defeat. AG suggests an interpretation of Wilson's intransigence that comprehends not only the rich historical evidence about Wilson's refusal to yield in certain political situations but also the data indicating his ability to compromise in other circumstances.

Also discussed in this chapter are methodological issues involved in making such interpretations as this one, and the suitability or lack of suitability of various personality types as subjects for psychologically oriented biography.

Alexander George is the author of Chapter 2, which is reprinted from Fred I. Greenstein and Michael Lerner, eds., *A Source Book for the Study of Personality and Politics*.[2]

In **Chapter 3**, which we wrote expressly for this book, we describe the reaction of specialists identified with various psychoanalytic schools to *Woodrow Wilson and Colonel House*. Some analysts, including

Erik Erikson and Robert Coles, found considerable merit in our interpretation.[3] Others suggested that viewing the data about Wilson in the light of the particular psychoanalytic theory they favor (e.g., that of Karen Horney, Alfred Adler, Heinz Kohut, Erik Erikson) would yield better interpretations than ours of some aspects of Wilson's personality, its origins and development, and the role it played in some of his political behavior.

Our purpose in Chapter 3 is not so much to assess the validity and contribution of these reinterpretations of Wilson as to use these reactions to our study in order to identify a number of theoretical and methodological problems inherent in efforts to apply psychodynamic theories in personality-oriented biography. As a case in point we offer the history of our own study of Wilson and of our decision to produce a nontechnical narrative of his life in the light of Harold Lasswell's very general theoretical propositions, which capture the basic commonality of thought that runs through various schools of psychoanalytic theory concerning the psychological development of human beings.

We emphasize the need to avoid psychological reductionism and suggest that this be done by broadening the use of any psychodynamic model of personality to take into account institutional, situational, and political role variables as well as aspects of political culture that are either internalized by an individual during the course of his or her political socialization or at least taken into account during the performance of political tasks.

We caution also on the danger of *medical* reductionism, which may be found in the work of even careful, truth-seeking physician-scholars. Writings about Wilson furnish our illustrative materials.

We contributed equally as authors of Chapter 3.

Chapter 4, "*Woodrow Wilson and Colonel House:* A Reply to Weinstein, Anderson, and Link," is the text, published here in full for the first time, of our reply to an article entitled "Woodrow Wilson's Political Personality: A Reappraisal," by Edwin A. Weinstein, M.D. (a psychiatrist and neurologist), James William Anderson (a psychologist), and Arthur S. Link (unquestionably this generation's preeminent Wilson scholar). Their article appeared in the Winter 1978–1979 issue of *Political Science Quarterly* and was a broadside attack on our book.

Weinstein, Anderson, and Link found our research inadequate and our interpretations incorrect. A third major deficiency, they said, was that we "ignore Wilson's neurological disorders as conditions affecting his behavior"—i.e., strokes that they unequivocally assert occurred in 1896 (Wilson's "first known stroke," Weinstein later characterized it), 1900, 1904, 1906 and 1907. (The alleged strokes of 1906 and 1907 played a role, they claim, in Wilson's defeat while president of Princeton University in his famously bitter battle with Dean Andrew Fleming West.) In early April 1919, at the Paris Peace Conference following World War I, Weinstein, Anderson, and Link (abandoning Weinstein's earlier diagnosis of another stroke) diagnose a viral encephalopathy, which, superimposed on the brain damage that they claim previous neurological disease had inflicted, supposedly affected Wilson's behavior in negotiating the peace treaty.

All the foregoing, of course, makes for a seamless logical progression to Weinstein, Anderson, and Link's contention that mental attitudes and personality changes produced by Wilson's stroke of October 1919 (the major stroke that he certainly suffered on October 2, 1919) were important factors in his failure to obtain ratification of the Treaty of Versailles—that is, his defeat at the hands of Senator Henry Cabot Lodge. This was a defeat that had fateful repercussions on world history, for it kept the United States out of the League of Nations. Wilson's behavior in his battle with Henry Cabot Lodge and the Senate, therefore, is relevant not only to Wilson scholars but also to researchers interested in the more general study of presidential decision-making as well as of questions concerning the health of presidents and related issues. Clearly, correct historical facts are the *sine qua non* for worthwhile research into all of these matters.

In order to evaluate Weinstein, Anderson, and Link's criticism, we spent three years reviewing our work and studying a great deal of manuscript material that had become available since publication of our book. We also examined closely the *published* historical record that had become available, thirty-seven (of the eventual total of sixty-nine) volumes of *The Papers of Woodrow Wilson*, edited by Professor Link.

From the first, we surmised that Weinstein, Anderson, and Link were unjustified in their unequivocal assertion of the alleged early "strokes." In the original research for our book we had come upon many accounts of what Wilson habitually referred to as his neuritis or "writer's cramp," which, in 1896, worsened to the point that he was unable for some time to use his right hand for writing. The documentation that his symptoms in 1907 signified a flare-up of neuritis also seemed to us convincing, as apparently it had to previous biographers who mentioned these ailments. We certainly never saw evidence of the "personality changes" that Weinstein, Anderson, and Link claimed to have occurred as a result of the "strokes." Yet it seemed unthinkable that these scholars would flatly assert the occurrence of multiple strokes unless they had reliable evidence that such strokes in fact had occurred.

We combed through the manuscript materials and the documents printed in *The Papers of Woodrow Wilson* in search of evidence that Wilson had suffered strokes in 1896, 1900, 1904, 1906 or 1907. We did not find in all this massive material a single mention of stroke. Yet in editorial comments by Link and his associates scattered through nine volumes of *The Papers of Woodrow Wilson* there were dozens of unequivocal, unqualified references to "strokes" in 1896, 1906, and 1907. In the historical documents themselves we found only additional evidence of Wilson's complaints of neuritis and writer's cramp that he, his doctors, and his family attributed to the overuse of his hand in writing out the prodigious number of books, essays, speeches, and letters that he produced in the 1890s.

An undoubtedly serious medical event did occur in 1906 when Wilson awoke one morning in May unable to see out of his left eye. Dr. George E. de Schweinitz, the distinguished ophthalmologist to whose office in Philadelphia Wilson's friend John Grier Hibben accompanied him, diagnosed a retinal hemorrhage.

Link, referring to this incident in the introduction to volume 16 of the *Papers*, wrote that Wilson had suffered a "major stroke." In an editorial note later in volume 16 he added the word "very," calling it a "very severe stroke," and referred readers to an article by Weinstein in which Weinstein said that this event gave "clear evidence of brain damage" caused by "occlusive disease," a "blocking of the internal carotid artery."[4] We were perplexed by Weinstein's diagnosis of arterial *occlusion* in the face of all the historical evidence that Wilson had suffered a retinal *hemorrhage*, which seemed to us a different matter. Our perplexity and doubts were reinforced when we learned of comments on Weinstein's article by Robert T. Monroe, a Boston internist and gerontologist who taught at the Harvard Medical School, indicating disagreement with Weinstein. Monroe wrote: "The event in May 1896 was not, in my view, due to brain damage. . . . Today this affair likely would be treated as pinched nerves in the neck [cervical arthritis], with stretching and a collar. The left eye blindness in 1906 is not necessarily evidence of cerebral arteriosclerosis. The hemorrhage may have come from a retinal vein, or a separation of the retina."[5]

A copy of Monroe's comments was sent to Link in 1971, and Link passed them on to Weinstein, who summarily rejected them, saying that it was his impression that Monroe did not recognize the syndrome of carotid artery occlusion.[6] Link did not print Monroe's comments or allude to them in the *Papers*, and he continued to include unqualified assertions of "strokes" in his editorial notes. (Volume 16, in which he asserted the "major stroke" and the "very severe stroke" of 1906, appeared in 1973.)

It was in these circumstances that we resolved to place all the medical and historical records at the disposal of competent medical authority for independent review. We count ourselves extremely fortunate that Michael F. Marmor, M.D., a Harvard-trained professor of ophthalmology at the Stanford University School of Medicine whose specialty is diseases of the retina, accepted our invitation to review all the available data bearing on Wilson's illnesses throughout his career and Weinstein's diagnoses of them as strokes dating back to 1896, with special attention to the episode of 1906. After exhaustive study, Marmor sent us a written opinion questioning both the medical interpretations of Dr. Weinstein and the propriety of presenting such views as historical fact, and he published his findings in the *New England Journal of Medicine*.[7]

Our response to Weinstein, Anderson, and Link addressed all three of the major "deficiencies" that they attributed to our book. We presented new evidence in support of our hypothesis that personality factors largely shaped Wilson's ruinously self-defeating behavior when, as president of Princeton, he was confronted with the challenge to his authority posed by Dean West and later, when as president of the United States, he was confronted with a sneering challenge to his authority by Senator Lodge. (Lodge later wrote a book in which he detailed how he utilized Wilson's hatred of him to achieve the result that he desired—Wilson's failure to obtain Senate ratification of the Treaty of Versailles, and thus Wilson's failure to achieve his supreme goal, U.S. participation in the League of Nations.)[8]

We expressed particular concern that Weinstein, Anderson, and Link had elevated their hypothesis that Wilson suffered "strokes" in 1896, 1900, 1904, 1906, and 1907 to the status of proven historical fact. We expressed our dismay that Link had referred to "strokes" in 1896,

1906, and 1907 as fact in editorial matter of the *Papers*, thereby, in our judgment, compromising the objectivity of that series, lending unfair weight to his preferred interpretation of Wilson's behavior, and reducing the ability of researchers to give fair consideration to alternative interpretations, such as ours.

The paper that follows as Chapter 4 in this book is the "long version" of our response to Weinstein, Anderson, and Link. Juliette George presented it in June 1981 at the annual meeting of the International Society of Political Psychology. A condensation appeared in the Winter 1981–1982 issue of *Political Science Quarterly* shortly after a book by Weinstein, *Woodrow Wilson: A Medical and Psychological Biography*, was published. In his book Weinstein carried representation of his conjectures as though they were established fact to new heights.

Juliette George is the primary author of Chapter 4.

In **Chapter 5** we turn to the broader issue of the character and psychological suitability of candidates for the presidency, which has received increasing attention in the past few decades. The question we raise is whether knowledge of such matters has advanced sufficiently to permit reliable assessments of this kind and whether acceptable procedures for doing so can be devised. The development of interest in assessing the psychological (as well as the medical) suitability of candidates has roots in historical trends that have shaped the modern presidency. The duties, responsibilities, and expectations of the president have grown enormously in magnitude and complexity since the Great Depression, a development given added impetus by World War II and the greatly expanded role of the United States in world affairs since then. This trend was accompanied by the belief that we must look to the president as the "engine of progress," the savior of the political system, the fulcrum of the entire governmental system. However, the misuse and abuse of presidential power charged to Lyndon B. Johnson for the way in which he involved the country in Vietnam and, later, to Richard Nixon over the Watergate scandal brought into focus a gloomy view of the presidency as a job that seemed to bring out the worst in each new incumbent.

These two historical developments—the trend toward a much more demanding set of presidential duties and the dismay generated by gross misuse and abuse of presidential power—do much to explain the tendency of many voters to regard character as perhaps a critical if not the most important requirement of candidates for the presidency.

Character has become for many the answer to the difficult question as to what is the essential qualification for dealing with the enhanced, complex responsibilities of the presidency. And "character flaws" seem to provide an explanation for tendencies to misuse presidential power in ways that may lead to policy disasters.

It is not surprising, therefore, that numerous efforts have been made in past presidential elections by journalists and others to assess the character and personality of aspirants to that office. These efforts, however, encounter fundamental difficulties that place into question the objectivity and validity of such assessments and the reliability of character-based predictions of the performance of a candidate if elected to the presidency.[9]

Similarly, it is not surprising that specialists on the presidency should have attempted to develop more scholarly ways of assessing presidential character and the psychological suitability for the presidency of candidates for that office. One of the earliest efforts of this kind, and perhaps the best-known, was the book by James David Barber, *The Presidential Character: Predicting Performance in the White House,* first published in 1972 and followed by several updated editions. Barber identified four character types that he constructed from two dimensions of character—"activity-passivity" and "positive-negative affect towards one's activity." Acknowledging that these two dimensions "are crude clues to character," he nonetheless combined them to identify four basic character types: the "active-positive," the "active-negative," the "passive-positive," and the "passive-negative." According to Barber's theory, a set of expectations regarding performance in the presidency is associated with each character type. Barber diagnosed past presidents as exemplifying one or another of these four types and used that diagnosis to help explain aspects of each president's performance in office. He regarded Richard Nixon as an example of the "active-negative" type and capped his study, published in 1972 prior to Nixon's campaign for reelection, by predicting a major character-induced catastrophe in his second term, were he reelected.

Alexander George published a review of Barber's book in *World Politics* (January 1974). It is reprinted here as Chapter 5.

The importance of a president's "style" in structuring and managing the policymaking process is referred to briefly in Chapter 5. In Chapter 6 AG presents a more detailed analysis of different types of presidential style and of the way in which personal styles of different presidents influence how they structure and manage the policymaking process. Three aspects of personality appear to be of particular importance in shaping a president's style: (1) the president's "cognitive style"—that is, the way in which he defines informational needs for purposes of making decisions and his preferred ways of acquiring and utilizing information and advice from others; (2) the individual's "sense of efficacy and competence" as it relates to decisionmaking and political tasks; and (3) the individual's general "orientation toward political conflict."

These three components of personality combine to influence how a new president will structure and manage the policymaking system around him, and how he will define his own role in that system and that of others in it. In Chapter 6, differences are noted in these three personality variables among presidents since Franklin D. Roosevelt, and it is suggested how these personality differences help to explain their preferences for different management models.

Chapter 6 is coauthored. The first part is taken from Alexander George's *Presidential Decisionmaking in Foreign Policy: The Effective Use of Information and Advice* (Boulder: Westview Press, 1980; chapter 8). The sections on Presidents Carter and Reagan were written for the present book largely by Eric Stern (Political Science Department, Stockholm University); he is also the sole author of the sections on Presidents Bush and Clinton.

The performance of presidential duties will be affected also by other personality characteristics that are not discussed in this book. A president and his advisers often must make important decisions on the basis of inadequate information and insufficient general knowledge by means of which to assess the utility of different options. In addition, major policy issues typically engage many values and interests. Often these cannot be harmonized and reduced to a single criterion but require the president to make difficult trade-offs among competing values. The need to act on important matters that are characterized by uncertainty and value complexity can be the source of considerable stress for a president.

How well do different individuals deal with decisional stress and how can the ways in which they attempt to cope with it affect their performance? AG has identified a number of analytical and psychological devices that individuals resort to when confronted with decisional stress, and he has assessed the impact that each of these coping devices is likely to have on the quality of decisions taken.[10]

We live in an era of great promise for increasing our knowledge of human development and of how the various factors that together produce human behavior interact with one another. May some of the readers of this volume, in the light of emerging discoveries, contribute to deeper insights into the actions of political leaders. If this book serves even in a modest way to stimulate their thinking, we will have accomplished our purpose.

Alexander L. George
Juliette L. George
Stanford, California
October, 1997

Notes

1. Alexander L. George and Juliette L. George, *Woodrow Wilson and Colonel House: A Personality Study* (New York: John Day Company, 1956; Dover Publications, 1964), Dover edition, v–xiv.

2. Fred I. Greenstein and Michael Lerner, *A Source Book for the Study of Personality and Politics* (Chicago: Markham Publishing Company, 1971), pp. 78–98.

3. Robert Coles, "How Good Is Psycho-History?" *New York Review of Books* (February 22, 1973); Erik Erikson, "The Strange Case of Freud, Bullitt, and Woodrow Wilson," *New York Review of Books* (February 9, 1967).

4. Arthur S. Link et al., eds., *Papers of Woodrow Wilson* (Princeton: Princeton University Press, 1973), vol. 16, pp. vii, 412. Edwin A. Weinstein, "Woodrow Wilson's Neurological Illness," *Journal of American History,* vol. 57 (1970), pp. 334 and 336.

5. Robert T. Monroe, M.D., "Comments on 'Woodrow Wilson's Neurological Illness' by Dr. E. A. Weinstein," Papers of Arthur Walworth (Yale University Library, New Haven, Conn.).

6. E. A. Weinstein to A. S. Link, October 26, 1971, Walworth Papers. See also Walworth to Robert T. Monroe, July 21 and November 7, 1971; Monroe to Walworth, July 30, 1971, and January 9, 1972; and Link to Walworth, November 3, 1971, all in Walworth Papers.

7. Michael F. Marmor, "Wilson, Strokes, and Zebras," *The New England Journal of Medicine,* vol. 307, no. 9 (August 26, 1982), pp. 528–534. See Marmor and Weinstein's ensuing correspondence in ibid., vol. 308 (1983), p. 164. See also Marmor, "A Bad Case of History: *Woodrow Wilson: A Medical and Psychological Biography,*" *The Sciences* (published by the New York Academy of Sciences), vol. 23 (January-February 1983), pp. 36–38; correspondence from Weinstein

and Marmor, *The Sciences* (September-October 1983), pp. 2, 4, 6; "Comments on 'Woodrow Wilson Re-examined: The Mind-Body Controversy Redux and Other Disputations,'" *Political Psychology*, vol. 4, no. 2 (June 1993), pp. 325-327; "The Eyes of Woodrow Wilson: Retinal Vascular Disease and George de Schweinitz," *Ophthalmology*, vol. 92, no. 3 (March 1985).

8. Henry Cabot Lodge, *The Senate and the League of Nations* (New York: Charles Scribner's Sons, 1925), pp. 212–213, 218–219, 226.

9. For a sophisticated discussion of character and its bearing on performance in the presidency, see the study by Stanley Renshon, who is both a Ph.D. in political science and a practicing psychoanalyst: *The Psychological Assessment of Presidential Candidates* (New York and London: New York University Press, 1996).

10. For a discussion of these aspects of presidential decisionmaking, see "Psychological Aspects of Decisionmaking: Adaptation to Constraints on Rational Decisionmaking," chapter 2 in A. L. George, *Presidential Decisionmaking in Foreign Policy: The Effective Use of Information and Advice* (Boulder: Westview Press, 1980).

1

The Psychoanalyst and the Biographer

Juliette L. George and Alexander L. George

WE WELCOME THE OPPORTUNITY afforded by publication of this new edition of our effort to study the life of Woodrow Wilson in the light of psychoanalytic theory to set down a few thoughts on the general problem of the relevance of psychoanalysis to the biographer's work.

It has often been noted that there exists a gap, which can never be bridged, between the range of data available to the psychoanalyst and that available to the biographer. For this reason, some have concluded that biographers cannot make effective use of psychoanalysis.

The analyst has the opportunity of learning in detail from the patient himself the unconscious feelings, wishes and fantasies which are the wellspring of his behavior. He has the object of his inquiry on his couch, providing the necessary material in the form of descriptions of his life experience, transference reactions, dreams and free associations.

The biographer, on the other hand, has no such access to his subject's intimate thoughts through personal contact. In those rare cases in which his subject is alive and willing to provide him information, the biographer who ventured to ask for the sort of personal revelation which the analyst routinely requires of his patient doubtless, and un-

Chapter 1 was originally published as the preface to the second edition of *Woodrow Wilson and Colonel House: A Personality Study* (New York: Dover Publications, 1964). Our work has been aided by a grant from the Foundations' Fund for Research in Psychiatry.

derstandably, would be given short shrift indeed. Almost always even when his subject is alive and always when he is dead, the biographer is at the mercy of a finite and distressingly incomplete body of information.

The force of this argument cannot be denied. It must be admitted that no biographer can "psychoanalyze" his subject because he is not in possession of that data pertaining to the subject's unconscious without which psychoanalysis in the classical sense is not possible. However, those who rely on this obvious point to substantiate the argument that psychoanalysis is therefore of no use in the biographer's enterprise overlook two important facts. They overlook, first, that "psychoanalysis" refers not only to a therapy for personality disorders: it also denotes a theoretical system of psychology, based on empirical clinical observation, which accounts for the structure, functioning and development of human personality. They overlook, second, that there is a crucial difference in the respective tasks of the psychoanalyst and the biographer, a difference which makes it possible for the biographer to work effectively on the basis of data which would not suffice for the purposes of the psychoanalyst.

The psychoanalyst is bent upon a therapeutic result with his patient, upon a reawakening in the analytic situation of unresolved conflicts with a view to providing the patient an opportunity to achieve more satisfactory solutions than those he originally adopted. The biographer, on the other hand, is spared the difficult task of attempting to alter his subject's personality. He wishes only to comprehend it and to transmit his comprehension to an audience of readers by means of a written narrative. These two facts are of paramount importance in the controversy about the feasibility of applying psychoanalytic theory to biographical material.

Psychoanalytic psychology comprehends individual human behavior in terms of the history and development and the past and present relationships of the id, the ego and the superego which, it claims, comprise the human psyche. By now, psychoanalysts have studied these complex relationships in thousands of cases in which patients have provided data about their unconscious processes and in which the psychoanalytic procedure has served as a method of research as well as a method of cure.

Certain types of readily observable behavior have been related to certain causal factors and varieties of conflict. Adequate understanding of analytic theory and experience sensitizes the biographer (as well as the analyst in *his* task) to the types of material to watch for as he examines the data available to him. The large body of published clinical data gathered by psychoanalysts over the past few generations puts at the biographer's disposal clues as to the possible significance of certain patterns of behavior or habits or traits of character of which he might otherwise take no notice.

The biographer's need is satisfied by this access to diagnostic hypotheses. The therapist's task, however, only begins with diagnosis, for he has the job of helping his patient achieve a more satisfactory distribution of his instinctual energies, one which will eliminate the need to invest so large a proportion of his emotional capital in maintaining repressions and struggling, consciously or unconsciously, to realize unrealizable infantile fantasies. To achieve this goal, he embarks with his patient upon an exploration of the patient's unconscious. If the therapeutic collaboration is successful, the patient will become aware of his repressed impulses and will learn to deal with them more expeditiously, consciously. The analyst's relentless pursuit of his patient's unconscious fantasies is necessitated by the fact that in order to renounce the unattainable infantile pleasures around which are woven the fantasies which hold him in thrall, the patient must confront his past and his deepest impulses with courage and feeling.

For his part, the analyst has in most instances long since known what ails his patient. Their intensive work together is not primarily to provide material for the analyst's diagnosis—although undoubtedly his diagnosis becomes more exact as the material unfolds—but to enable the patient to grow and change.

Indeed, psychoanalysts are usually able to perceive the essential dynamics of the patient's personality and the general nature of his problems very early in the treatment situation, even before the patient has produced the dreams, free associations and transference reactions which reveal in detail the contents of his unconscious.

Freud once remarked that, try as he may, a person cannot conceal what is motivating him—all manner of surface behavior expresses the basic constellation of unconscious impulses. Again, in a paper on analytic technique, Freud noted that "it is not difficult for a skilled analyst to read the patient's hidden wishes plainly between the lines of his complaints and the story of his illness." Some contemporary training analysts—e.g., Franz Alexander and Leon Saul—hold that the analyst

can and should discern the patient's central conflict and the basic out-
lines of his personality in the very first interview or, at the most, in the
first few interviews, which usually consist largely in the patient's account of his difficulties and an initial narrative of significant life experiences.

For the analyst, then, to "read" the patient's unconscious and to understand what his problems are is apparently the least onerous part of
his task. The real challenge is to induce the patient to change, and it is in
connection with that part of the analytic endeavor that the patient must
come to know the contents of his unconscious. (Some analysts claim
that even for therapeutic purposes, it is often unnecessary to reconstruct
the patient's unconscious infantile past; that, however, is strictly a point
of therapeutic technique and not of concern in this context.)

A biographer, unless he is singularly unfortunate (in which case
even a conventional biography will prove difficult), usually has considerable data about the way his subject feels and reacts to the problems of life, and he has even more detailed knowledge about his subject's actions in various situations. Indeed, he has available to him
material which the analyst customarily does not have relating to the
actual impact of his subject on other people, and he has more accurate
evidence of how his subject actually interacts with others in reality
since his materials include not only his subject's impressions of certain
sequences of events but those of other people as well. In short, he often has at his disposal considerable data of a character which is mean-
ingful in terms of psychoanalytic hypotheses, and these can be an in-
valuable aid to interpretation.

To argue the possibility of the fruitful application of psychoanalytic
theory to biography is by no means to suggest that all biographers can
or should attempt it. To master psychoanalytic theory takes many
years of study. To apply it to biographical materials in a useful fashion
is an extraordinarily difficult task which makes many demands upon
the biographer not only as a scholar but as a human being.

The biographer's raw material customarily is locked up in books
and files. There will usually be letters to and from the great man—the
scrawl of the schoolboy writing to his parents, the ardent letters of the
young man to his wife-to-be or perhaps to a friend in whom he con-
fides his views of the world and his notion of his own place in it, the
workaday correspondence with those associated with him in the con-

duct of his business. There will be newspaper accounts of his activities, memoranda by contemporaries, both friend and foe, telling the story of their association with the great man. If the political figure be of the mid-twentieth century or later, the biographer will be able to see and hear him at first hand by means of recordings and films, to study his gestures, his facial expressions, and personally to experience the impact of his public "style." Perhaps there are books written by the subject, or diaries revealing secret hopes and preoccupations. There will be official records—transcripts of meetings in which the great man participated and of speeches he made. There will be books of reminiscences by people who stood in various relationships to the biographical subject—adviser, wife, political rival, political supporter, journalist, friend. Each may have encountered a different facet of the great man so that he emerges in many different lights, and there is the further complication that each account will be colored by the idiosyncrasies of its author and also by his motives for undertaking to write it.

All this mass of material the biographer lets flow freely into him. He is the medium through whom the chaotic raw data is digested, ultimately to be rendered back in an orderly verbal re-creation of an intelligible human being, his individuality revealed. Insofar as the biographer correctly perceives and succeeds in expressing the logical connections among disparate facts, the subject of his biography will achieve a new life, vouchsafed to any who care to read about it. Only the biographer who has been able to filter the data through his own personality without in the end distorting it in consequence of its tortuous passage can perform this creative task.

It is, indeed, an extraordinary function that the biographer sets out to fulfill in relation to his subject. To perform it satisfactorily, he must possess, in addition to that devotion to diligent scholarship the need for which has been abundantly discussed in works of historiography, qualities of mind and spirit which have been less thoroughly explicated. Certainly biographers have been told often enough that they ought to be "unbiased" and that they ought to aim at presenting the "truth." The actual processes involved, however, the vicissitudes of the data between the time the biographer first encounters them and the time he finally transmutes them into a synthesized account, generally have been left untackled on the theory that these are manifestations of artistic creativity and that the essence of artistic creativity defies analysis. In short, the most vital aspect of the biographer's enterprise, the nature of the processes involved in his perception and digestion of the data, has been neglected.

The biographer wishes to *understand* the man whose life he is studying. In order to grasp why his subject behaved as he did in various situations, the biographer wishes to know him emotionally, to be able to experience vicariously the feelings which his subject experienced at various junctures of his life. He wishes to be able to participate in his subject's emotional experience sufficiently to comprehend it, but not to become so intensely involved that he is unable to stand back and dispassionately evaluate that experience in the full context of reality. In order to achieve his objective of conveying some truth about the human being he is studying, the biographer, as the psychoanalyst, must have the capacity for both involvement with and detachment from his subject. He must be involved in order to gain understanding of his subject's reactions; he must be detached in order to evaluate and analyze.

As the data flow into him, the biographer gradually builds a picture of what kind of person his subject was, what his characteristic attitudes and defenses were and how they developed, what made him anxious, what gratified him, what goals and values he adopted, how he went about pursuing them and so on.

At first, the biographer's picture of his subject is vague and sketchy, but as he becomes steeped in the data, more and more details are limned in, providing increasing points of reference. Then when he comes upon a situation in which the subject's behavior is somewhat puzzling, he pauses and attempts to project himself into his subject via the personality picture of him he has formed: how would a given situation or problem—perhaps it is some sort of political challenge or provocation—*feel* to the subject? The biographer, having saturated himself in knowledge of the times in which his subject lived and the external realities of his situation, now "listens" to the data from the inside, as it were, from the point of view of the interior reactions of his subject. If his image of the subject's personality has been well and sensitively derived and his insight into the nature of the problem at hand is accurate, the biographer is likely to achieve an understanding of how the subject experienced the external problem. The behavior, perhaps previously unfathomable, will then seem logical in terms of the inner psychological reality which produced it.

By empathizing, the biographer reaches his subject's feelings in a given situation. Giving free rein to his faculties, both conscious and unconscious, he next tries to grasp the logical connections between the emotions thus perceived and the subject's whole life history. Now he must subject the inferences which his intuition has yielded to strict, rational scrutiny in an attempt to evaluate their validity.

If his data are sufficient and he has functioned well in empathizing, in intuiting and finally in rigorously examining his conclusions, the biographer is now in a position to interpret the bit of historical evidence to which he has been addressing himself. The interpretation will be consonant with all that he knows about his subject, and it, and all the insights which contributed to its formulation, will enable him to develop and refine his mental image of his subject. That, in turn, will improve his ability to cope with the next problem of interpretation, for he will face it with an enriched awareness of his subject.

This is an iterative process. The biographer is constantly re-examining and revising his earlier interpretations of his subject's behavior with improved hypotheses gained from his expanding familiarity with and understanding of the data. His view of his subject gradually achieves an internal consistency as he works and reworks the material.

The foregoing account of the way in which the biographer goes about his work applies also to the way the psychoanalyst works—this aspect of his functioning has been fully described in psychoanalytic literature.[1] Many historians, however, undoubtedly would consider it merely word juggling: of course the biographer must empathize and intuit, they might reply. The real question is, how do you do it? What, since erudition alone obviously is not the answer, makes some people good at it and others inept? It is all very well to say that the biographer has in mind a picture of his subject's personality and that if this picture has been sensitively derived he will be able to project his own consciousness into his subject's feelings. The riddle lies precisely in what has been glossed over in the phrase, "if this picture has been sensitively derived": what, indeed, contributes and what detracts from the biographer's ability to be sensitive?

In this area, psychoanalysis has much to offer the historian which is novel to his accustomed way of thinking. Everything which psychoanalysts have discovered about what impairs or facilitates an analyst's ability to "see" his patient—all the phenomena of what is known in psychoanalytic theory as countertransference—holds also for what impairs or facilitates a biographer's ability to "see" his subject truly and fully.

In order to understand his subject, the biographer must maintain that same attitude of freely hovering attention that Freud prescribed for analysts vis-à-vis their patients. If an analyst's capacity to maintain that attitude is impaired by anxious, hostile or guilty reactions to the patient deriving from unresolved problems of his own life experience, his understanding of the patient is impeded by his countertransference reactions. So too is the biographer's understanding of his subject reduced when the materials at hand elicit irrational irruptions from his own past. If that happens he is likely to produce that familiar phenomenon—the biography more revealing of its author than of its subject.

Analyst and biographer both must be able to participate without inhibition in the feelings of their subjects and this ability depends upon the range and quality of their emotional resonance as well as upon their rational equipment. Non- or even anti-psychoanalytically oriented biographers perforce also use their emotional endowment but, being unaware of that fact or denying it, they are in a poorer position to engage in full self-scrutiny for the purpose of eliminating distortions of perception and interpretation arising out of their own idiosyncrasies.

The psychoanalytic theory of human development is widely recognized as a rich source of hypotheses concerning human behavior. Within the past few generations, the fields of education, sociology, psychology and anthropology have been transformed by the impact of analytic conceptions. It would seem natural, then, that the historian and biographer, who wish not merely to describe but to account for the behavior of people individually and collectively, would seek to absorb and make use of this new body of knowledge. Some half century after Freud's formulation of the basic tenets of psychoanalytic theory, however, it must be conceded that there have been few noteworthy psychoanalytically oriented biographies. Why is this so?

For one thing, there are few first-rate psychoanalysts with the time and interest to do full-length biographical studies (Erik Erikson, who wrote an excellent biography of Luther, is one of the notable few); and there are few first-rate biographers with the time, interest and capacity to master analytic theory. Psychoanalytic theory cannot be used successfully by analysts as a short cut which reduces the need for painstaking historical research and the most scrupulous attention to the social setting in which the biographical subject lived. Nor can biographers inadequately grounded in psychoanalytic theory successfully appropriate bits and pieces of it to "explain" their protagonists. Numerous biographical atrocities committed particularly during the 1920s and 1930s, and quite properly dismissed by serious scholars as mockeries of the biographer's art, testify to this fact.

Another impediment to the development of a fruitful union between psychoanalytic theory and biographical research is the persistence of mutual suspicion between many psychoanalysts and many historians. A serious biographer, seeking to obtain research training in psychoanalytic theory with a view not to becoming a therapist but to applying analytic concepts to historical materials, will find the doors of the major psychoanalytic institutes closed to him. Nonmedical "outsiders" are rarely accepted as students for intensive training. To social scientists desiring to gain the technical competence required for the responsible use of analytic theory in their own disciplines, this bar to the privilege of formal instruction seems unreasonable.

Similarly, historians, as a group, regard psychoanalysis with an attitude of hostile skepticism. In 1957, the distinguished diplomatic historian, Professor William Langer of Harvard, then president of the American Historical Association, called attention to this fact in his presidential address to the Association. Professor Langer's talk was entitled "The Next Assignment," and this he identified as the exploitation by historians of the concepts and findings of psychoanalysis. He urged his colleagues to abandon their "almost completely negative attitude toward the teachings of psychoanalysis" and open their minds to analytic theory as the most promising key to further progress in historical study. It is hardly surprising that few historians to date have chosen to run the gantlet of their fraternity's scorn and possibly even to jeopardize their careers by attempting interdisciplinary work along lines so unsympathetically regarded.

These barriers to communication, however, are already giving way under the pressure of the quest for truth, and there are many hopeful beginnings of cooperative effort between psychoanalysts and social scientists. The psychoanalytically oriented biographer is likely to gain for his work today a fairer hearing than he could ever have hoped for in the past. His task remains difficult, but the promise of a deeper understanding of his subject is an irresistible lure and any success he achieves in this direction is a reward justifying his best effort.

Notes

1. An excellent exposition, to which we are greatly indebted, is Dr. Ralph Greenson's paper "Empathy and Its Vicissitudes," read at the 1959 meeting of the International Psycho-Analytical Association and published in the *International Journal of Psycho-Analysis,* vol. 41, July–October, 1960.

2

Some Uses of Dynamic Psychology in Political Biography: Case Materials on WoodrowWilson

Alexander L. George

MORE SO THAN HISTORICAL WRITING at large, biography is selective. By choosing a single individual as his concern, the biographer can focus on those aspects of the historical process which interacted most directly with his subject. The nature of this interaction and, particularly, the extent to which it is reciprocal, is one of the central problems of biography. To what extent was the behavior of the subject culturally and situationally determined? To what extent did it reflect the individuality of his personality? Though variously worded by different writers, this twofold task of the biographer is a familiar and perplexing one.

In a brief but acute statement of the problem, the Committee on Historiography emphasized that the writing of biography requires both a systematic field theory of personality and hypotheses as to social roles.[1] While agreeing with this twofold emphasis, we have chosen for several reasons to focus attention in the present article upon the need

From Fred I. Greenstein and Michael Lerner (eds.) *A Source Book for the Study of Personality and Politics* (Chicago: Markham Co., 1971). The author's acknowledgement in George's 1960 essay: In preparing this paper I benefited from opportunities for study and discussion as a fellow of the Center for Advanced Study in the Behavioral Sciences, 1956–57, and more recently from a research grant from the Foundations' Fund for Research in Psychiatry.

23

for a systematic approach to personality factors. First, it would appear that historians generally are already more favorably disposed to the cultural approach, and better prepared to employ it, than to a systematic handling of personality components in biography. Second, we wish to show by introducing concrete case materials that a systematic personality approach may be necessary and particularly rewarding in the biographical study of innovating leaders, those who attempt to reinterpret and expand the functions of existing roles or to create new roles. We are particularly interested, that is, in "role-determining" as against "role-determined" leadership. At the same time, we agree that the creation or reinterpretation of leadership roles can only be understood in the context of social-historical dynamics and the institutional setting. The "great leader," as Gerth and Mills observe, has often been a man who has successfully managed such institutional dynamics and created new roles of leadership.[2]

We shall draw upon our previously reported study of Woodrow Wilson[3] in order to demonstrate how the personality component in a biography may be handled in a systematic fashion. And we shall attempt to show that dynamic psychology provides a number of hypotheses which can supplement a cultural or role analysis of Wilson's interest in constitution-writing and which permit the biographer to view the relationship between his "Presbyterian conscience" and his political stubbornness in a new light.

Some Deficiencies of Psychological Biographies

In the past three or four decades historians have occasionally turned to the new field of dynamic psychology for assistance in this task. At the same time, specialists in psychology, especially psychoanalysts, have themselves occasionally attempted to apply the insights and theories of their practice to historical figures.[4] The results of such efforts, from both sides, to merge history and psychology in the writing of political biography have not been encouraging. Even when their purpose was not to debunk a historical figure, most psychoanalytical biographies suffered from pronounced and basic deficiencies.

Three major deficiencies in this type of biography may be briefly mentioned. In the first place, in varying degrees such biographies exaggerate the purely psychological determinants of the political behavior of their subjects. In the cruder of these studies, the subject is represented as if in the grip of powerful unconscious and irrational drives which dictate his every thought and action. Even in more discriminating analyses, the revelation of human motive resulting from incisive insights into the subject's personality can easily oversimplify the complexity of motivation and political action.

Secondly, in viewing adult character and behavior as the legacy of certain early childhood experiences, psychological biographies often oversimplify the process of personality formation and the intricacy of personality structure and functioning. Such a psychological approach is by today's standards inadequate for it overlooks the relevance of important developments in "ego psychology" in the past few decades.[5] Contemporary students of personality emphasize that in the course of his development the individual develops a variety of defenses against underlying anxieties and hostilities. He may learn ways of curbing and controlling tendencies which handicap him in various situations; and he may even devise *constructive* strategies for harnessing personal needs and motivations and directing them into fruitful channels. In other words, the individual attempts to cope simultaneously with the demands of impulse, conscience and reality in developing a philosophy of life, a system of values, a set of attitudes and interests, and in choosing in various situations from among alternative courses of action.[6]

And, finally, to conclude this brief review of the major deficiencies encountered in psychological biographies, one is struck by the fact that the actions of the subject are often interpreted in ways which seem highly speculative and arbitrary. Few investigators in this field have come to grips with the admittedly difficult problem of making rigorous reconstructions of personality factors and plausible interpretations of their role in behavior from the types of historical materials usually available to the biographer. The result is that the use which the biographer makes of dynamic psychology often appears to consist in little more than borrowing certain terms and hypotheses, and superimposing them, more or less arbitrarily upon a smattering of the available historical materials concerning the subject.

Personality Types: The Problem of Diagnosis and Classification

Typologies of personality or character are provided by most of the various schools of psychoanalysis and dynamic psychology. The depiction of a type is usually on the basis of one or more traits, or behavioral tendencies. Often, the characterization of types also includes some indication of the origins and underlying psychodynamics of that type of behavior, which enhances the usefulness of the typology to the biographer. We do not propose to review these typologies here or to attempt to assess their relative worth to the biographer.[7] Rather we wish to consider the status or nature of these personality types and some of the problems which arise in efforts to utilize them in biography.

Most of the types in question are to be understood as being general constructs, or *ideal types*. Though derived from empirical observation, they abstract and deliberately oversimplify reality.[8] Accordingly, their value to the biographer is necessarily limited, since his task is to describe and explain a particular individual in all his concreteness and complexity.

The biographer cannot be satisfied merely to label his subject as constituting an instance of, or bearing a certain resemblance to, a certain personality or character type. To do so oversimplifies the task of making fruitful use of the theories and findings of dynamic psychology and yields results of a limited and disappointing character. Many investigators whose initial attempt to use a personality approach in biography is of this character become disillusioned and abandon the task. They sense that to type their subject, as a "compulsive" for example, tends to caricature him rather than to explain very much of the richness, complexity and variety of his behavior throughout his career.

We are concerned here with a problem not always clearly recognized in the writing of psychological biographies. *Classification* is often confused with *diagnosis*. To tag the subject of the biography with a label or to pigeonhole him in one of a number of existing categories does not in itself provide what the biographer will need most: namely, a discriminating "theory," i.e., a set of assumptions or hypotheses, as to the structure and dynamics of his subject's personality system.

The "diagnosis *vs.* classification" problem also exists in clinical psychiatry where a distinction is sometimes made between the "sponge" and the "file-drawer" clinician.[9] The "sponge"-type clinician attempts to approach his patient with a relatively open mind, trying to derive a theory about that particular patient from an intensive analysis of his behavior and case history. In contrast, the "file-drawer"-type of clinician is more inclined to orient himself to the patient on the basis of general theories and past experience. The one attempts to construct a theory about the patient *de nouveau*, a theory that, as a result, may be highly particularistic; the other stresses gaining insight into the patient by making an astute classification of him on the basis of accumulated theory and experience.

The difference between these clinical approaches is mentioned here in order to point up alternative approaches available to the biographer. As will become clear, we are suggesting that though the biographer should indeed be familiar with available personality theories, he should nonetheless approach his subject as does the "sponge"-type clinician and undertake to develop as discriminating and refined a theory as possible of that particular personality.

In attempting to account for the subject's actions throughout his career, the biographer will have to make specific diagnoses of the operative state of his personality system in numerous situations. To this end, the biographer starts with as good a theory of the subject's personality as he can derive from secondary accounts and from a preliminary inspection of historical materials. Then he reviews chronologically, or developmentally, the history of his subject's behavior, attempting to assess the role that situational and personality factors played in specific instances.[10]

In utilizing a preliminary theory of the subject's personality to make specific diagnoses the biographer in a real sense also "tests" that theory. Detailed analysis of the subject's actions in a variety of individual situations provides new insights into the motivational dynamics of the subject's behavior; these insights, in turn, enable the biographer to progressively refine and improve the theory of the subject's personality with which he started. What the biographer hopes to achieve eventually is an account of the subject's personality that gives coherence and depth to the explanation of his behavior in a variety of situations and that illuminates the more subtle patterns that underlie whatever seeming "inconsistencies" of character and behavior he has displayed.

Two Uses of Personality Types in Biography

Despite the general nature of personality and character types, they may be of substantial use to the biographer in several ways. First, knowledge of these types assists the biographer in developing the kind of *preliminary* theory about the personality of his subject to which reference has already been made. Second, familiarity with the psycho-

dynamics of behavior associated with a particular personality or character type provides the biographer with hypotheses for consideration
in attempting to account for the actions of his subject, especially those
that cannot be easily explained as adequate responses to the situation
which confronted him. Let us consider these two general uses in somewhat greater detail.

A major shortcoming in many conventional biographies, including
those of Wilson, is that they lack a systematic theory about the subject's personality and motivations. The biographer is usually satisfied
to catalogue individual traits exhibited by the subject without exploring their possible interrelationship and their functional significance
within the personality as a whole.[11] Various of Wilson's biographers,[12]
for example, have called attention to his marked "conscientiousness,"
"stubbornness," "single-track mind," and various other traits. They
have done so, however, without indicating awareness that, according
to Freudian theory, these traits are commonly exhibited by "compulsive" persons.

The term "compulsive" today is commonly applied to persons
whose lives are regulated by a strict super-ego, or conscience, which
dominates their personalities. Perhaps not generally known, however,
is the fact that this type of behavior has been carefully studied over a
period of many years by many clinicians; as a result, there are a number of detailed analyses and theories of compulsiveness and the compulsive type that attempt to account for the genesis and underlying
dynamics of this type of behavior. Later in this paper we shall attempt
to show how this rich body of observation and theory can be used by
the biographer. It suffices here to observe that biographers of Wilson,
being generally unfamiliar with such materials, have not been in a position to assess the significance of individual traits displayed by Wilson in terms of their underlying dynamics.[13]

Occasionally biographers of Wilson have been able, on the basis of
an intensive analysis of a particularly well-documented episode in
Wilson's career, to infer or to suggest that his choice of action in a particular situation was apparently governed by personal motives other
than the aims and values which he was publicly espousing.[14] But generally they have hesitated to make diagnoses of the operative state of
Wilson's personality system in specific situations, to explore in any
systematic fashion the complexity and deeper levels of his motivation,
or to postulate in detail the role of his personality in his political be-

havior. Therefore, while these biographers have sensed Wilson's personal involvement in politics and called attention to his many contradictions, their portraits of Wilson's personality are inevitably somewhat flat, even though accurately depicting behavioral tendencies at a surface level.

A familiarity with personality and character types identified in the literature of dynamic psychology will assist the biographer to construct a *preliminary* theory, or model, as to the structure and functioning of his subject's personality. For this purpose there are available to the biographer a variety of typologies of personality and character. Some of these are predominantly sociopsychological rather than clinical in their conception and orientation. Not all typologies of personality are comparable, since they have been constructed from different theoretical standpoints, for different purposes and applications. An overlapping can be noted, however, particularly among some of the typologies provided by various schools of psychoanalysis. Thus, for example, the "aggressive" person in Karen Horney's system bears a substantial resemblance to the Freudian concept of the compulsive type. Similarly, Alfred Adler's central emphasis upon the drive to power and superiority as a means of compensation for real or imagined defects finds a place in many other personality theories as well.

Given the variety of alternative typologies available, the biographer must obviously consider a number of them before choosing the type or types that seem most appropriate to his subject and most useful for the specific questions about the subject's motivations and behavior he is trying to clarify.

Personality theorists, Freudian and non-Freudian, have emphasized that the type-constructs formulated by them are not pure types. Rather, they view the personality functioning of an individual as a mixture of several trends, or types, in a more or less dynamic relationship to each other. This observation applies with particular force to Wilson, in whom several diverse trends can be detected.[15] Nonetheless, the present account is limited to discussing the applicability of the compulsive type to Wilson, partly because of limitations of space and partly because we feel that the compulsive component of his personality is particularly important for illuminating the self-defeating aspects of his behavior.

In any case, having found much evidence of compulsiveness and of the compulsive syndrome in the historical accounts of his life and career, we felt justified in adopting as a tentative working theory that Wilson had a compulsive personality.

We then considered his development and behavior in detail from this standpoint, examining the voluminous documentation of his career that is available to the biographer. In doing so, we encountered increasing evidence of behavior on his part that could not easily be subsumed under the simple model of the compulsive type. This forced us to refine and elaborate the theory as to his compulsiveness, and to attempt to state the *conditions* and to characterize the *situations* in which he did and did not behave in a way (for example, stubbornly) that was in accord with the expectations explicit or implicit in the personality model with which we were working.[16]

Gradually, then, the general construct of the compulsive type (which, as already mentioned, is to be taken as an abstraction and deliberate oversimplification of reality) was modified and brought into consonance with the complexities encountered in the individual case at hand. The point was reached when the picture of Wilson's personality that was emerging became too complex to be retained within the bounds of the compulsive model with which we had started. What remained of that model or theory was the notion of an important compulsive component in his personality and functioning. This component, we shall attempt to show, remained of considerable value as an explanatory principle for some of Wilson's political behavior that has puzzled and distressed many of his contemporaries and biographers.

Another major use of typologies and theories of personality to the biographer is that of providing alternative hypotheses for consideration in attempting to account for the actions and behavioral patterns of his subject. Such general hypotheses are not ready-made explanations to be employed arbitrarily or to be superimposed upon the data. Rather, as a statement of the dynamics of behavior and motivation often or typically associated with a certain personality type, they may serve to orient the biographer's effort to explain the actions of his subject.[17] A familiarity with such hypotheses broadens and deepens the biographer's assessment of the aims and values that the subject pursues in a given situation or in a series of situations. Furthermore, it sensitizes him to historical evidence of the possible operation of unconscious or unstated motives he might otherwise overlook.

During the preparation of our study of Wilson we combed the technical literature for hypotheses about the dynamics of motivation and behavior associated with compulsiveness that might illuminate the nature of Wilson's personal involvement in political activities.[18] We hoped to find clues to certain inept and apparently irrational actions on his part and to discover, if possible, a consistent pattern or thread in the various inconsistencies of behavior and character he displayed.

If Wilson is not the simple clinical stereotype of a compulsive, neither can he be regarded as a full-blown neurotic. True, one cannot read, for example, Karen Horney's insightful and penetrating descriptions of neurotic drives and of the neurotic character structure without being struck by the applicability of much of what she says to Wilson. But these descriptions are applicable only to a certain point and, upon reflection, one is on balance equally or more impressed with the extent to which Wilson's behavior and career *diverge* from those of her patients. This divergence from the clinical picture concerns precisely the critical question whether the neurotically disposed individual is able to deal adequately with his conflicts and hence retains the ability to function effectively.

For Wilson was, after all, a highly successful person. He was able to overcome a severe disturbance in childhood development; thereafter, not only did he keep fairly well in check the compulsive and neurotic components of his personality but he succeeded in large measure in harnessing them constructively to the achievement of socially productive purposes.[19] To the clinical psychologist, therefore, Wilson is interesting as much because he was able to overcome childhood difficulties and to perform as successfully as he did in public life, as he is because of the pathological pattern of self-defeating behavior he tended to repeat on several occasions during his public career.[20]

Compulsiveness and the Compulsive Type

To indicate briefly what is meant by compulsiveness and the compulsive type of personality is not an easy task since these concepts are employed somewhat differently within the various theoretical schools which comprise dynamic psychology. The point to be made here is that the existence of different theoretical orientations and, particularly, of important lacunae in knowledge and theory within the field of dynamic psychology need not prevent the biographer from making fruitful use of systematic personality theory as a source of hypotheses that serve to orient and give direction to his own research.[21]

In any case, the usefulness of the technical literature to the biographer will be enhanced if the distinction is kept in mind between the question of the *origins* of compulsiveness and compulsive traits, about which there are various views, and the *dynamics* of such behavior, about which there is less disagreement. Similarly, the biographer will observe that specialists seem able to agree more readily on a characterization of the quality of compulsive behavior than on a list of specific traits common to all compulsive persons.

In Freudian theory various correlations are predicted between disturbances of different stages in libido development and the emergence of certain adult character traits. Disturbances in one of these stages of development leads, according to the theory, to the presence of orderliness, stinginess, and stubbornness in adult behavior.[22] These are general traits, or broad tendencies, that manifest themselves more specifically in a variety of ways. By combing the technical literature one can easily construct a richer, more elaborate list of traits which together comprise the syndrome or constellation.[23]

Thus, for example, the general trait "orderliness" may manifest itself in (a) "cleanliness" (corporeal, symbolic); (b) "conscientiousness" (single-track mind, concentration, drive, pedantism, reliability, punctuality, punctiliousness and thoroughness); (c) "regularity" (according to spatial and temporal aspects); (d) "plannedness"; (e) "norm conformity."[24]

Most personality and character types are usually described, at least in the first instance, in terms of certain manifest behavioral traits such as those that have been listed. If the description of a type does not link the traits in question with a theory of personality structure and motivational dynamics, the type-construct will obviously be of little value for motivational and situational analysis of an individual's behavior. At the same time, however, it is overly sanguine to expect that relationships between most manifest behavior traits and their inner, subjective functions for the personality will be of a simple one-to-one character. For, as clinical psychologists have particularly emphasized, the same item of manifest behavior may fulfill different functions for different personalities or, at different times, for the same individual. Particularly the political and social behavior of an individual, in which the biographer is most interested, is not likely to reflect single motives; it is more likely to be the outcome of a complex interplay of several motives and of efforts on the part of the person to adjust inner needs and strivings to one another as well as to external reality considerations.

A personality type construct is potentially more useful, therefore, if it is associated with a more or less distinctive type of motivational dynamics, whether or not this be invariably accompanied by a set of distinctive behavioral traits. From this standpoint, leaving aside for the present the question of its validity, the Freudian concept of the compulsive type is a particularly rich one in that it includes, in addition to the syndrome of traits already noted, a rather explicit and detailed set of structural-dynamic hypotheses of this kind.

We shall not attempt to recapitulate the rather involved and technical set of structural-dynamic hypotheses associated with the compulsive type in Freudian theory. Of immediate interest here is the fact that orderliness and stubbornness in persons of this type are said to derive in part from a desire for power or domination, which in turn is said to be related to a more basic need for self-esteem, or security.[25] Thus, according to the technical literature compulsives often show a marked interest in imposing orderly systems upon others, an activity from which they derive a sense of power. They also hold fast obstinately to their own way of doing things. They dislike to accommodate themselves to arrangements imposed from without, but expect immediate compliance from other people as soon as they have worked out a definite arrangement, plan or proposal of their own.

In the spheres of activity in which they seek power gratifications, compulsives are sensitive to interference. They may take advice badly (or only under special circumstances). Often they exhibit difficulties in deputing work to others, being convinced at bottom that they can do everything (in this sphere) better than others. This conviction is sometimes exaggerated to the point that they believe they are unique. Negativeness, secretiveness and vindictiveness are traits often displayed by compulsives. (Considerable evidence of most of these traits and tendencies, too, can be found in the historical materials on Wilson, many of them being noted by contemporaries and biographers.)[26]

While particularly that aspect of Freudian theory that regards interferences with libido development as the genesis of adult character traits has been criticized, the existence of certain constellations of adult traits, as in this instance, is less controversial and, in fact, appears to enjoy some empirical support.[27]

In revisions and elaborations of Freudian theory somewhat less emphasis is often placed upon specifying a distinctive content of compulsive behavior. Karen Horney, for example, regards compulsiveness as a characteristic quality of all neurotic needs. Thus, the craving for affection, power and prestige, and the ambition, submissiveness and withdrawal which different neurotics manifest all have a desperate, rigid, indiscriminate and insatiable quality, i.e., the quality of compulsiveness.[28]

Much that is common to various of these formulations has been summarized in Harold D. Lasswell's account of the functional role of the compulsive dynamism in the personality system and of the general character of the circumstances in which it is adopted.[29] Thus, the compulsive dynamism is one of several possible defensive measures a child may adopt as a way out of an acute tension-producing situation that may arise during the course of socialization and learning. Tension is produced when a relatively elaborate set of requirements are imposed upon the child and reinforced by a system of rewards and punishments of a special intensity and applied in such manner so that deprivations and indulgences are balanced. One possible defensive measure against the ensuing tension is the adoption of a blind urge to act with intensity and rigidity, i.e., the dynamism of compulsiveness.

The reasons and conditions for the emergence of compulsiveness are, as has been suggested, somewhat difficult to formulate precisely. However, in making use of available knowledge of the compulsive personality for purposes of political biography, an answer to the causal question is not essential. Whatever creates a given personality dynamism, the dynamism itself—which is what interests the biographer the most—can be fairly readily identified in accounts of the subject's behavior.

In Wilson's case, even the circumstances under which the compulsive dynamism was adopted are richly suggested in materials collected by the official biographer.[30] Thus, accounts of early efforts at the boy's education, in which the father played a leading role, strongly suggest the sort of acute tension-producing situation that, we have already noted, is considered by specialists as predisposing to the adoption of the compulsive dynamism. This, however, evidently was not Wilson's initial method of coping with the tension-inducing situation; rather, for quite a while his method of defense took the form of a tendency to withdraw from the situation. For the time being the boy was unable, perhaps out of fear of failure, or unwilling, perhaps out of resentment, to cooperate with his father's efforts to advance his intellectual development. Wilson's early "slowness" (which specialists today might well consider a case of reading retardation based on emotional factors) was a matter of considerable concern to his family; it manifested itself most strikingly in his not learning his letters until he was nine and not learning to read readily until the age of eleven.[31]

At about this time the boy showed signs of beginning to cooperate actively with his father's efforts to tutor him and to make prodigious efforts to satisfy the perfectionist demands that the Presbyterian minister levied upon his son.[32] One can only speculate at the reasons for the change at this time; possibly it was connected with the birth of a younger brother when Wilson was ten. (Wilson had two older sisters but no younger brothers or sisters until this time; he himself recalled that he had clung to his mother and was laughed at as a "mama's boy" until he was a great big fellow.)

In any case, it is easy thereafter to find evidence of a compulsive bent to the young adolescent's personality. It requires no great familiarity with the technical literature on such matters to detect indications of compulsiveness in the youth's extreme conscientiousness, the manner in which he drove himself repeatedly to physical breakdowns, and the singleness of purpose he displayed in applying himself to the task of achieving knowledge and skill in the sphere of competence—politics and oratory—with which he quickly identified his ambitions.[33]

Wilson's Interest in Constitutions

In the remainder of this paper we should like to develop the case, mainly by way of illustrative materials from the study of Wilson, for supplementing cultural and historical components in biography by an intensive and relatively systematic appraisal of personality.

A number of Wilson's biographers, including the official biographer,[34] have been struck by the interest in constitutions he displayed from early youth. Beginning in his fourteenth year he wrote or revised a half dozen constitutions, an activity that culminated in the Covenant of the League of Nations. It is our thesis that this activity on his part reflects the type of interest in order and power that compulsive persons often display. In other words, he was motivated in part (though not exclusively) by a desire to impose orderly systems upon others, deriving therefrom a sense of power or domination.

The historian will quickly object, and rightly so, offering a more obvious counter-hypothesis, which is certainly plausible; namely that Wilson's interest in writing constitutions was culturally determined. After all, it was part of the belief system of the age that progress in human affairs was to be achieved by such instrumentalities as better constitutions, institutional reform, etc. The fact that Wilson wrote or revised many constitutions, therefore, does not necessarily attest to a personal interest in order and power.

Is it possible to demonstrate that Wilson's motivation in the matter did not stem exclusively from identification with a role that was socially approved? Or is such a question entirely out of the reach of the historian? In the following remarks we shall attempt to show that such questions are capable of being dealt with on the basis of the materials and method of the historian.

First, why Wilson and not someone else? Why, in other words, did the belief system in question impress itself particularly on Wilson? Is it not more than a coincidence that in every club he joined as a youth he seized the earliest opportunity, often making it the first order of business, to revise its constitution in order to transform the club into a miniature House of Commons? Granted that constitution-making was part of the existing cultural and political ethos and that admiration for the British system was already widespread among American students of government, why should the task of revising the constitution and political structure of these groups always fall to Wilson? Why were none of these constitutions revised along desirable lines by others, before Wilson joined these clubs? It would seem that among his contemporaries it was Wilson who found constitution-making a particularly attractive occupation. The readiness with which he accepted for himself a role that was, to be sure, culturally sanctioned makes the inference plausible that personal motives were strongly engaged by the possibility that constitution writing afforded of ordering the relations of his fellow-beings.[35]

Secondly, what evidence can be found of an unconscious motive or need to impose orderly systems upon others? If such a motive exists, we may expect appropriate pleasurable feelings to ensue from its gratification. However, we cannot reasonably expect that the pleasure experienced by the individual in such instances will be fully articulated under ordinary circumstances. Hence, in the type of historical materials on the subject's inner life usually available to the biographer we can expect only episodic and fragmentary evidence of the fact that an activity on his part has satisfied deeply felt personality needs. This is in fact what we find in this case. For example, after rewriting the constitution of the Johns Hopkins debating society and transforming it into a "House of Commons," Wilson reported to his fiancee the great pleasure he had derived from the project: "It is characteristic of my whole self that I take so much pleasure in these proceedings of this society. . . . I have a sense of power in dealing with men collectively that I do not feel always in dealing with them singly."[36]

That constitution-writing had a deep personal meaning for Wilson is further suggested by the fact that such activities were always instrumental to his desire to exercise strong leadership. It is rather obvious even from historical accounts that rewriting constitutions was for Wilson a means of restructuring those institutional environments in which *he* wanted to exercise strong leadership. He wished to restructure the political arena in these instances in order to enhance the possibility of influencing and controlling others by means of oratory. This was a skill in which he was already adept as an adolescent and to the perfection of which he assiduously labored for years. In the model House of Commons which Wilson created, and in which as the outstanding debater he usually became "Prime Minister," independent leadership was possible and, as Wilson had foreseen, the skillful, inspirational orator could make his will prevail.[37]

From an early age, then, Wilson's scholarly interest in the workings of American political institutions was an adjunct of his ambition to become a great statesman. He wished to exercise power with great initiative and freedom from crippling controls or interference. The relationship between Wilson's theories of leadership and his own ambitions and changing life situation, which we cannot recapitulate here, is revealing in this respect.[38] Suffice it to say that when Wilson's career development is studied from this standpoint considerable light is thrown on the intriguing question of the role of personal motivations in political inventiveness and creativity. Political psychologists have hypothesized that a compulsive interest in order and power is often to be found in strong political leaders who were great institution-builders and who made it their task to transform society. The case study of Wilson lends support to this general hypothesis.

To posit such personal, unconscious components in the political motivation of some leaders by no means excludes the simultaneous operation of cultural determinants There is no doubt in Wilson's case that his personal interest in order and power was defined and channelized by the cultural and political matrix of the times. Moreover, concrete opportunities to rewrite constitutions and to exercise and perfect his talents as orator-leader were provided by existing situations in which he found himself or that he actively sought out.

Thus, the external situation in which the individual exists necessarily defines and delimits the field in which personality develops and in which personality needs and traits find expression. On the other hand, the interaction between the personality of a political leader and the milieu in which he operates may be, in an important sense, a reciprocal one. A leader's basic needs and values, his motives and dispositions, shape his perception of the situations that confront him and influence his definition and evaluation of the choices of action open to him.[39]

What is gained by attributing motivations of this character to a political leader? In this case, what difference does it make whether Wilson's interest in writing constitutions had the type of personal motivation in question? The postulate of a deep-seated, unconscious interest in imposing orderly systems upon others as a means of achieving a sense of power, we believe, accounts in part (but only in part) for Wilson's peculiar involvement in the League Covenant and in the making of the peace, the many strands of which we have attempted to document in our book. The biographer who is sensitive to the possible role of unconscious motivation is struck, for example, by the fact that it was Wilson's constant concern to reserve to himself final authorship of the Covenant, even though none of the ideas that entered into it were original with him, and that he appeared to derive peculiar pleasure from giving his own stamp to the phraseology of the document.[40]

Similarly, the postulate that Wilson derived from constitution-writing gratification of unconscious personal needs for power and domination may account in part (again only in part) for the tenacity with which he resisted efforts by various Senators to rewrite parts of the Covenant, which in some cases amounted merely to an alteration of its wording. Wilson appears to have subconsciously experienced all such efforts as attempts to "interfere" with or "dominate" him in a sphere of competence that he regarded as his own preserve.

Such an interpretation, taken alone, will seem highly speculative. The reader, we hope, will find it more plausible in the context of the theory of Wilson's personality that we have worked out and utilized in detail for purposes of analyzing Wilson's entire development and career. Briefly paraphrased here, the theory is that political leadership was a sphere of competence Wilson carved out for himself (from early adolescence on!) in order to derive therefrom compensation for the damaged self-esteem branded into his spirit as a child. Particularly when performing in his favored role as interpreter and instrument of the moral aspirations of the people, he considered himself as uniquely endowed and virtually infallible. His personality needs were such that in the sphere of competence, which he regarded as peculiarly his own, he had to function "independently" and without "interference" in order to gain the compensatory gratification he sought from the political arena. These we believe to have been the underlying dynamics of his somewhat autocratic style of leadership to which many contemporaries and biographers have called attention.[41]

The Relationship Between
Wilson's Morality and His Stubbornness

The extraordinary role of "conscience" and "stubbornness" in Wilson's political behavior has been noted by numerous of his contemporaries and biographers. It has often been said that Wilson's refusal to compromise on certain notable occasions, particularly as President of Princeton and as President of the United States, was a reflection of his "Presbyterian conscience." When great principles were at stake, as on these occasions, he could not bring himself to compromise. In such situations Wilson characteristically portrayed himself as confronted by a choice between dishonorable compromise of principles and an uncompromising struggle for moral political goals. Accordingly, for him, there could be no alternative but to fight for truth and morality against all opposition, whatever the consequences.

No matter that others (including careful historians such as Arthur S. Link)[42] find his characterization of the situation in these terms unconvincing; that in fact Wilson was not really confronted by such an unpleasant either-or choice. The fact remains that *Wilson* saw it thus. However much one may deplore the political consequences of his refusal to compromise, so the argument goes, surely the only valid conclusion that can be drawn is that Wilson was possessed by an unusually strong sense of morality and rectitude that exercised a determining influence upon his political behavior.

It has seemed plausible, therefore, to attribute great importance to the Presbyterian culture in which Wilson was reared and from which, to condense this familiar thesis, he derived his unusual conscience and sense of morality.

Such a thesis must cope with various questions that can be legitimately raised. For example: If Wilson's refusal to compromise in certain instances is simply a matter of his Presbyterian conscience, then what of the numerous instances in which that same conscience was no bar to highly expedient, if not opportunistic, political behavior on his part?[43] Clearly, at the very least a more refined theory as to the nature of the Presbyterian conscience and of its influence on political behavior is needed.

This general question is merely posed here. Instead of pursuing it further on this occasion let us consider, rather, the usefulness of looking at the relationship between Wilson's morality and his political stubbornness in terms of what is known about the dynamics of the compulsive type. To examine the problem of Wilson in these terms is not to deny the importance of his Presbyterian upbringing or related cultural factors. Nor does it thereby ignore the possibility, which need not be explored here, that compulsive personalities are or were frequently to be found among members of the Presbyterian subculture. Indeed, the Presbyterian ethos no doubt provided reinforcement and rationalization for Wilson's stubbornness. We have elsewhere observed that such a creed produces men of conviction who find it possible to cling to their principles no matter what the opposition. The feeling that they are responsible, through their conscience, only to God, gives them a sense of freedom from temporal authority and the opinions of their fellow men.[44]

The problem of Wilson's convictions that he was "right" in refusing to compromise, and was acting in conformity with moral standards, however, is more complex than it appears at first glance, as we will try to show.

The analysis of "stubborn" behavior in compulsive personalities indicates that it is often a form of aggression. Thus aggressive tendencies, usually repressed, find expression in situations that actually comprise, or can be represented by the individual to himself as comprising, struggles on behalf of goals that receive strong endorsement by the conscience. The operative mechanism is referred to as "idealization" and has been described in the following terms: "The realization that an ideal requirement is going to be fulfilled brings to the ego an increase in self-esteem. This may delude it into ignoring the fact that through the idealized actions there is an expression of instincts that ordinarily would have been repressed. . . . the ego relaxes its ordinary testing of reality and of impulses so that instinctual [in this case, aggressive] impulses may emerge relatively uncensored."[45] One is reminded in this connection of Wilson's repeated expressions of his "pleasure" and "delight" at an opportunity for a good fight on behalf of a good cause, and his highly aggressive outbursts against opponents who blocked his high moral purposes. The instinctual nature of these eruptions is suggested by their extreme and intemperate quality; they were often personally unbecoming as well as politically inexpedient, and on occasion left Wilson shortly thereafter much chagrined at his loss of self-control.

Whatever the satisfactions of an uncompromising fight for what is "right," it may lead the compulsive person into essentially immoral behavior, behavior which strongly conflicts with role requirements and expectations. Given a culture in which political power is shared and in which the rules of the game enjoin compromise among those who participate in making political decisions for the community, to insist stubbornly that others submit to your own conception of what is truth and morality may in fact contravene political morality. The "right" thing for Wilson to do in the critical phases of his struggles at Princeton and with the Senate in the League matter, in terms of the prevailing political mores, was to have worked together with others who legitimately held power in order to advance as far as possible towards desirable political goals.

Wilson was well aware of this requirement. As a historian and astute student of American political institutions, he knew very well that the "right" thing for a statesman to do is to be practical and accomplish what he can. And he had expressed himself often on this very problem. In an address before the McCormick Theological Seminary, in the fall of 1909, for example, he had said: "I have often preached in my political utterances the doctrine of expediency, and I am an unabashed disciple of that doctrine. What I mean to say is, you cannot carry the world forward as fast as a few select individuals think. The individuals who have the vigor to lead must content themselves with a slackened pace and go only so fast as they can be followed. They must not be impractical. They must not be impossible. They must not insist upon getting at once what they know they cannot get."[46]

However, at several critical junctures in his public career, when he found his righteous purposes blocked by opponents who would not bend to his will, Wilson did not do the "right" thing; he did not compromise or accommodate, even when friends and political associates enjoined him to do so. Rather, he stubbornly persisted in his course and helped bring about his own personal defeat and the defeat of worthwhile measures which he was championing.

It seems, then, that we are confronted here by a form of self-defeating behavior in which the role of "conscience" in political stubbornness is perhaps much more complex than is implied in the familiar thesis of Wilson's "Presbyterian conscience" and his stiff-necked "morality."

But why must stubborn refusal to compromise be pushed to the point of self-defeat and the frustration of desirable legislation if not for Wilson's stated reason that he would have found it immoral to compromise great principles? Once again the literature on compulsiveness provides an alternative set of hypotheses with which to assess the available historical data. It is our thesis, which we have tried to document elsewhere,[47] that Wilson's stubborn refusals to compromise in situations where true morality and the requirements of his role demanded accommodation created feelings of guilt within him. He was vaguely disturbed by what he subconsciously sensed to be his own personal involvement in the fights with his opponents. The greater the stubbornness (a form of aggression against his opponents), the greater the inner anxiety at violating the moral injunction to compromise, which was a very real requirement of his political conscience.

This predicament was worked out in the following manner: stubborn refusal to compromise was maintained to the point where Wilson could demonstrate his "moral superiority" over his opponents. This could be achieved by manipulating the situation so that his opponents were also involved in "immoral" behavior, for example, by permitting their dislike of Wilson to warp their political good sense, by conspiring to defeat Wilson despite the merits of the issue at stake, by refusing to support desirable proposals just because he was championing them, etc. Thus, stubbornness was maintained so that, should it not succeed in forcing the capitulation of his opponents, it would provoke his defeat by selfish and immoral opponents. Thereby, he could at least assuage his anxiety and guilt for, whatever his "crime," it was outweighed by the demonstration in defeat of his "moral superiority" over his opponents.

These, we believe, were the underlying dynamics of the search for martyrdom which other writers[48] as well have seen in Wilson's ill-fated Western speaking tour on behalf of the League of Nations. Whether the available historical materials which we have cited in support of this thesis render it sufficiently plausible and convincing must be left to individual judgment. Instead of rephrasing the evidence and reasoning already presented on its behalf in our book, we shall confine ourselves here to noting that the mechanisms described above, as underlying the possible quest for martyrdom, are very well described in the literature on compulsive stubbornness.

> ... What is usually called stubbornness in the behavior of adult persons is an attempt to use other persons as instruments in the struggle with the super-ego. By provoking people to be unjust, they strive for a feeling of moral superiority which is needed to increase their self-esteem as a counter-balance against the pressure of the super-ego.[49]
>
> ... The stubborn behavior is maintained the more obstinately, the more an inner feeling exists that it is impossible to prove what needs to be proven, and that one is actually in the wrong. ... The feeling, "Whatever I do is still less wicked than what has been done to me," is needed as a weapon against the super-ego and, if successful, may bring relief from feelings of guilt.[50]

In brief, therefore, the very "morality" in terms of which Wilson could initially legitimize the open expression of pent-up aggression and hostility ensnared him in profoundly immoral political behavior. His repeated protestations as the struggle with his opponents wore on that he had to do what was "right" and what conscience demanded were, in fact, a cloak for activity that was contrary to the requirements of his leadership role and some of the demands of his own conscience. The repeated protestations that he was acting merely as an instrument of the people's will and had no personal stakes in the battle were the external manifestation of desperate efforts to still inner doubts of the purity of his motivation in refusing compromise and to controvert the knowledge that gnawed from within that he was obstructing his own cause.[51] We have here an instance not of stern morality but of a type of rationalization which has been labelled the "moralization" mechanism, i.e., a tendency to interpret things as if they were in accord with ethical standards when they are actually (and subconsciously known to be) in striking contrast to them.[52]

Thus did Wilson go down to tragic defeat. A subtle personal involvement in political struggle prevented him from anchoring his actions in the profound wisdom of the maxim: "There comes a time in the life of every man when he must give up his principles and do what he knows is right."[53]

The Self-Defeating Pattern in Wilson's Career

The thesis of a self-defeating dynamism in Wilson's personality gains in plausibility from evidence that it was part of a pattern which tended to repeat itself under similar conditions during his career.[54] A number of Wilson's biographers have noted that Wilson's defeat in the fight for the League fits into a pattern of behavior he had displayed earlier in public life. Thus, after a painstaking analysis of the bitter and unsuccessful struggle Wilson waged with his opponents at Princeton, Professor Link was led to remark that "a political observer, had he studied carefully Wilson's career as president of Princeton University, might have forecast accurately the shape of things to come during the period when Wilson was president of the United States." Calling the former period a microcosm of the latter, Link ascribed to Wilson's uncompromising battles both in the graduate college controversy and in the League of Nations battle with the Senate "the character and proportions of a Greek tragedy."[55]

Similarly, writing many years before, Edmund Wilson, the distinguished man of letters, saw in the same events of Wilson's career evidence of a curious cyclical pattern that can be detected in the lives of other historical figures as well:

> It is possible to observe in certain lives, where conspicuously superior abilities are united with serious deficiencies, not the progress in a career or vocation that carries the talented man to a solid position or a definite goal, but a curve plotted over and over again and always dropping from some flight of achievement to a steep descent into failure.[56]

The type of enigmatic personality described here by a humanist is one which has been of long-standing interest to the clinician as well. Influenced by Freud's earlier description and analysis of neurotic careers, Franz Alexander in 1930 presented what has become a classical psychoanalytical account of this general character type.[57] In many cases, driven by unconscious motives, persons of this type alternate between committing a transgression and then seeking punishment. Thereby, their careers may exhibit "alternating phases of rise and abrupt collapse," a pattern indicating that "aggressive and self-destructive tendencies" run along together. "The neurotic character," Alexander continues, "has fired the literary imagination since time immemorial. They are nearly all strong individualities who struggle in vain to hold the anti-social tendencies of their nature in check. They are born heroes who are predestined to a tragic fate."

Let us examine more closely the repetitive pattern of behavior that observers working from different standpoints have detected in his career.[58] As President of Princeton, Governor of New Jersey, and President of the United States, Wilson gained impressive early successes only to encounter equally impressive political deadlocks or set-backs later on. He entered each of these offices at a time when reform was the order of the day, and with a substantial fund of goodwill to draw upon. In each case there was an initial period during which the type of strong leadership he exercised in response to his inner needs coincided sufficiently with the type of leadership the external situation required for impressive accomplishment. He drove the faculty and trustees at Princeton to accomplish an unprecedented series of reforms. The New Jersey legislature of 1911 was a triumph of productivity in his hands. Later, he exacted a brilliant performance from the Sixty-Third Congress of the United States.

We are forced to recognize, therefore, that Wilson's personal involvements contributed importantly to the measure of political accomplishment he attained. In each position, however, his compulsive ambition and imperious methods helped in time to generate the type of bitter opposition that blocked further successes and threatened him with serious defeats. Wilson was skillful in the tactics of leadership only so long as it was possible to get exactly what he wanted from the trustees or the legislature. He could be adept and inventive in finding ways of mobilizing potential support. He could be, as in the first year of the Governorship and in the "honeymoon" period of the Presidency, extremely cordial, if firm; gracious, if determined; and generally willing to go through the motions of consulting and granting deference to legislators whose support he needed. It is this phase of his party leadership that excited the admiration of contemporaries, historians, and political scientists alike. It is essential to note, however, that Wilson's skillfulness in these situations always rested somewhat insecurely upon the expectation that he would be able to push through his proposed legislation in essentially unadulterated form. (As Wilson often put it, he was willing to accept alterations of "detail," but not of the "principles" of his legislative proposals.)

Once opposition crystalized in sufficient force to threaten the defeat or marked alteration of his proposed legislation, however, Wilson was faced with a different type of situation. Skillful political behavior—the logic of the situation—now demanded genuine consultation to explore the basis of disagreement and to arrive at mutual concessions, bargains, and formulas that would ensure passage of necessary legislation. In this type of situation Wilson found it difficult to operate on the basis of expediential considerations and at times proved singularly gauche as a politician. Once faced with genuine and effective opposition to a legislative proposal *to which he had committed his leadership aspirations,* Wilson became rigidly stubborn and tried to force through his measure without compromising it.[59] The greater the opposition, the greater his determination not to yield. He must win on his own terms or not at all!

Personally involved in these struggles, Wilson was incapable of realistically assessing the situation and of contriving skillful strategies for dividing the opposition and winning over a sufficient number to his side. Both at Princeton and later in the battle with the Senate over ratification of the treaty, Wilson was incapable of dealing effectively in his own interest with the more moderate of his opponents. In the heat of the battle, he could tolerate no ambiguity and could recognize no legitimate intermediate position. He tended to lump together all of his opponents. In such crises, therefore, his leadership was strongly divisive rather than unifying. He alienated the potential support of moderate elements who strongly sympathized with his general aims but felt some modification of his proposals to be necessary. Instead of modest concessions to win a sufficient number of moderates over, he stubbornly insisted upon his own position and rudely rebuffed their overtures, thus driving them into the arms of his most bitter and extreme opponents.[60] It was his singular ineptness in the art of political accommodation, once the battle was joined, which was at bottom responsible for some of Wilson's major political defeats at Princeton and in the Presidency.

In these situations—when opposition crystalized and threatened to block Wilson's plan—the desire to succeed in achieving a worthwhile goal, in essence if not in exact form, became of less importance than to maintain equilibrium of the personality system. He seems to have experienced opposition to his will in such situations as an unbearable threat to his self-esteem. To compromise in these circumstances was to submit to domination in the very sphere of power and political leadership in which he sought to repair his damaged self-esteem. Opposition to his will, therefore, set into motion disruptive anxieties and brought to the surface long-smouldering aggressive feelings that, as a child, he had not dared to express. The ensuing struggle for his self-esteem led, on the political level, to the type of stubborn, self-defeating behavior and the search for moral superiority over his opponents that we have already described.

Notes

1. *The Social Sciences in Historical Study: A Report of the Committee on Historiography,* Social Science Research Council, Bulletin 64, 1954, pp. 153–54. By "field theory of personality" the Committee had in mind one which takes into account the fact that "'external factors,' not just childhood training, set norms and incentives and influence motivation and codes of conduct." (See also *Ibid.,* p. 61.)

2. Hans Gerth and C. Wright Mills, *Character and Social Structure* (New York, 1953), chapter xiv, "The Sociology of Leadership." See also fn. 35, pp. 87, 88.

3. A. L. George and J. L. George, *Woodrow Wilson and Colonel House: A Personality Study* (New York, 1956). (Hereafter referred to as *WW & CH.*)

4. For a recent review of such studies see John A. Garraty, "The Interrelations of Psychology and Biography," *Psychological Bulletin* 51, No. 6 (1954): 569–82. See also Gordon W. Allport, *The Use of Personal Documents in Psychological Science,* Social Science Research Council Bulletin 49, 1942.

5. For a brief review of this development see Calvin S. Hall and Gardner Lindzey, *Theories of Personality* (New York, 1957), pp. 64–65, 271–72.

6. For a useful statement of major trends in social psychology and personality theory see Chapter 2, "Converging Approaches," in Smith, Bruner and White, *Opinions and Personality* (New York, 1956). For a useful summary and synthesis of the ways in which unconscious needs find expression in political behavior see Robert E. Lane, *Political Life* (Glencoe, IL, 1959), chapter 9.

7. Useful accounts of some of these typologies, and others drawn partly from social-psychological standpoints, are available in Ruth L. Monroe, *Schools of Psychoanalytic Thought* (New York, 1955); Harold D. Lasswell, *Power and Personality* (New York, 1948); Robert E. Lane, "Political Character and Political Analysis," *Psychiatry* 16 (1953): 387–98. On trends in the study of politi-

cal leadership, see Lester G. Seligman, "The Study of Political Leadership," *American Political Science Review* 44 (December 1950): 904–15.

8. On this general point, see Gardner Murphy, *Personality: A Biosocial Approach to Origins and Structure* (New York and London, 1947), pp. 749–52.

9. I am indebted to Dr. David Hamburg, Chairman, Psychiatry Department, Stanford University, for bringing this to my attention.

10. The need for developmental analysis of personality that starts with some preliminary theory, or set of hypotheses, has been frequently emphasized by those writing on the problems of biography. See, for example, the following statement by the historian Thomas C. Cochran: "Faced with the task of constructing an interpretive biography, the investigator trained in psychological methods would formulate hypotheses as he started work on the early life of his subject—hypotheses as to what sort of person the man would prove to be when he later became involved in different types of situations. A systematic testing of these hypotheses against the evidence provided at different stages in the life history would not only provide clues to the understanding of motives but would also focus the biography sharply on the processes of personality development." (In *The Social Sciences in Historical Study: A Report of the Committee on Historiography*, Social Science Research Council, Bulletin 64, 1954, p. 67.)

11. Much dissatisfaction has been expressed in recent times with the conventional "trait" approach to the study of personality and leadership. See, for example, Cecil A. Gibb, "The Principles and Traits of Leadership," *Journal of Abnormal and Social Psychology* 42 (1947): 267–84; Alvin Gouldner, *Studies in Leadership* (New York, 1950).

12. Among the many useful personality sketches and interpretations of Wilson see particularly those recently provided by Arthur S. Link, *Wilson: The New Freedom* (Princeton, 1956), pp. 61 ff., 93–144; John A. Garraty, "Woodrow Wilson: A Study in Personality," *The South Atlantic Quarterly* 56, No. 2 (April, 1957): 176–85; John Morton Blum, *Woodrow Wilson and the Politics of Morality* (Boston, 1956).

13. Thus Blum refers only parenthetically to Wilson's "compulsiveness" and his "obsessive sense of unrest" (*op. cit.*, pp. 5, 11, 75). Though he has explored the technical literature on compulsive behavior, Blum did not attempt a methodical exploitation of it in preparing his study of Wilson. (Personal communication to the author.)

The compulsive nature of Wilson's ambition and political style, his inability to pace his demands for reform more expediently, was earlier grasped by the official biographer (Ray Stannard Baker, *Woodrow Wilson: Life and Letters* [New York, 1927], II, pp. 153, 244–45; V, p. 119); Link (see for example *Wilson: The Road to the White House* [Princeton, 1947], pp. viii-ix, 45, 90); by Edmund Wilson, "Woodrow Wilson at Princeton," *Shores of Light* (New York, 1952), pp. 312–13; and by Edward S. Corwin, in *Woodrow Wilson: Some Princeton Memories*, ed. William Starr Meyers, pp. 34–35.

14. See, for example, Arthur S. Link's perceptive account of Wilson's highly revealing reaction when his opponents at Princeton unexpectedly offered to

accept a compromise proposal to which he had earlier committed himself. (*Op. cit.*, pp. 69–71, 75–76; see also *WW & CH*, pp. 42–43.)

15. Thus, a fuller statement of the personality trends or types that can be detected in Wilson's personality would, in Freudian terms, probably have to include reference to the "oral character" and the "neurotic character" (see pp. 92, 93), as well as to the compulsive type. Similarly, if Karen Horney's typology is employed, Wilson would probably have to be described as an amalgam of her "compliant," "aggressive" and "detached" personality types. See K. Horney, *Our Inner Conflicts* (New York, 1945).

It should be noted that some of the "contradictions" in Wilson's character, often noted by contemporaries and biographers, can be understood in terms of the combination of trends, or types, of which his personality was composed.

16. See *WW & CH*, pp. 115–22.

17. I have omitted from this paper a discussion of the historian's method for explaining the "subjective" side of action (the "logic-of-the-situation" approach), and of the prospects for merging it with that of the clinician's. These prospects are not unfavorable, though the task is admittedly difficult. Both the historian and the clinician (as well as the political scientist!) are interested in intensive causal analysis of the single case and employ for this purpose a variant of the same type of interpretive procedure.

18. A useful, detailed summary of theories about the dynamics of behavior in compulsives is provided in Otto Fenichel, *The Psychoanalytic Theory of Neurosis* (New York, 1945), pp. 268–310, 487–88, 530–31.

19. On this point see also *WW & CH*, p. 320.

20. We must reserve for another occasion an effort to account for Wilson's development of a viable personality organization and the ability to function as successfully as he did.

21. The fact that there are various specialized terminologies within the field of dynamic psychology and that members of the various schools at times state their differences polemically tends to obscure the wide area of fundamental agreement among them and the fact that an important body of knowledge and insight into human behavior has been gradually developed around a common dynamic point of view. Moreover, dynamic psychology has based itself more recently upon a core of assumptions common to a number of approaches to the study of behavior: psychoanalysis, social anthropology, social psychology and learning theory. (See, for example, O.H. Mowrer and C. Kluckhohn, "Dynamic Theory of Personality," in J. McV. Hunt, ed., *Personality and the Behavior Disorders*, I (New York, 1944), pp. 69–135.)

22. These traits, comprising the so-called "anal" or "anal compulsive" character, are sometimes formulated in different terms as instances of sublimations or reaction formations. Freud's statement of the type appears in his "Character and Anal Erotism," *Collected Works*, II (London, 1950), pp. 45–50. For more recent formulations, see Fenichel, *loc. cit.*, especially pp. 278–84.

An important restatement and interpretation of Freud's libido theory is provided by Erik H. Erikson in his *Childhood and Society* (New York, 1950). See also the attempt to clarify and elaborate operationally the Freudian character types in Henry A. Murray, *Explorations in Personality* (New York, 1938), pp. 361–85.

23. For this purpose, in addition to the sources cited in the preceding footnote, see for example, William Healy and Augusta F. Bronner, *The Structure and Meaning of Psychoanalysis as Related to Personality and Behavior* (New York, 1930); William C. Menninger, "Characterologic and Symptomatic Expressions Related to the Anal Phase of Psychosexual Development," *Psychoanalytic Quarterly* 12, 1943: 161–93.

24. In the initial phase of our research we collected a large amount of evidence of the presence of most of these orderly traits in Wilson. Contemporaries and biographers have been impressed by various orderly traits in Wilson. For example, Wilson was "a stickler for accuracy" (David Lawrence, *The True Story of Woodrow Wilson*, p. 342); he had an extraordinary ability to concentrate and compartmentalize (Baker, *op. cit.*, II, p. 44) and himself often referred to his "single-track" mind (Alfred Maurice Low, *Woodrow Wilson—An Interpretation*, p. 282); he attempted to rigidly separate thinking and emotions and leaned over backwards to prevent private and personal considerations from interfering with public duties (Baker, *op. cit.*, II, p. 2; III, pp. 160–61; Edith Bolling Wilson, *My Memoir*, p. 162; Joseph Tumulty, *Woodrow Wilson As I Know Him*, pp. 473–74); he was pedantic, dogmatic and fastidious as a teacher (C. W. Mosher, Jr., "Woodrow Wilson's Methods in the Classroom," *Current History* 32 [June 1930]: 502–03; Baker, *op. cit.*, II, p. 13); he was reliable and scrupulous in keeping his word, no matter what the inconvenience (E. B. Wilson, *op. cit.*, p. 171; Tumulty, *op. cit.*, p. 469); his punctuality was well-known and it was said that one could set one's watch from his comings and goings (Eleanor Wilson McAdoo, *The Woodrow Wilsons*, pp. 22, 60, 213; Lawrence, *op. cit.*, p. 126); he was punctilious, thorough and methodical (Baker, *op. cit.*, I, pp. 86–87, 182; E. W. McAdoo, *op. cit.*, pp. 24, 188; E. B. Wilson, *op. cit.*, pp. 90, 307, 347; A. S. Link, *Wilson: The Road to the White House*, p. 94); he was strikingly neat, orderly and regular in personal working habits (Baker, *op. cit.*, II, p. 46; V, p. 138; E. W. McAdoo, *op. cit.*, p. 20; E. B. Wilson, *op. cit.*, p. 79).

25. The hypothesis that certain types of (compulsive or neurotic) personalities pursue power as a means of obtaining compensation for low self-esteem can be and has been divorced from the distinctive structural-dynamic framework and terminology of the Freudian school. Various versions of a similar hypothesis are provided by other schools of dynamic psychology.

26. In his personality profile of Wilson, Arthur S. Link, for example, identifies the following traits: a demand for unquestioning loyalty, egotism and a belief in the infallibility of his own judgment, vanity and a belief in his own superior wisdom and virtue, inability to rely upon others, indulgence in narrow prejudices and vindictiveness, intolerance of advice and resentment of criticism, a tendency to equate political opposition with personal antagonism, susceptibility to flattery. (*Wilson: The New Freedom*, pp. 67–68.) In his *Wilson: The Road to the White House*, the same biographer referred to his subject as possessing an "imperious will and intense conviction," a "headstrong and deter-

mined man who was usually able to rationalize his actions in terms of the moral law and to identify his position with the divine will" (p. ix).

In compulsives, too, an overevaluation and high development of the intellect is often found. At the same time, however, intellectualization is curiously combined with archaic features (superstitiousness and magical beliefs). It is noteworthy, therefore, that many writers (e.g., *ibid.*, p. 94) have been struck by the curious streak of superstitiousness in Wilson, a man otherwise noted for his emphasis on the intellect and on being guided by reason.

27. See, for example, Robert R. Sears, *Survey of Objective Studies of Psychoanalytic Concepts*, Social Science Research Council Bulletin 51, 1943, pp. 67–70.

28. Karen Horney, *The Neurotic Personality of Our Time* (New York, 1937); *Our Inner Conflicts* (New York, 1945).

29. H. D. Lasswell, *Power and Personality* (New York, 1948), pp. 44–49.

30. Some of these materials are presented in volume I (pp. 36 ff.) of Ray Stannard Baker, *Woodrow Wilson: Life and Letters* (New York, 1927). However, other relevant materials on Wilson's childhood, and, especially, on his relationship with his father were not included in the official biography and are to be found in the Baker Papers, Library of Congress. A fuller summary and interpretation of this material than is possible here is given in *WW & CH*, Chapter I.

31. The significance of this childhood developmental problem has been overlooked in the otherwise authoritative biography by Arthur S. Link. There is no reference to it in Link's account of Wilson's formative years. On the contrary, Link asserts that "Wilson's boyhood was notable, if for nothing else, because of his normal development." (*Wilson: The Road to the White House*, p. 2.) The fact of Wilson's "slowness" is also omitted in the biographies by Garraty and Blum, though it is mentioned (and glossed over) by Baker, *op. cit.*, I, pp. 36–37. The stern, domineering and caustic manner of Wilson's father, a source of acute tension and discomfort for Wilson, is also muted in Baker's published account, though not in the materials which Baker collected for his biography. (See the preceding footnote.)

32. A belated identification with his father appears to have accompanied Wilson's adoption of the compulsive dynamism at this time. The identification with the father was extremely strong on the manifest level and was rigidly maintained throughout Wilson's lifetime. At the same time, however, feelings of inferiority vis à vis the father, who had been the chief instrument of Wilson's damaged self-esteem, persisted throughout Wilson's life. For this and other reasons, accordingly, we have felt it necessary to postulate that the father-son conflict persisted in Wilson at an unconscious level. (Readers familiar with the technical literature will be reminded of the Freudian theory of the Oedipal basis of the inferiority complex.)

We have also postulated that aspects of Wilson's behavior in the struggles with Dean West and Senator Lodge constituted a displacement, or "acting out," of the unconscious hostility that he had experienced towards his father as a child but had not dared to express. (For a fuller statement of the thesis concerning the father-son relationship, see *WW & CH*, Chapter I, also pp. 46,

114–15, 270–73.) On the conditions under which Wilson's latent aggressive impulses could find overt expression against political opponents, see the discussion of "idealization," p. 90.

33. Baker, *op. cit.*, I.

34. Baker, *op. cit.*, I, pp. 45, 75–76, 94, 123–24, 148, 198–200, 302–03.

35. In more general terms we are asserting the possibility that personality needs and motives of an unconscious character may govern an individual's selection of social and political roles and that these needs and motives may infuse themselves into the individual's performance of those roles. The fact that a person's behavior *can* be interpreted in terms of role theory, therefore, does not relieve the investigator from considering the possibility that aspects of basic personality are also expressing themselves in such behavior. It is incorrect, therefore, to define the problem as some proponents of role theory tend to do in terms of "role *vs.* personality." Rather, the interplay of role and personality needs to be considered.

36. Baker, *op. cit.*, I, p. 199; *WW & CH*, p. 22.

37. *Ibid.*

38. See *WW & CH*, p. 144–48, 321–22.

39. *WW & CH*, p. xvii.

40. See *WW & CH*, p. 208–10, 223, 226–28.

41. This theory is a special application of a general hypothesis concerning the pursuit of power as a means of compensation for low self-estimates, which Harold D. Lasswell has extracted from the findings and theories of various schools of dynamic psychology. (See his *Power and Personality*, p. 39 ff.) The hypothesis is evidently of wide, though not universal, application in the study of political leaders.

We have discussed some of the problems of applying this general hypothesis to someone like Wilson, who pursued other values as well as power, in *WW & CH*, pp. 319–22, and in the paper, "Woodrow Wilson: Personality and Political Behavior," presented before a panel of the American Political Science Association, Washington, D.C., September, 1956.

As already noted, the pervasiveness of power strivings as compensation for organic or imagined defects was given early emphasis by Alfred Adler. The fruitfulness of Adler's theories for subsequent social psychological approaches to personality is now widely recognized. See, for example, Gardner Murphy, *op. cit.*, Chapter 24, "Compensation for Inferiority."

42. *Wilson: The Road to the White House*, p. 76.

43. See particularly Arthur S. Link, *Wilson: The Road to the White House*, and *WW & CH*, Chapters III and IV.

44. *WW & CH*, pp. 4–5.

45. Otto Fenichel, *Psychoanalytic Theory of Neurosis*, pp. 485–86.

46. Baker, *op. cit.*, II, p. 307.

47. *WW & CH*, pp. 290–98.

48. See, for example, Richard Hofstadter, *The American Political Tradition*, 2nd ed. (New York, 1954), pp. 281–82; Thomas A. Bailey, *Woodrow Wilson and the Great Betrayal* (New York, 1945).

49. Fenichel, *op. cit.*, p. 279.

50. *Ibid.*, p. 497. See also Christine Olden, "The Psychology of Obstinacy," *Psychoanalytic Quarterly* 12, (1943): 240–55.

51. *WW & CH*, pp. 297–98.

52. See, for example, Fenichel, *op. cit.*, p. 486.

53. It might be added that we have encountered no evidence that Wilson subsequently ever expressed or experienced any self-doubts as to the wisdom or correctness of his refusal to compromise in the struggle to ratify the peace treaty. On the contrary, his defeat and physical breakdown seem to have provided relief from the feelings of uneasiness experienced at the time.

54. It should be emphasized that whether, to what extent, and how often the self-defeating dynamism referred to here finds expression depends upon the character of the situations encountered by the subject during his lifetime. Similarly, we have postulated that this destructive tendency was held in check to some extent by the development in Wilson's personality system of a constructive strategy whereby he generally committed his need for domination and achievement only to political projects which were about ready for realization. (On this point, not discussed further in this paper, see *WW & CH*, pp. 118, 320–22.)

55. Arthur S. Link, *Wilson: The Road to the White House*, pp. 90–91. A similar observation is made by Blum, *op. cit.*, p. 36.

56. Edmund Wilson, "Woodrow Wilson at Princeton," reprinted in his *Shores of Light* (New York, 1952), p. 322.

57. "The Neurotic Character," *International Journal of Psychoanalysis* 11 (1930): 292–311. In contrast to true neurotics who squander their energy in futile inactivity, Alexander noted, persons of this character type live active and eventful lives, they "act out" repressed unconscious motives that are unacceptable to their ego. The neurotic element in such persons appears, that is, not so much in the form of circumscribed symptoms but permeates the personality and influences their entire behavior.

58. The following paragraphs are a brief paraphrase of materials presented in *WW & CH*, pp. 116–21, 320–22, and in a paper at the meetings of the American Political Science Association, Washington, D.C., September, 1956.

59. The italicized phrase is an important qualification to the general proposition. In the case of legislative proposals which were not "his" or to which he had not committed his aspirations for high achievement, for example the military "preparedness" legislation of 1915–16, Wilson was more flexible when confronted by effective Congressional opposition. (*WW & CH*, pp. 116, 121.)

60. *WW & CH*, pp. 38, 45; Chapter XIV, especially 286–89.

3

Writing Psychobiography: Some Theoretical and Methodological Issues

Alexander L. George and Juliette L. George

ONE OF THE REACTIONS that came from several quarters generally appreciative of *Woodrow Wilson and Colonel House: A Personality Study* was that our study of Wilson's personality and its effect on his political behavior would have been more incisive and in some respects different had we been guided by various psychodynamic theories that their respective proponents urged upon us.

In an article entitled "The Georges' Wilson Reexamined: An Essay on Psychobiography," Professor Robert Tucker of Princeton University argued that Karen Horney's writings on the neurotic personality better illuminate the data about Wilson presented in our book than Harold Lasswell's very general hypothesis, on which we had chosen to build.[1]

At academic meetings there were usually a few participants who told us that the key to understanding Wilson lies in the theories of Heinz Kohut and that we ought revise our work accordingly. A Chicago psychiatrist, Dr. Joseph Bongiorno, sent us his essay, "Woodrow Wilson Revisited: The Pre-political Years," in which he proposes that Wilson suffered problems in the regulation of tension and self-esteem that are better understood in terms of Kohut's studies of the self than through our interpretation.

Dr. H. L. Ansbacher, editor of the *Journal of Individual Psychology*, a publication devoted to the discussion of Alfred Adler's theories, wrote in a letter to us that he fully agreed with our interpretation, that indeed Lasswell's hypothesis closely resembles one of Adler's, a debt that Lasswell had only "to some extent" acknowledged. Ansbacher invited us to write about the common ground between Lasswell and Adler in the pages of his journal and urged us to make use of Adlerian concepts in our ongoing work.[2]

Admirers of Erik Erikson's thinking suggested to us that Erikson's formulations concerning the eight stages in the development of personality from infancy to maturity would have furnished us an excellent theoretical framework for studying Wilson's life. In particular, Erikson's elaboration of the impact on the developing personality of the manner in which the growing individual resolves the focal psychological conflict characteristic of each of the successive stages seemed to them especially suited to analyzing the available data about Wilson's boyhood and youth.

Many of the statements about Wilson's personality that were couched in the diverse language of differing psychodynamic theoretical systems seemed to us (and continue to seem) plausible. Moreover, we agree that an examination of the data about Wilson from different psychodynamic perspectives might indeed lead to deeper understanding of the man in all his complexity.

It may be useful at this point to say something about how our study came into being and how we set about our work. *Woodrow Wilson and Colonel House: A Personality Study* originated in a term paper that Alexander George (AG) wrote in 1941 for a graduate course in personality and politics taught by Nathan Leites at the University of Chicago. Leites and his colleague Harold Lasswell were promulgating the then novel idea that the insights of depth psychology are relevant to the study of political leadership.[3] Leites's lectures about psychoanalytic theory caught AG's interest. The case histories that Leites presented convinced him that this approach indeed added valuable insights into the behavior of the public figures under discussion. AG began to study psychoanalytic and related literature.

Leites's assignment to the class was to research the life of a political leader in order to assess the usefulness of examining his or her career in the light of depth psychological theory. AG decided to choose a U.S. president as his subject. His reading about various presidents led him first to consider studying Theodore Roosevelt. Then he encountered biographies and memoirs about Woodrow Wilson and was struck by the recognition that ran through them that at the supreme crisis of his public life—his battle with the U.S. Senate over ratification of the Versailles peace treaty, on which depended U.S. entry into the League of Nations—Wilson engaged in stubborn, self-defeating behavior obvious at the time to friend and foe, perplexing afterward to generations of historians, and of portentous impact on the course of world history. AG was struck also by the fact that Wilson's battle with the Senate in 1919 and 1920 was reminiscent of an equally bitter, peculiarly personal clash a decade earlier that had led to defeat and to his resignation as president of Princeton University. In that situation too, Wilson's refusal to compromise with those who disagreed with him seemed even to many of his friends to be driven by some inexplicable inner problem that thwarted the achievement of his own goals. AG decided to make Wilson the subject of his paper. Leites thought well of the result and urged him to expand it. World War II intervened. AG put his Wilson study aside and was otherwise occupied for the next several years.

In 1948, a few months after we were married, AG disinterred his term paper and invited Juliette George (JG) to have a look at it. Thus began our collaboration. There ensued several years of much reading of psychoanalytic and psychodynamic theory, which sensitized us to the kinds of data that would be relevant to our study of Wilson's development and led us to consider a variety of possible interpretations of his political behavior. We also continued the research that AG had begun in 1941, expanding it to include the most extensive manuscript collection then available to us about Wilson, the papers of Ray Stannard Baker at the Library of Congress.[4] We explored this rich and voluminous collection, which is still indispensable to Wilson scholars, for several years.

It was an exciting enterprise. The more we learned, the more finely detailed and more internally consistent a picture of Woodrow Wilson emerged that made more comprehensible his seemingly perplexing behavior during his battle at Princeton and later with the U.S. Senate over the League of Nations.

In 1950 we had the good fortune to be among the first to whom Charles Seymour, president emeritus of Yale University and curator of the papers of Edward M. House, granted access to Colonel House's diary. House had been Wilson's closest adviser and confidant throughout Wilson's first term as president of the United States and for most of his second term as well. In 1919 Wilson ended their friendship. The cause of the celebrated break occasioned the speculation of many journalists at the time and of historians in later years. Seymour had published four volumes of House's papers, including extensive portions of his diary. JG, who spent several months reading the complete diary and related manuscript materials in the House Collection in the Sterling Memorial Library at Yale, discovered that Seymour had omitted from his published volumes numerous passages of extraordinary interest. These unpublished passages of House's diary shed light on the dynamics of the relationship between the two men in a way that revealed Wilson's style of decisionmaking, the conditions under which he accepted advice, his unusually intense need of approval and affection and, in certain circumstances of idiosyncratic psychological significance, his unwillingness to share power and inability to yield to opponents.

By 1952 we felt that we had the makings of a book. The question of how best to convey the understanding that we thought we had achieved came to the fore. We knew that by and large historians would look askance at a biography of Woodrow Wilson that explicitly drew on psychoanalytic theory to interpret his behavior at critical junctures in his political career. Yet it was those who best knew the historical record that we most hoped would find our interpretation persuasive. We must write a readable narrative, free of jargon. We must so present our psychodynamically informed account that open-minded readers, especially historians and other social scientists, would find Wilson's behavior consistently comprehensible rather than puzzling, and a cause for pity at the self-induced defeat of a very great man.

Given the style that we had prescribed for ourselves, it was necessary to find a way of skirting the controversies in which, in the late 1940s and early 1950s, even as now, contending factions in the field of psychoanalysis were embroiled. Such analysts as Alfred Adler, Otto Rank, Karen Horney, Erich Fromm, Franz Alexander, Carl Rogers, Harry Stack Sullivan, Heinz Hartmann, and Erik Erikson, or their followers, in one way or another were amending, reformulating, or extending Freud's theories concerning methods of conducting therapy and also concerning human development. Orthodox Freudians continued to dominate the field, but even within that group, theoretical (not to mention personal!) rifts flourished. The disputes about therapeutic methods were not relevant to our project, but the burgeoning discussions of personality and how it develops and influences behavior were of central interest. We, who are neither psychoanalysts nor psychologists, were confronted with a variety of hypotheses in a veritable Babel of terminology, which was yet further expanded by the contributions of child psychologist/analysts (e.g., Piaget, Anna Freud), learning theorists (e.g., Neal Miller and John Dollard), and others who had incorporated some elements of psychoanalytic theory into their work.

Notwithstanding all the differing language and varied approaches, there runs through psychoanalytic theory some basic commonality of thought concerning the psychological development of human beings. It was these areas of agreement that Harold Lasswell captured in his very general, relatively nontechnical developmental hypothesis, which has special relevance to the study of political leaders.

In *Power and Personality*, Lasswell posits that under certain conditions an adolescent will develop an intense striving for power and achievement as a way of compensating for damage to self-esteem in childhood and as a way of coping with the tension induced by the child's experiencing at the hands of demanding parents severe deprivation on the one hand and extreme indulgence on the other.[5]

Lasswell characterizes such parents. They are likely to be "ambitious and loving," often middle-class professionals, especially "clergymen and teachers," whose homes are "hothouses of ambition, holding their children to high standards of achievement. . . . "[6] He elaborates the conditions that favor the emergence from such an environment of the person who seeks compensatory power: "*Compensation is favored when the deprivation is not overwhelming . . . [and] when they [deprivations] are accompanied by some indulgences.*"[7] If deprivations (punishments) too greatly outweigh indulgences (rewards), the child may react by withdrawing from active participation in human relationships rather than with compensatory strivings. Lasswell refines this point as follows:

> An essential factor is the balancing of deprivation by indulgence; and, more particularly, the tensions arising from extremes of both. Without a compensating flow of affection and admiration, deprivations may appear too overwhelming to justify the exertions necessary to acquire the skills essential to eventual success. . . . One of the tension-inducing environments is created when affection, respect and other values are (or are felt to be) contingent upon the acquisition and exercise of skills. . . .

A special form is given to this type of tension-inducing environment, Lasswell writes, "when the young person is exposed to a relatively elaborate set of requirements, which are rewarded or punished with special intensity. Almost all learning of set tasks gives rise to characteristic deprivations. One must practice grammar, for instance, at a set time whether one is in the mood or not."

What are the consequences of submitting to such requirements and inhibiting impulses to engage in play or other preferred activity? The young person often experiences "rage reactions, reactions which may never rise to full expression in what is said and done or even thought." And if not "even thought," additional tension develops, to cope with which defensive measures are taken, one such measure being to become rigid and compulsive.

What of such a young person's self-image? On the one hand, Lasswell writes, he may appear to himself "loving and admired." On the other, he may seem to himself to be "unloved, shameful, guilty and weak. Pessimism may rest on the idea that one is loved only 'conditionally'; that is, that love can only be received as part of a bargain or a battle."[8]

We found Lasswell's exposition remarkably descriptive of the familial environment in which Wilson grew up, a case of theory providing an excellent empirical fit with historical data. It had the virtue of cutting across and being at least compatible with many systems of psychoanalytic thought. We decided to cite Lasswell's hypothesis and write of Wilson's life in relatively nontechnical language. Such insight as our study of various psychodynamic theories had placed at our disposal would implicitly inform our narrative. The historical facts would be available to adherents of the different psychoanalytic schools of thought, and they, if they wished, could formulate interpretations cast in their preferred terms. In fact, as we have already indicated, this is what happened after the publication of our book.

Others can address more objectively than we the obvious question of whether and to what extent these reinterpretations cast new light on Wilson and deepen understanding of the impact of his personality on his political functioning. William Friedman has provided one such evaluation which seems to us to be fair-minded, constructive, and deserving of close scrutiny. He concludes that indeed "there is potential for new accounts of Wilson, stimulated by new theory," but he also cautions against "applying to a historical figure personality constructs that may be most applicable to contemporary character types." He notes that Jerrold Post offers an important reformulation that refines and adds to the Georges' thesis that Wilson saw in certain figures in his career (West, Lodge) the image of his father, and defied them as he wished he could have defied the original. Post adds to this—reflecting a contemporary "object relations" orientation, rather than the "drive theory" of classical Freudian analytical thinking—the concept that Wilson was not just reacting *against* his experience of his father, but was acting out his identification *with* him. . . . To this the Georges respond that "[Post's] discussion of the nature of Wilson's identification with his father . . . strikes us as having captured the truth. It accords with everything we know of the data and illuminates them."[9]

We should like to raise five issues relevant to assessing the relative merits of alternative psychodynamic explanations of the behavior of individuals who are subjects of psychodynamically oriented biography.

I. Are Alternative Psychodynamic Interpretations of a Leader Genuinely Different?

We suggest that it is useful to distinguish among three different types of explanations offered as alternative interpretations:

- First, formulations may be advanced as alternatives that are little more than translations of the original interpretation under consideration into the language of a preferred psychodynamic theory. Such a translation can have value if it is understood and conveyed as such.
- Second, an alternative interpretation or approach can be advanced that substantively adds to the model under consideration without undermining that model.
- Third (and most interesting), an alternative interpretation can be advanced that claims that some important part of, or the entire model under consideration is incorrect and needs to be replaced by a different one based on a particular psychodynamic theory.

Each of these three types of alternative interpretations can be useful, and the more so if those who offer them clarify both for themselves and for their readers which of the three they are putting forward. It seems to us that clarity on this point is often lacking.

II. Does the Alternative Interpretation Offer a Comprehensive Model of the Biographee's Personality, or Is the Alternative Narrower in Scope?

It is relatively easy to offer an ad hoc interpretation or reinterpretation of a particular circumscribed aspect of a biographee's personality and behavior. Again, such an effort gains in utility if its limited nature is explicitly recognized. Both more difficult and more useful is to offer a comprehensive model of the biographee's personality and demonstrate that this model resolves apparent behavioral inconsistencies and can explain the biographee's behavior as a whole, successes as well as failures.

We attempted to develop such a model of Wilson's personality, one that has explanatory power as to both his successful performance as a political leader *and* the repetitive (infrequently triggered but disastrous) pattern of self-induced defeat. The same personality model enabled us to make sense of the perplexing contradictions and inconsistencies in his political behavior—the fact that in *certain* situations he could shrewdly identify his objectives and behave opportunistically (despite his strict Presbyterian conscience!) to accomplish them, whereas in certain other situations in which cherished goals were at stake aspects of that *same* personality contributed to deficient reality testing, poor judgment, rigidity, and ruinous stubbornness that contributed to defeat.[10]

We do not think that there has yet appeared a fully developed alternative to our psychodynamic interpretation of Wilson. Were we in a position to redo our study, we think we might choose to draw also on Erik Erikson's theory of human development.

Friedman, in his article, points to the value of some of the alternative psychodynamic interpretations of Wilson that have been suggested, but he also points to some of the difficulties that in his judgment their proponents have not surmounted. For example, he notes that whereas "the Georges seem most interested in understanding Wilson psychodynamically and are willing to use whatever theoretical constructs seem to work best," Joseph Bongiorno "is trained in Kohut's theory, and has already decided which is the most advanced psychological theory. . . . " In "Woodrow Wilson Revisited," Friedman suggests, Bongiorno "is using Wilson as an exercise in applied [Kohutian] self-psychology. . . . It is probably fair to say that, in addition to scholarly judgment, there are myriad factors that make particular psychological theories 'ego syntonic' . . . [and] there are subtle ways in which theoretical favoritism can color a particular argument. . . . In Bongiorno's excellent paper, in the several places where he compares oedipal level interpretations to self-psychological ones, it is clear that his scholarly passion is in the latter. The former are not presented in a distorted manner, but they are bland, without creative juice, and this casts a particular tone to the comparison."[11]

III. Must a Psychodynamically Oriented Biography Attempt to Identify the Origins of the Subject's Behavior Patterns?

The answer, we believe, is no. Often data are lacking even to speculate sensibly as to the etiology of certain readily observable personality traits or patterns. Sometimes, however, the data seem so compelling that even though proof is never possible, cautious speculation as to etiology, presented as speculation, is legitimate and interesting.

We worked with the familiar model in psychodynamic psychology that identifies and attempts to link three levels of observation and analysis:

- At the first level, the subject's "presenting" or manifest behavioral characteristics can be observed and described. To present a good description of a political leader's readily discernible behavior is in itself a useful contribution. Indeed, it may be the most appropriate effort in the case of living political figures, where questions of privacy and good taste are involved.
- At the second level, the data may permit a description of the psychodynamic patterns that appear to underlie various aspects of manifest behavior.
- At the third level, which is the most difficult and problematical to address, possible developmental causes for the patterns of behavior identified at the second level may be suggested.[12]

In a paper (written in 1960, published in 1971, and reproduced as Chapter 2 in this book), AG made the commonplace point that identifying a biographee's readily observable personality characteristics is a much easier task for the biographer than that of identifying or inferring the underlying psychodynamic patterns, and that, in turn, is less precarious than venturing to suggest the etiology of the psychodynamic patterns. He also noted that it is fallacious to assume that a one-to-one linear relationship exists between the first level (manifest behavior) and either of the other two levels. Thus, for example, as noted in Chapter 2, readily observable stubbornness can have a variety of psychodynamic explanations as well as explanations that are *not* psychodynamic in character.

From a methodological standpoint, it is important for the biographer to take great care when attempting to infer from a subject's "presenting characteristics" what the underlying psychodynamic patterns might be, let alone when venturing to suggest what the etiology of those patterns might be. In the absence of sufficient data, or when dealing with a living subject, the biographer may well decide not to attempt the deepest (i.e., the third) level of analysis. It may be best to go no further than suggesting what the subject's psychodynamic patterns are without speculating about their cause.

Readers may wonder how it happened that we, who had all of the preceding caveats firmly in mind, ventured into the minefield of the third level of analysis and had the temerity in *Woodrow Wilson and Colonel House* to suggest the etiology of the personality dynamisms that brought Wilson to such grief during the two great crises of his career. We did not do it lightly. In fact, for several months we debated about whether or not to suggest that underlying Wilson's overtly idyllic relationship with his exceedingly demanding father there may have been a deep, unconscious ambivalence that ultimately found expression in Wilson's intransigence and defeat in his peculiarly personal battles with Dean Andrew Fleming West at Princeton and later with Henry Cabot Lodge in the U.S. Senate over ratification of the Treaty of Versailles. (The treaty, of course, contained Wilson's supremely prized Covenant of the League of Nations. Its defeat agonized him.)

This third level of "deep" interpretation constituted the most hypothetical interpretive leap to be found in our book. For the rest, we settled for a relatively "shallow" personality model of the development and workings of Wilson's personality, one that permitted easy linkage of theory to available historical data. In his article, Friedman correctly represents our view when he observes that our "shallow" model "assumes that it is not necessary to have insights into the most buried and primitive layers of Wilson's unconscious in order to sufficiently understand his political dynamics." We also accept Friedman's observation that our interpretation "can only be considered relatively, not absolutely, non-technical" since it reflects "a somewhat more classical psychoanalytical orientation."[13]

The central concepts of our personality model were "self" and "self-esteem" which, indeed, are important concepts in all psychodynamic theories. Lasswell's focus on damaged self-esteem and efforts to compensate for it made his developmental hypothesis particularly useful as a major element in our "shallow" model of Wilson's personality.

Our study of the Wilson materials prompted AG to elaborate on Lasswell's general developmental model. Lasswell had noted that the individual seeking power or bent on some other great achievement as a way of overcoming low self-estimates must develop skills appropriate to the attainment of the chosen objective. AG added to this that successful compensation for damaged self-esteem requires an individual to develop a "sphere of competence." Evidence abounds of the determination and iron discipline with which during his adolescence and early adulthood Wilson applied himself to the task of developing the skills and knowledge that would equip him to become a political leader and fulfill his longing, as he once put it in a letter to his wife, "to do immortal work."[14]

The boy who did not learn his letters until he was nine years old assiduously practiced writing, penmanship as well as composition, until he perfected a style that even his demanding father found it possible to compliment. The boy who could not read until he was eleven and suffered the humiliation of being at the bottom of his class at school studied history books, read biography, plowed through mountains of dull texts in order to become a lawyer—all to prepare himself for the greatness to which he aspired. We referred to this as Wilson's carving out for himself a "sphere of competence" and noted that doing so and performing well within that sphere enabled him to replace the low self-estimates of his childhood with self-confidence and high self-estimates. This revised self-image, as we see it, was serviceable in most circumstances but, because of its compensatory nature, vulnerable in circumstances that awakened the feelings of inadequacy that had dogged him throughout his childhood and adolescence.[15]

Ample evidence exists that Wilson's father was a powerful, often intimidating figure, a perfectionist concerned about the early seeming
backwardness of his, at that time, only son ("Josie" was not born until
"Tommy" was almost eleven), a man with a stinging wit that sometimes targeted young "Tommy," and an erudite man who loved the
English language and drilled his son in its correct usage. Ample evidence also exists that Wilson considered himself inferior in many
ways to "my incomparable father." Even in adulthood he referred to
his father as superior to himself in looks, as a writer and speaker, and
in accomplishment.[16]

It was our judgment that the data about Wilson's childhood nicely
"fit" Lasswell's hypothesis about the psychological circumstances that
foster the adoption by an adolescent of the compensation mechanism
and, further, that the data about Wilson's adolescence just as power-
fully indicate that in fact he *did* adopt the compensation mechanism.
Given that Lasswell's hypothesis and the data that so richly support it
both resonate with so many other psychodynamic formulations about
human development, JG became convinced that Wilson's damaged
self-esteem had its origins in his relationship with his loving, well-
meaning, but overly strict and demanding father. Though he felt that
this interpretation truly "fit," AG was for some time reluctant to include it in our narrative. We both knew that it would be a lightning
rod for wrathful criticism, but we eventually agreed that Wilson's was
one of the doubtless rare cases in which the historical data justify the
articulation of a conjecture, identified as such, about etiology. With
this and the other interpretations that we offered throughout the book
in mind we wrote in *Woodrow Wilson and Colonel House:*

> The validity of the foregoing interpretation and of others that follow is
> necessarily a matter of opinion. No incontrovertible proof can be offered.
> Nor can any one incident be relied upon to sustain this or any other the-
> ory of Wilson's motivation. It is only when the man's career is viewed as
> a whole that a repetition of certain basically similar behavior is dis-
> cernible. Let the reader consider whether these patterns of behavior be-
> come more consistently comprehensible in terms of the explanations
> herein offered than in terms of other explanations. That will be the best
> test of their usefulness.[17]

We also said:

> If Dr. Wilson [Wilson's father] was a martinet, there were other facets to
> his personality as well. He could be full of fun. There are tales of tag be-

tween the dignified minister and his young son, the participants progressing noisily from the study to the garden, to the delighted consternation of the female contingent of the family. The two played chess and billiards together. They took long walks and Dr. Wilson spoke to the boy without condescension of his hopes and problems. He was free in his expression of affection. He often greeted his son with a kiss. 'My Precious Son,' his letters generally began. His ambition for his son was boundless. Long before it seemed likely that Wilson would enter politics, Dr. Wilson regarded him as presidential timber. . . .

Dr. Wilson communicated to his son a solid sense of belonging, both to a religious tradition and to his family. He truly nurtured his son, perhaps unwisely in some respects, but with an unflinching acceptance of his responsibilities. It is a fact of fundamental significance that Dr. Wilson's strict training of his son was conducted in the context of genuine concern for the boy and pride in him. If it is necessary in order to understand some of Wilson's later difficulties to postulate a subterranean hostility between Wilson and his father, it is certainly also necessary in order to understand the man as a whole, to underscore the positive influence of the elder Wilson.[18]

Notwithstanding all the controversy that our admittedly speculative treatment of Wilson's relationship with his father engendered, we continue to believe that we were justified in writing as we did. We continue to believe that our level-three hypothesis reflects a truth that is central to understanding Woodrow Wilson.

IV. Avoiding Reductionism

However relevant the above-described three-level model, the theoretical framework it provides is not broad enough for studying the role that personality plays in a leader's performance in the political arena. What needs to be added are *institutional* variables, *situational* variables, and those aspects of the *political culture* that the leader has internalized during the course of his or her political socialization or that affect his or her performance even if not internalized. Institutional variables and political culture shape the *role requirements* of leadership positions to which the individual must adapt in some way. In addition, role requirements and the manner in which the leader understands and complies with them are sensitive to situational variables.[19]

It is useful, indeed necessary, to consider the "fit"—or lack of fit—between, on the one hand, different aspects of an individual's personality and style and, on the other, particular role requirements of the leadership position that he or she occupies or has occupied. A leader's personality "fits" some role requirements of the position better than it does other role requirements. A leader is likely to be energized when experiencing a good "fit" with certain role requirements and is apt to spend more time and energy in fulfilling these than in trying to satisfy less congenial requirements of the position.

Creative leaders often attempt to reshape institutions and roles to make them more suited to their personality needs, leadership skills, and strengths. From an early age Wilson, for example, rewrote the constitutions of the many clubs to which he belonged. His goal was to convert them into parliamentary-type institutional structures within which the oratorical skills that he had assiduously cultivated could be used to greatest advantage as a means of gaining and exercising leadership. The Covenant of the League of Nations was but the last of several constitutions he devoted himself to composing.

Why do we emphasize the need to broaden the theoretical framework within which to undertake the enormously complex task of understanding the role of personality in a political leader's public behavior? It is because not to do so increases the likelihood of focusing too narrowly on the relevance of psychological theories for explanation and lapsing unwittingly into psychological reductionism. The resulting work will present a caricature of the biographical subject and will fail to illuminate the historical data, to which it will have a faulty (if any) connection.

A similar danger arises when medical specialists attempt to apply their medical knowledge to historical materials. In an essay (invited by Professor Arthur S. Link, editor of *The Papers of Woodrow Wilson*, and published in volume 58 of that series) about the possible impact of illness on Wilson during the peace negotiations in Paris following World War I, Dr. Bert Park, himself a medical specialist, explicitly warns against "the risk of falling prey to retrospective medical reductionism."[20] He notes that his extensive review of the extant sources on Wilson's performance at the Paris Peace Conference "casts doubt on the supposition" that Wilson's health problems "adversely affected what transpired" or "impacted negatively on what was agreed to [by Wilson] at Paris."[21] Although Park does not name the scholars guilty of medical reductionism, he clearly dissociates himself from efforts by Link and his longtime medical guru, Dr. Edwin A. Weinstein, a neurologist, to find a medical explanation for what they considered to be inadequacies and flaws in Wilson's diplomacy in Paris. As Park put it,

"Contrary to previous accounts (including my own), the evidence does not then conclusively support the hypothesis that illness [Wilson's bout with influenza in early April 1919] played a major role in any of the alleged concessions Wilson made to the Allies during this period. . . . "[22]

Park also examined the evidence presented by Link and his coeditors in *The Papers of Woodrow Wilson* that "from late April to about mid-May 1919 . . . Wilson was undergoing some kind of crisis in his health." It was, they claimed, "so serious that, at times, it rendered him incompetent." They suggest that at a meeting of the Big Four on May 1, he was "in a daze and did not know what was going on," and that on May 8, in the midst of a speech, he "became disoriented" and "forgot where he was." The editors suspected "a 'slight' stroke, or lacunar infarction, on or about April 28, and additional bleeding in the brain during the next two weeks or so." Park concluded that this proposition "falls short of the necessary criteria to argue the case with conviction."[23] (Having studied the record of Wilson's activities day by day during that period as well as collateral data, we cannot refrain from adding that Park's mild statement must rank among the most tactful and notable understatements in academic literature.)

We think that Park is a courageous truth-seeker and that his essay performs a signal service in questioning the validity of Link and Weinstein's too-confidently expressed opinion that Wilson was in an impaired mental state during the negotiation of the Treaty of Versailles. We further believe, however, that Park's conclusion that by May 1919 Wilson can be diagnosed as suffering from dementia relies heavily on so-called evidence that Wilson's behavior underwent morbid "changes" and that he engaged in medically significant bizarre behavior in Paris.[24] We believe that the "changes" and allegedly strange behavior are myths that, variously proposed and embraced by Link and Weinstein, have become firmly entrenched in the secondary literature and continue to mislead conscientious scholars, such as Park.

We believe that Link himself has been misled by Weinstein over the years and that Weinstein has done egregious disservice to Wilson scholarship by persistently presenting as historical *fact* his mere *conjecture* that Wilson suffered strokes dating back to 1896 that adversely affected his political behavior at various critical junctures in his career.

Perhaps one day scholars with no involvement in today's differences of view will fully examine the rich historical materials that document

Wilson's life from his youth to his death (including much manuscript material that, understandably, because of constraints of space, does not appear in *The Papers of Woodrow Wilson*). Perhaps they will emerge to render thoroughly grounded accounts that will serve to validate or invalidate some of this generation's interpretations of Wilson, or perhaps to advance new ones the nature of which no one can foretell.

V. Formulating and Testing Hypotheses

A problem arises from the failure of many psychobiographical efforts to deal adequately with the basic distinction between hypothesis formation and hypothesis testing. Indeed, a biographer can employ *any* theory—psychological, medical, "bureaucratic politics," or anything else that he or she believes to be a source of insight—to generate interesting (and often beguiling) hypotheses. Biographers, including psychobiographers, face a more difficult task when it comes to assessing and testing the hypotheses so generated.

All too often one sees in psychobiography the absence of a serious effort to evaluate the validity of a hypothesis that has been imported from a prestigious psychological theory and used to explain some aspect of the biographee's behavior. The distinction between hypothesis formation and hypothesis testing has been blurred. The biographer's subjective certainty of the validity of a particular hypothetical explanation is confused with, and substituted for, the task of addressing the requirements for testing that hypothesis. This shortcoming helps to account for the frequently heard criticism that biographies influenced by psychodynamic theory are much too speculative, that is, that they contain interpretations of (or worse, flat assertions about) the biographee's behavior without convincing evidence that the biographer has subjected them to a disciplined assessment.

The biographer sensitive to psychodynamic theory and prepared to undertake the arduous task of using it to best advantage must understand and make use of techniques for developing promising hypotheses. As noted in Chapter 1, this involves the biographer's ability to *empathize* with the subject (a process similar to that employed by psychoanalysts as they seek to discern the inner feelings of patients), to be aware of and manage *countertransference* reactions, and to maintain that *detachment* from the subject necessary for the rigorous evaluation of the hunches, guesses, and hypotheses that this process engenders. We shall consider each of these requirements in turn.

The psychobiographer proceeds to the task of forming hypotheses about the behavior of the biographee by empathizing with that individual. Many historians, too, have long recognized the need to empathize with biographees in order to gain insight into their behavior. In *Laws and Explanation in History*, William Dray writes of a widely, though not unanimously, shared view among his colleagues that the historian

> must *penetrate* behind appearances, achieve *insight* into the situation, *identify* himself sympathetically with the protagonist, *project* himself imaginatively into his situation. He must *revive, reenact, re-think, re-experience* the hopes, fears, plans, desires, views, intentions, &c., of those he seeks to understand.[25]

Characterizing Sir Herbert Butterfield's views as representative of the views of a large group of his colleagues, Dray then quotes from Butterfield's *History and Human Relations* regarding personalities of the past:

> Our traditional historical writing . . . insists that the story cannot be told correctly unless we see the personalities from the inside, feeling with them as an actor might feel the part he is playing—thinking their thoughts over again and sitting in the position not of the observer but of the doer of the action. If it is argued that this is impossible—as indeed it is—not merely does it still remain the thing to aspire to, but in any case the historian must put himself in the place of the historical personage, must feel his predicament, must think as though he were that man. Without this art not only is it impossible to tell the story correctly but it is impossible to interpret the very documents on which the reconstruction depends.[26]

By *empathizing* with the individual under study, therefore, the analytically oriented biographer and the conventional historian each tries to gain insight into the personality and behavior of that individual. Each will begin to guess under what circumstances this individual behaves in particular ways, and each may begin to speculate about the more ambitious question—the *cause* of a particular act or pattern of behavior. In short, each will begin to develop hypotheses that subjectively ring true.

Assuming that both scholars are dedicated to the truth and that both are excellent researchers who bring to their work ever-increasing

knowledge of the details of the subject's life and of the external circumstances in which that individual acts, we suggest that the one who
has absorbed the findings of depth psychology is likely to be the more
successful in generating broadly perceptive hypotheses. The reason is
that the psychoanalytically aware biographer presumably will be familiar with the phenomenon of *countertransference* and with the problem that misperceptions of a biographee may arise from a biographer's reactions to the data. The analytically informed biographer
who has good insight into his or her own inner world and the wish to
eliminate obstacles to true understanding of the life being studied is
more likely to recognize, examine, and correct such misperceptions
than the biographer who has not contemplated these matters.

Further, the psychologically informed biographer brings to the task
knowledge of a discipline that has explored the role of the unconscious in human behavior as well as the relation of childhood experience to adult conduct. That biographer is likely to be more sensitive
than the conventional historian to clues that may indicate the unconscious sources of overt behavior. The biographee may have been entirely unaware of the wellspring of certain of his or her actions and attitudes, having repressed the knowledge, but if the data permit, a
biographer free of the biographee's anxieties may be able to form impressions of the subject's deeper motivations.

Even while empathizing with the biographee, the analytically oriented biographer is aware of the necessity of maintaining the *detachment* that enables reality-based evaluation of the validity of the hypotheses that he or she has formed concerning the behavior of the
biographee. As indicated earlier, an important component of that detachment is a self-awareness—ideally, ever present—that enables the
biographer to "see" the biographee accurately, without subjective dis-
tortion.

In summary: The better the ability of the biographer to empathize
with the subject, to discipline empathy with detachment, and to avoid
the misperceptions and misinterpretations arising from countertransference reactions, the better is likely to be the quality of the working
hypotheses that emerge from this process.

Though of great help to the biographer in formulating hypotheses,
psychoanalytic and other psychodynamic theories are of little help
when it comes to the critically important task of testing those hypotheses. In the clinical setting, the therapist's hypotheses (advanced as in-

terpretations) may be validated by the patient's recognition that the interpretation "fits" and illuminates some aspect of a theretofore unperceived aspect of his or her behavior or feeling. The psychobiographer's subject, on the other hand, is not available for such direct interaction. Only data concerning that person's life are available. It is indeed on the data themselves that the biographer must rely to confirm or invalidate the various hunches, conjectures and hypotheses formed in the course of becoming familiar with the biographee's life. The biographer must comb and recomb through the facts of the biographee's life to determine whether they "fit" and thus validate a particular hypothesis. If the facts do *not* fit, the hypothesis must be discarded or, if the mismatch is minor enough to lend itself to that possibility, it must be refined. The biographer must continue to subject his or her hunches, conjectures, and hypotheses to rigorous scrutiny until, through a process of constant refinement of the theoretical structure that thus evolves, there remain no data about the biographee's behavior that defy subsumption into that structure. At that point, some truth about the biographee will have been attained. Through the repetition of this painstaking process a diligent biographer will attempt to learn many truths that, in sum, afford a measure of genuine understanding of the biographee.

In the foregoing, we have described an ideal biographer, one possessed of great knowledge both of depth psychology and history, one of absolute integrity, uncommon wisdom, and dedication solely to the discovery and presentation of the truth, no matter how many years such an endeavor takes. In reality, we know of no biographer who has entirely succeeded in living up to these standards. To strive to do so, however, is worthy of any scholar's best efforts.

Notes

1. Robert C. Tucker, "The Georges' Wilson Reexamined: An Essay on Psychobiography," *American Political Science Review,* vol. 71 (June 1977), 606–618.

2. Letter from H. L. Ansbacher, editor of the *Journal of Individual Psychology,* to Alexander George, March 14, 1967.

3. See Harold D. Lasswell, *Psychopathology and Politics* (Chicago: University of Chicago Press, 1930).

4. In 1949 we sought access to the Wilson papers. Wilson's widow, Edith Bolling Wilson, denied our application. Shortly before publication of our book, Katherine Brand, Mrs. Wilson's representative in the Manuscript Divi-

sion of the Library of Congress, allowed us to read through the folders containing what she assured us was all the information then in the Wilson papers about Wilson's childhood. The contents of those folders merely confirmed information that we had obtained from other sources. Since Mrs. Wilson's death, the Wilson papers have become available to researchers and, of course, we have studied them.

5. Harold Lasswell, *Power and Personality* (New York: W. W. Norton & Company, 1948), 39, 44–45.

6. Ibid., 43, 47–48.

7. Ibid., 40–41; italics in original.

8. Ibid., 44–46.

9. William Friedman, "*Woodrow Wilson and Colonel House* and Political Psychobiography," *Political Psychology*, vol. 15, no. 1 (March 1994), 35–59. For the passage quoted, see 51–52, 55–56.

10. See Alexander L. George and Juliette L. George, *Woodrow Wilson and Colonel House: A Personality Study* (New York: The John Day Company, 1956; Dover Publications, 1964), Dover edition, 57–59, 61–63, 71–72, chapter 7, and the "Research Note," 319–322. See also Alexander L. George, "Power as a Compensatory Value for Political Leaders," *Journal of Social Issues*, vol. 24, no. 3 (July 1968), 38–43; and Alexander L. George, "Some Uses of Dynamic Psychology in Political Biography: Case Materials on Woodrow Wilson," in Fred I. Greenstein and Michael Lerner, eds., *A Sourcebook for the Study of Personality and Politics* (Chicago: Markham Publishing Company, 1971), 78–98. The latter essay appears in this book as Chapter 2.

11. Friedman, *op. cit.*, 49–50. Friedman regards Robert Tucker's essay as "a good example of the Georges' relatively non-technical formulations being translated into a preferred theory" (i.e., into Karen Horney's theory.)

12. These three levels of analysis, identified in Alexander L. George, "Some Uses of Dynamic Psychology," were elaborated in much useful detail by Fred Greenstein in his important work, *Personality and Politics: Problems of Evidence, Inference, and Conceptualization* (Chicago: Markham Publishing Company, 1969), chapter Three, 63–93.

13. Friedman, *op. cit.*, 47, 49.

14. Ray Stannard Baker, *Woodrow Wilson: Life and Letters* (New York: Doubleday, Page, 1927) vol. 1, 242. AG first articulated the concept of carving out a sphere of competence and its applicability to Wilson's development in an unpublished seminar paper at the University of Chicago in 1950, then in a paper given at the annual meetings of the American Political Science Association in 1956, and finally in Alexander L. George, "Some Uses of Dynamic Psychology in Political Biography," in Fred I. Greenstein and Michael Lerner, eds., *A Sourcebook for the Study of Personality and Politics*, 88–89. See also Alexander L. George, "Power as a Compensatory Value for Political Leaders," 38–40.

15. Another addition that AG made to Lasswell's general model was to call attention to the fact that the compensatory mechanism adopted by Wilson in his adolescence persisted as a psychodynamic pattern in his political decision-making as an adult. In "Power as a Compensatory Value for Political Lead-

ers," 46–47, AG noted the characteristic replacement of low self-estimates and uncertainty during the initial phase of Wilson's decisionmaking process with high self-estimates, often bordering on arrogant self-confidence, regarding the correctness and morality of his eventual decision. The similarity of AG's concept of "carving out a sphere of competence" to Erikson's resolution of the identity crisis could occur to us only later, when we became familiar with his theory of the stages of psychosocial development.

16. Ray Stannard Baker, *op. cit.*, 31, 46; Alexander L. George and Juliette L. George, *Woodrow Wilson and Colonel House*, 6; Alexander L. George, "Power as a Compensatory Value for Political Leaders," 34.

17. Alexander L. George and Juliette L. George, *Woodrow Wilson and Colonel House*, 12.

18. Ibid., 12–13. There are now many accounts of Wilson's childhood and adolescence. We continue to admire most the chapters written by Wilson's first great biographer, Ray Stannard Baker, because they convey so empathically both the warmth of the Wilson household and the intimidating demands that were made on young "Tommy." See Baker, *op. cit.*, vol. 1, 28–80. See also John M. Mulder, *Woodrow Wilson: The years of Preparation* (Princeton: Princeton University Press, 1978).

19. The following discussion is based on Alexander L. George, "Assessing Presidential Character," *World Politics*, vol. 26, no. 2 (January 1974), 234–282. This article is reproduced as Chapter 5 of this book.

20. In Arthur S. Link et al., eds., *The Papers of Woodrow Wilson* (Princeton: Princeton University Press, 1966–1994), vol. 58, 621, 630.

21. Ibid., 627, 630.

22. Ibid., 625.

23. Ibid., vol. 56, 558; vol. 58, 278, 600, 606, 629.

24. We comment briefly in Chapter 4 on these widely disseminated stories. We have a fuller discussion in preparation.

25. William Dray, *Laws and Explanation in History* (London: Oxford University Press, 1957), 119.

26. Ibid., quoting from Sir Herbert Butterfield, *History and Human Relations* (New York: Macmillan, 1952), 145–146. See also 116–117.

4

Woodrow Wilson and Colonel House: A Reply to Weinstein, Anderson, and Link

Juliette L. George and Alexander L. George

PROFESSOR ARTHUR S. LINK of Princeton University has devoted some forty years to the study of Woodrow Wilson's life. He is Editor of *The Papers of Woodrow Wilson* of which, through 1980, thirty-five volumes had been published. He has authored five volumes, with more projected, of a widely acclaimed biography of Woodrow Wilson, as well as a number of books about various aspects of Wilson's career. Professor Link, by common consent, is the pre-eminent Wilson scholar of our time. It behooves any authors whose interpretations of Wilson Professor Link finds sadly wanting to re-examine their work in the light of his criticisms. Such authors are we, whose *Woodrow Wilson and Colonel House: A Personality Study*[2] Professor Link, Dr. Edwin A. Weinstein (a psychiatrist and neurologist who has been studying and writing about Wilson for almost fifteen years), and Professor James William Anderson (a clinical psychologist) jointly pronounced, in an article in *Political*

Juliette George presented this paper at the fourth annual meeting of the International Society of Political Psychology, Mannheim, Germany, June 22–June 27, 1981. It is published here in full for the first time. A condensation appeared in the Winter 1981–1982 issue of *Political Science Quarterly*. Copyright © 1998 Alexander L. George and Juliette L. George.

Science Quarterly, "an essentially incorrect interpretation of the personality of Woodrow Wilson and its effect on his career."[3]

Over the past two years, therefore, we have reviewed our work, and incorporated into our research a great deal of manuscript material that has become available since publication of *Woodrow Wilson and Colonel House.* This review in the light of all the evidence, old and new, has served to confirm our belief, notwithstanding the criticisms levelled at us by Weinstein, Anderson, and Link, in the essential validity of the interpretation of Wilson that we offered in *Woodrow Wilson and Colonel House.* Indeed, the data now available permit a much fuller delineation of the relationship between Wilson and his father—of the extraordinary bond that existed between them, the very intensity of which, in our view, is related to the intensity of Wilson's early self-doubt, his suffering and need for approval (all of which now also may be more fully documented). We continue to view Wilson as a great tragic figure whose "tragic flaw"—a ruinously self-defeating refusal to compromise with his opponents—evolved out of low self-estimates that we believe (though, as we have always freely conceded, such a proposition is not susceptible of conclusive proof) he developed as a child in response to his father's demands.

We consider it unfortunate, moreover, that Weinstein, Anderson, and Link present as though it were an indisputable fact Dr. Weinstein's mere *hypothesis*—a hypothesis that is demonstrably controversial amongst physicians—that Woodrow Wilson suffered strokes dating back to 1896 and, further, that these alleged strokes produced brain damage that significantly and adversely affected his political functioning even so early as during his Princeton presidency. Much more serious in our judgment than such statements in the pages of *Political Science Quarterly,* however, is the fact that Professor Link has permitted himself to state unequivocally in numerous notes and other editorial apparatus in various volumes of *The Papers of Woodrow Wilson* that Wilson suffered small strokes in 1896 and 1907 and a "major stroke" in 1906.[4] We believe he has thereby compromised the objectivity and therefore the value to historians, both present and future, of that otherwise superb series.

Woodrow Wilson and Colonel House, Weinstein, Anderson, and Link state:

> . . . suffers from three major deficiencies, which, taken together, result in an inaccurate portrayal of Wilson's personality. The principal failing of the book is that the research on which it rests is inadequate. Second, the Georges fail to recognize the limitations of their psychological model and

misrepresent evidence to fit their theory. Third, they ignore Wilson's neurological disorders as conditions affecting his behavior.[5]

We shall address these criticisms in turn.

I. Source Materials for *Woodrow Wilson and Colonel House*

Weinstein, Anderson, and Link disparage our research—*Woodrow Wilson and Colonel House* furnishes "'deep' interpretations of the work of others."[6] In our book, we characterize our work as "largely a synthesis and reinterpretation of well-known facts of Wilson's career."[7] Even at the time we were gathering data in the 1940s and 1950s a voluminous literature about Wilson was available. We acknowledge that we combed through it assiduously and extracted a great deal of useful information. We did not claim to be historians nor was it our aim to uncover new data: rather, we hoped to cast a fresh eye on that which was already known. Further, we are willing to argue that there is a legitimate place for interpretive historical studies based on secondary sources. However, that would be a digression. For the fact is that we were unwilling to rely only on secondary sources. We were concerned with the possibility that other writers might have overlooked or discarded information that we might find significant. We therefore decided to study primary source materials too.

The three principal relevant manuscript collections were: the Wilson papers at the Library of Congress, the papers of Ray Stannard Baker at the Library of Congress, and the papers of Colonel House at the Sterling Memorial Library at Yale University. Access to the Wilson papers was controlled at that time by Wilson's widow, who was notoriously chary of granting access to scholars. We applied in 1949 and were promptly turned down because, Katharine E. Brand (Mrs. Wilson's representative in the Manuscript Division of the Library of Congress) told us, our approach did not commend itself to Mrs. Wilson. We periodically renewed our request and finally, when our study was almost complete, were allowed to read a series of documents which, Miss Brand assured us, was all the collection contained for the years of Wilson's childhood and youth. We found little of significance in what we were allowed to see that Baker had not already published.

Miss Brand herself, who had been Baker's assistant for many years and was his literary executor, had charge of his papers and she granted us access to them. We studied the Baker papers over a period of years, to the great enrichment of our comprehension of Woodrow Wilson. For Baker, with Mrs. Wilson's help, had collected the reminiscences of scores of Wilson's family, friends and associates. Baker's commitment to seeking the truth about Wilson illuminates his correspondence, his journal, indeed the whole record of his prodigious work. His papers remain an indispensable source for Wilson researchers.

Access to Colonel House's papers was controlled by Charles Seymour, President-Emeritus of Yale, who after his retirement became curator of the House Collection. Shortly after Mr. Seymour announced that Colonel House's diary would be open to scholars, we applied for permission, which he granted, to read it, and spent the first half of 1951 doing so. We[8] came to the House papers eager to read House's original diary entries for a number of particular dates on which he had written passages that Seymour in his *Intimate Papers of Colonel House* had omitted, substituting for them tantalizing ellipses, thus: " . . . " From the context of the deleted passages we suspected, correctly as it turned out in many instances, that they contained highly revealing expressions by House of his attitude toward Wilson.

It is a source of abiding satisfaction to us that, although we do not fancy ourselves historians, we found and published for the first time several illuminating passages from House's diary. What Seymour had omitted were a number of indications of House's calculated and manipulative approach to Wilson and of a certain disrespect for and irritation with his patron. Inga Floto, whose book *Colonel House in Paris: A Study of American Policy at the Paris Peace Conference 1919,*[9] Weinstein, Anderson, and Link refer to as "the most authoritative study of House at the Paris Peace Conference"[10] characterizes *Woodrow Wilson and Colonel House* as "epoch making," a "'coup' from an historian's point of view." We find it awkward to cite her generous praise but consider the disparagement of our research by Weinstein, Anderson, and Link justification for doing so. *Woodrow Wilson and Colonel House*, Floto writes, is "the first attempt at a consistent utilization of House's voluminous diary in its full, chronological scope" and she credits us with having made available material of "decisive importance."[11]

Weinstein, Anderson, and Link make no reference whatever to our use of primary source materials, let alone to the fact that we unearthed new data. We consider this an unfair omission and their criticism of our research unjustified.

That we defend our research does not mean that we were—or are, even after all the materials we have subsequently read—satisfied with the data. Weinstein, Anderson, and Link find it "almost incredible"[12] that we make so little mention of Wilson's mother. We ourselves called attention to the deficiencies of the data about Janet Woodrow Wilson[13]; and even a decade after *Woodrow Wilson and Colonel House* had been published, Link stated in the introduction to the first volume of *The Papers of Woodrow Wilson:* "The Wilsonian documentary record before 1873 is virtually nonexistent."[14] The Wilson papers now do contain richly revealing letters to Wilson from his mother and father, sisters and brother (but unfortunately, with only a couple of exceptions, not his to them) starting from the time he went away to college, as well as an enormous and fascinating correspondence between Wilson and his wife from the time of their engagement. Most of the former were not even added to the collection, and access to the latter was entirely restricted until well after the publication of our book. Also unavailable to us before our book appeared but freely accessible to scholars now was the correspondence between Wilson and the second Mrs. Wilson before their marriage in 1915.

If we said little about Wilson's mother—to return to our critics' incredulity at our having written so little about her—it is because we felt the data were lacking even to suggest a hypothesis relevant to Wilson's political functioning. The question naturally arises, *would* we have said more about Janet Woodrow Wilson had we had at our disposal at the time we were writing *Woodrow Wilson and Colonel House* the material that we have subsequently seen? Indeed the question is a broader one: would our interpretation of Woodrow Wilson now be significantly different from that published in *Woodrow Wilson and Colonel House?*

Of course were we writing now with fuller information at hand and with the benefit of what we hope is the added wisdom of our years, we would no doubt write somewhat differently. We now might well strive to trace the development of Wilson's greatness in as much detail as the flaw in that greatness. Such a broader design would result in the presentation of more detail about Dr. Joseph Wilson's central role in spurring his son to heroic achievements as well as, we continue to believe, in engendering in him those feelings of inadequacy that led to the development of self-defeating patterns of behavior and tragic defeat. No matter how we might choose to frame our portrait of Wilson, however, our interpretation would remain substantially the same: that power for Woodrow Wilson was a compensatory value, a means of restoring self-esteem damaged in childhood. It remains our conviction that this hypothesis, applied to the vast body of data concerning Woodrow Wilson, has consistent explanatory power. It also remains our conviction that his self-defeating behavior in the two great crises of his public career (at Princeton and vis-à-vis the Senate over ratification of the peace treaty) was the logical manifestation of deeply rooted personality patterns developed in consequence of low self-estimates.

In short, we consider that the research upon which *Woodrow Wilson and Colonel House* was based was conscientious and that the data that have since become available, so far from confuting its interpretation, permit a richer documentation of its validity.

II. Woodrow Wilson's Personality

We turn now to the second of our "principal failings": ". . . the Georges fail to recognize the limitations of their psychological model and misrepresent evidence to fit their theory."[15] It seems to us that we were not only aware but scrupulous to convey to readers an awareness that what we were presenting for their consideration is an interpretation of Wilson based on certain hypotheses, which we articulated and invited them to examine on the basis of data, which we also presented. We explicitly stated in our book that the validity of our interpretations is necessarily a matter of opinion:

> No incontrovertible proof can be offered. Nor can any one incident be relied upon to sustain this or any other theory of Wilson's motivation. It is only when the man's career is viewed as a whole that a repetition of certain basically similar behavior is discernible. Let the reader consider whether these patterns of behavior become more consistently comprehensible in terms of the explanations herein offered than in terms of other explanations. That will be the best test of their usefulness.[16]

Weinstein, Anderson, and Link evince no such restraint in the presentation of their hypotheses. Consider, for example, the way they conclude their statement concerning Wilson's inability to read until he was eleven, which they attribute to developmental dyslexia, physiologically determined, and which we, on the other hand, suggest in *Woodrow Wilson and Colonel House*[17] may have derived from feelings of inadequacy and been an unconscious expression of resentment of his father's perfectionist demands. Say Weinstein, Anderson, and Link:

> We do not have a good record of Wilson's childhood such as might be gained from contemporary letters, diaries, or autobiographies; like any other child, he may have felt insecurities. However, it is certain that they did not come about in the manner postulated by the Georges.[18]

Whence, in the absence of adequate data, these authors' certainty? Is peremptory assertion a substitute for reasoned argument? So apparently Weinstein, Anderson, and Link think; for so many of their interpretations and medical diagnoses are couched in categorical language—language that we consider inappropriate to the speculative nature of their enterprise.

Let us get down to specific cases: we do not think our hypothesis about Wilson's delayed acquisition of reading skills can be thus handily dispatched. Nor do we consider it irrelevant in evaluating Link's present certainty as to the cause of Wilson's reading problem that it follows decades of his failing to recognize that a problem requiring explanation even existed.

In *Wilson: The Road to the White House*, Link did not even refer to Wilson's early learning difficulties and wrote: ". . . Wilson's boyhood was notable, if for nothing else, because of his normal development."[19] (This notwithstanding that years before, Baker,[20] whose work Link cites, had specifically drawn attention to Wilson's early slow development. One may therefore reasonably conclude that Link had encountered the fact of Wilson's slow learning—which, indeed, he must also have come upon in the various manuscript materials—and dismissed it as of little consequence.) Twenty years later, in 1967—long after we, in *Woodrow Wilson and Colonel House*,[21] had again drawn attention to the data of Wilson's early learning problems and he himself had mentioned in passing that Wilson "was a late starter"—Link was still arguing that "all evidence indicates that Wilson had a normal boyhood, at least as normal as was possible for boys growing up in the South during the Civil War and Reconstruction."[22]

By 1968, Link was at least referring, however doubtfully, to the "family tradition" which "may or may not be correct" according to which Wilson "did not learn to read until he was nine." (Actually the data indicate he had learned only his letters when he was nine. He could not read until he was eleven.) To be sure, the boy "seems to have suffered from insecurity on account of his inability to achieve as rapidly as he thought he should," but it was "normal insecurity." Indeed "his personal advantages and precocity aside, Wilson seems to have been a remarkably normal person during the first forty years of his life. His childhood was serene. . . "[23]

The article in *Political Science Quarterly* by Weinstein, Anderson, and Link provides gratifying indication that Professor Link has at last taken notice of what he joins his colleagues in correctly describing as the "well-known" facts of Wilson's boyhood learning difficulties. However, the diagnosis he joins them in offering—developmental dyslexia—seems to us to collapse under scrutiny.

Before examining the evidence they offer, we should like to draw attention to these authors' undue certitude in introducing their hypothesis. Weinstein, Anderson, and Link speak of developmental dyslexia as if it were a now thoroughly understood disability of established etiology:

> Undiagnosed in Wilson's childhood, the condition was well-known to neurologists at the time that the Georges wrote their book. However, a number of psychiatrists and psychologists still believed that the condition was an emotional rather than a neurological problem, and the Georges simply chose an explanation that was currently popular. The condition is a frequent one, occurring in about 10 percent of the school population, significantly more frequently in boys. Research over the past seventy years indicates that developmental dyslexia is caused by a delay in the establishment of the dominance of one cerebral hemisphere—usually the left—for language.[24]

A far less confident tone about the nature of reading disabilities and various types of dyslexia is taken by several of the experts who participated in the conference on dyslexia conducted in 1977 by the National Institute of Mental Health. For example, Dr. Michael Rutter, a British psychiatrist, contends that the term "dyslexia" has not yet been even satisfactorily defined and that "the presumption of a neurological basis is just that—namely a presumption." He considers it "meaningless" at this time to attempt any estimate of the prevalence of dyslexia.[25] Dr. Arthur L. Benton of the Department of Neurology and Psychology, University of Iowa, speaks of "the rather scanty knowledge that exists about the neurological basis and genetic background" of developmental dyslexia, notwithstanding significant advances in recent years. Benton agrees with Rutter that "estimates of the prevalence of this disability depend upon how it is defined. . . "[26] While there is great interest in

the hypothesis that a delay in the acquisition of left-hemisphere dominance may be associated with some cases of reading difficulty, Rutter,
citing Benton, considers that "the evidence on this point remains incon-
clusive."[27] And Dr. John Hughes of the Department of Neurology, University of Illinois School of Medicine, writes: "Satz (1976) has summarized the data relating cerebral dominance and dyslexia and has
claimed that information is still lacking on this crucial issue."[28] As for
the etiology of reading disorders, a number of eminent psychiatrists
and psychologists *continue* to believe that emotional factors are the basis for some of them. For example, Dr. Leon Eisenberg, Professor of
Psychiatry at the Harvard University Medical School, addressing the
World Congress on Dyslexia at the Mayo Clinic in 1974, described one
kind of parent-child interaction in which

> reading becomes the arena in which parent-child conflicts are fought out.
> For parents with a high stake in their child's school success, his almost
> deliberate sabotage of their inordinate expectations is a dramatic mode of
> retaliation against their demands.[29]

We continue to believe that Wilson's reading problem was of this
nature.

Our purpose in citing the continuing perplexities of specialists in
dyslexia research is to counter the impression that readers might well
gain from Weinstein, Anderson, and Link that medical research has
solved the mystery of reading disabilities and that psychological explanations have been eliminated for all varieties. According to Rutter the
very concept of developmental dyslexia "constitutes a hypothesis—the
hypothesis that within the large overall group of disabled readers there
is a subgroup with a distinct constitutionally determined condition."[30]
Very well. Weinstein, Anderson, and Link claim that "Tommy" Wilson
was such an intrinsically impaired child. What is their evidence?

"Specific evidence" of developmental dyslexia, Weinstein, Anderson, and Link claim, is that

> he was a slow reader into adult life. At the Johns Hopkins, the amount of
> assigned reading was his bane. "Steady reading," he wrote his fiancée,
> "always demands of me more expenditure of resolution and dogged en-
> ergy than any other sort of work."[31]

We believe that this statement by Wilson, when placed in context, reveals—not the aftermath of developmental dyslexia—but the after-

math of a heroic effort by a conscientious graduate student to plow through a mountain of required reading. It must be remembered that Wilson had a history of delighting in books that interested him and recoiling from the necessity of toiling through those that were merely required. He read slowly as a matter of choice. He himself once put it thus:

> I like to read *much* but not *many* things—at least, not many things *at once*. I go on the principle that father used to announce in very strong English to his pupils in Columbia, namely, that "the mind is not a prolix gut to be stuffed," but a thing of life to be stimulated to the exercise of its proper functions, to be strengthened, that is, to do its own thinking. I *can't* "cram"; I must eat slowly and assimilate, during intervals of rest and diversion. My chief ground of indictment against my professors here is that they give a man infinitely more than he can digest. If I were not discreet enough to refuse many of the things set before me, my mental digestion would soon be utterly ruined.[32]

The sentence from Wilson's letter to his fiancée, Ellen Axson, which Weinstein, Anderson, and Link quote in support of their thesis is incorrectly cited as having been written on March 29, 1884. This is an error of some consequence, since its correct date, *November* 29, 1884, places it within the period that Wilson was making an all-out effort to toil through the reading required for obtaining a Ph.D. It was an effort he detested, which only weeks before he had decided to abandon on the grounds, he had written Ellen Axson, that "a forced march through fourteen thousand pages of dry reading" would jeopardize his health. "I am quite sure that I shall profit much more substantially from a line of reading of my own choosing, in the lines of my own original work . . . "[33]

Nonetheless, in those days, as in these, a degree made a man more marketable. Wilson, avid to equip himself for a job that would give him the wherewithal to marry, reluctantly embarked on the hateful "forced march" almost immediately after he had renounced it. The drudgery was all but unbearable. The sentence preceding the one Weinstein, Anderson, and Link quote from his letter of November 29, 1884, reads: "My Thanksgiving 'vacation' has been a week of about the hardest work I've done in a twelvemonth." By the end of January, 1885, he was writing Ellen Axson:

> I have been reading the last three days with a keen consciousness that out-of-doors the world was radiant with sunshine and full of an air that

is like nectar to the lungs—and such a consciousness has not made Mr. [George] Bancroft seem a very charming writer. Imagine a fish in the stale waters of a close, dark tank hearing the cool, silvery plash of free sunlit waters just outside his prison-walls, a frisking horse in his cramped stall smelling the pastures outside . . . and you will have formed a sort of conception of what it has cost me to read, read, read . . . [34]

His letters to Ellen Axson during these weeks and until mid-February, 1885 chronicle his growing distress. He is tempted "to throw down these heavy volumes and run out into the glories of the open air." He berates himself for not accepting the necessity of "the compulsory drill of pupilage" but he cannot submit. "I often grow savagely out of humour with my present state of pupilage . . . "[35] To a friend he writes:

I am at present going through the not too exciting round of von Holst, Bancroft, Curtis, &c, which you possibly remember having taken yourself . . . and I call upon you for sympathy. It's a "demnition horrid grind" and, like grinding, it is wearing me out. I fear that the bloom upon my cheek has departed. I have shaved off my "siders" until cramming is no more![36]

Nor is reading for the Ph.D. the full measure of his problem: ". . . I am handicapped for my degree," he writes another friend, "because of the extra work with which I was indiscreet enough to saddle myself." He has committed himself to collaborate on a history of political economy with Dr. Ely, one of his professors. ". . . I am to wade—am wading, indeed—through innumerable American text writers . . . for the purpose of writing . . . about one-third of the projected treatise." As for the degree—"it's this year or never."[37]

The burden proves too great and on February 17, 1885, a crisis is at hand:

The long-gathering storm of worry at my so far unavailing efforts to work off the arrears of my degree reading has broken upon me, bringing headache and dire discouragement in its train . . . I can feel, from the strain of hurried, anxious work, that I am risking my health; and yet I know that if I don't take my degree, my position at Bryn Mawr will be one of just so much less estimation.[38]

Two days later he resolves the problem, at least for the time being: ". . . I have given up—this time conclusively—the struggle for the degree . . . Cramming kills me; reading in development of a subject improves and invigorates me."[39]

Is the sentence that Weinstein, Anderson, and Link pluck from one of the letters Wilson wrote in the midst of the struggle described above credible evidence of developmental dyslexia? We think not. That construction of it strikes us as tortured. Much more likely, it seems to us, is that Wilson's statement is simply one of many indications of his distress at the *kind* of reading that was being demanded of him and the crushing amount of it. Would Wilson's plaints not resonate in the hearts of many today who are Ph.D. candidates? Is developmental dyslexia rampant in our graduate schools?

If the record indicated that Wilson was generally a reluctant reader, slow because the very act of reading was difficult for him, the case for Weinstein, Anderson, and Link's hypothesis of developmental dyslexia would gain some ground. The record fails them, however. One has but to look through the diary Wilson kept during the summer after his freshman year at Princeton to see that he was in fact an omnivorous reader, provided only that he had a taste for the matter at hand: Macaulay, Shakespeare, Gibbon, Plutarch, Pepys, Dickens, novels, magazines, encyclopedia articles—all passed under his frequently enthusiastic but by preference unhurried scrutiny. An earlier diary and "Commonplace Book" also testify to the intensity of Wilson's appetite for books from which he felt he could learn that which interested him.[40] The argument may be summed up in a simple statistic: that it takes no less than *thirty pages* of quite fine print in the index to the first twelve volumes of *The Papers of Woodrow Wilson* to cover the subject category, "Woodrow Wilson—Reading."[41]

Weinstein, Anderson, and Link claim two other "groups" of "specific evidence that Wilson had developmental dyslexia." They are A) that he was "extremely poor in arithmetic," an ineptitude commonly associated with developmental dyslexia; and B) that he quickly "and without practice" mastered writing with his left hand when in 1896 (as the result of a stroke, they say, an assertion about which more later) he was unable to write with his right hand—an ability that "strongly suggests that he had mixed cerebral dominance for language."[42] In connection with A) we would point out first, that being "extremely poor in arithmetic" can have a score of explanations other than developmental dyslexia; and second, that whatever his difficulties with arithmetic, Wilson's capabilities ranged from keeping meticulous personal financial records to overseeing the formulation of national economic policy and the negotiation of intricate international economic questions. Would he have been able to function so efficiently if his difficulties in calculation were of such dimensions as to justify the diagnosis of a neurological disorder? As for B) it seems relevant to mention that Wilson had considerable artistic talent. A cousin, for example, recalls his passion as a boy of fifteen for drawing ships—hundreds of them, beautifully shaded. She also recalls: "About this time he had great admiration for my father's handwriting, and wrote pages every day, trying to imitate it. Both were examples of his intense perseverance in what interested him."[43] Given his artistic talents and perseverance, it is not surprising that he succeeded in learning to write with his left hand. The accomplishment did not come easily, however, as Weinstein, Anderson, and Link claim it did. We know from Stockton Axson's account that Wilson set about the task with "customary determination"[44]—a determination strengthened, no doubt, by a wish to be able to write to his wife from England where he was planning to spend the summer alone. We know from Wilson himself that he practiced "laboriously," notwithstanding which writing with his left hand remained "clumsy and uncertain," "awkward," "tedious," "a painfully slow process"—"it takes me half an hour to one of these pages."[45] In short, Wilson does not seem to have been naturally ambidextrous. That he trained himself to write with his left hand seems quite in character, and the evidence does not support that it was the effortless attainment which Weinstein, Anderson, and Link postulate in support of their thesis.

We believe, however, that Wilson's writing indeed bears on the hypothesis of developmental dyslexia, but in quite the opposite direction from that suggested by Weinstein, Anderson, and Link. "Disordered handwriting associated with developmental dyslexia has been noted from the earliest days of the century," Dr. Macdonald Critchley, President, World Federation of Neurology, tells us. Wilson's handwriting—as surely Weinstein, Anderson, and Link would agree—is a very model of beautiful penmanship. Even his check registers and drafts of articles look like copperplate. "Very occasionally," Dr. Critchley says, a "dyslexic" will write neatly but then characteristic errors—reversals of letters or syllables, all manner of transpositions, repetitions, omissions, intrusion of block capitals into the middle of a word, etc.—will be "conspicuously displayed." These writing disorders "are always considerable in cases of developmental dyslexia . . . "[46]

Most damaging of all to the dyslexia hypothesis: Wilson was an all but flawless speller. Summarizing research results to the mid-1970s, Rutter states: "Since the very earliest papers on developmental dyslexia, there has been an emphasis on the very strong association between reading difficulties and problems in spelling."[47]

Finally, it is worth noting that the profile experts on dyslexia have constructed of former "cases" seems without application to Wilson. Thus Critchley:

> What is the natural history of developmental dyslexia? What happens as dyslexic children grow up? . . . The usual end product of a fortunate patient is that he can manage. He can read magazines, newspapers, and notices on the wall. But he could not possibly read Tolstoy's *War and Peace;* nor would he choose to cope with any textbook of philosophy or any technical monograph . . . It is rather rare for an ex-dyslexic to be bookish, to be academically minded, or to attain a place in Oxford, Cambridge, or other such universities. Their principal continuing objective handicap consists in atrocious and bizarre spelling, which, as a rule, they never overcome.[48]

Obviously, in and of itself, such a broad description of the "typical" adult who has had dyslexia proves nothing about a particular case. There are, after all, many atypical cases and Wilson, it might be argued, was one of them. Yet an atypical outcome makes acceptance of the diagnosis contingent upon stronger supporting evidence in its behalf than if the outcome itself served to confirm the correctness of the diagnosis. In short, it seems to us that in order to be persuasive in their assertion that Wilson had developmental dyslexia, Weinstein, Anderson, and Link would have to present very strong evidence that such was the case. In our judgment they have failed to do so.

It is interesting, however, to pursue their train of thought. Let us for that purpose grant for a moment that "Tommy" Wilson suffered from some inborn defect, that it was indeed developmental dyslexia that impeded his learning to read. What would the psychological consequences of such a disability have been, both upon the boy and his parents? "Every poor reader has psychological problems," Dr. Eisenberg stated at the World Congress on Dyslexia:

> The "inevitability" of psychiatric disturbance in the poor reader stems from the pivotal role of success at school for the self-concept of the child. Schooling is, in the first instance, reading. Not only is this the major demand on the child in the early grades, but it is the fulcrum for the rest of

his learning. Reading has a multiplier effect, for good or bad, in every academic content area. In the school environment, reading is being. An inadequate reader is, in his mind's eye, an inadequate (that is, bad or stupid) person—and, all too often, in the eyes of his teachers, his parents and his peers as well.[49]

Dr. Drake D. Duane of the Department of Neurology at the Mayo Clinic commented that Eisenberg's observation that "every disabled reader is predisposed to an emotional problem is one with which on reflection all clinicians must concur."[50]

Weinstein, Anderson, and Link give passing recognition to the fact that "the reading disability affected Wilson's development and his relationship with his parents," but they immediately add "but hardly in the way that the Georges state." How, then, *was* the boy affected? "It probably made him more dependent on his family." Anything else? "Also, he may have feared that his reading problems indicated that he was stupid or lazy." What about his father's reaction? "The condition probably made Dr. Wilson more pedagogic and insistent on drilling his 'lazy' son." Having edged up to the dread explanation, Weinstein, Anderson, and Link hurry away and remove Dr. Wilson with them: during the Civil War he was sometimes away from home, other family members read to Wilson and he enjoyed that, and the data are lacking but whatever insecurities Wilson might have felt "it is certain they did not come about in the manner postulated by the Georges." Further: "To judge from Wilson's pleasant memories of having his family read to him, they seem to have been tolerant of his problem"[51]—a far too weighty conclusion, it seems to us, to hang on so tangentially relevant a recollection. That is the end of their analysis of the effects upon Wilson and his family of his reading problem. Weinstein, Anderson, and Link then continue their criticism of our interpretation of Wilson's relationship with his father.

We shall address their further criticisms, but first we must respectfully suggest that their account leaves some nagging loose ends that not only deserve but demand consideration. What would the effect be on a boy to fear that he was stupid or lazy—and, by the way, there is no "may have" about it: years later when he was President, Wilson often reminisced about his boyhood with his physician and friend, Dr. Cary Grayson, and Grayson recalls that "he often spoke of himself as being a lazy boy."[52] What attitudes toward himself would his father's "insistent drilling" have engendered—his father, a master of the English language, a brilliant expositor of Calvinist doctrine, which says

nothing about developmental dyslexia but a great deal about wicked-
ness and sin and dereliction of duty? Would this devoted father, a man
of his times, not have had an especially poignant stake in the intellectual progress of this, his third child but first son, and been frustrated
and disappointed at the boy's poor performance? And would
"Tommy" not have felt humiliated, unworthy, inadequate? In short,
would this family situation not have fostered the ripening in a boy's
heart of those low estimates of himself that these authors deny existed? It seems to us they refuse to draw the conclusion obvious even
from their prettified account of the family interaction.

For the sake of evaluating Weinstein, Anderson, and Link's thesis on
its own ground, we have thus far omitted the ingredient of Dr. Wilson's propensity for sarcasm and severe criticism and how these are
likely to have impinged upon his son's development.

"The Georges claim that Wilson suffered from a troubled relationship with his father," write Weinstein, Anderson, and Link, and they
reject the idea. Having attempted to subtract Wilson's reading problem as indication of father-son stress, they try to belittle the significance of the testimony of young family members that Joseph R. Wilson, a man of many virtues, to be sure, was nonetheless also a sarcastic
tease whose tongue could fall like a lash upon defenseless flesh.

Were his grandchildren afraid of him? They did not know him well
until cerebral arteriosclerosis had rendered him "testy and puerile,"
say Weinstein, Anderson, and Link. Did a niece, Helen Bones, remember "Uncle Joseph" as a "cruel tease, with a caustic wit and a sharp
tongue" and that her family used to "tell indignantly of how Cousin
Woodrow suffered under his teasing"? Her testimony must be dis-
counted, say Weinstein, Anderson, and Link, because, fiercely devoted
to Woodrow Wilson all her life, she probably would have exaggerated
and, besides, "there is evidence of bad blood" between her parents
and Dr. and Mrs. Wilson. Did Helen Bones's sister Jessie, Wilson's
childhood playmate, recall an example of Dr. Wilson's teasing which
caused a "painful flush" to come over "Tommy's" face? Weinstein,
Anderson, and Link dismiss it as a minor incident.[53]

The evidence is not susceptible of being eclipsed, however, although
its presentation necessitates subjecting the reader to unconscionable
detail: During the last fifteen years of his life, Joseph R. Wilson was a
more or less regular member of his son's household. The youngest of
Woodrow Wilson's three daughters was born some fourteen years be-

fore Joseph R. Wilson died. If therefore she (Eleanor Wilson MacAdoo) later wrote that the venerable Doctor was regarded by his grandchildren "with fearful respect" and "we were afraid of him," and her next older sister (Jessie Wilson Sayre) years afterward spoke of his sharp tongue and of being very much in awe of him, it was on the basis of considerable personal contact over the years as well as on an enormous amount of family lore.

To the Wilson girls' recollections of their awe-inspiring grandfather must be added those of another of Dr. Wilson's grandchildren—his daughter Annie's son George Howe. Young Howe also lived for several years with the Woodrow Wilsons in Princeton and there saw a good deal of his grandfather. He too told Ray Stannard Baker of Dr. Wilson's "painful teasing" which "sometimes left barbs in the wounds he made." Howe too spoke of Joseph Wilson's "gift of repartee that was often devastating."[54]

As for devaluing Helen Bones's recollections of Joseph Wilson's acerbity on the grounds that her views came from her parents and there was "bad blood" between the Wilsons and the Bones'—Weinstein, Anderson, and Link are grasping at a straw: the evidence is that ties of blood and friendship united these two families in lifelong mutual devotion. Joseph Wilson and James Bones (who were married to the Woodrow sisters), and another brother-in-law, Thomas Woodrow, were close friends from their early manhood. Helen Bones later recalled that her father "always loved and admired Dr. Wilson."[55] Thomas Woodrow's son, too, left recollections of jolly summers the three families spent together and of the close relationship of all the parents which "endured until the death of the elders."[56] The only recorded shadow that fell between the Wilsons and the Bones's did not involve Joseph Wilson at all: it involved some property that Mrs. Wilson and Mrs. Bones inherited from their older brother William Woodrow and which James Bones, a notoriously poor businessman, was managing (or, as Mrs. Wilson came to fear—apparently with good reason—mismanaging, though with honest intent), for the two sisters. In the early 1880s Mrs. Wilson engaged her son Woodrow, then a fledgling and otherwise clientless attorney, to prevail upon James Bones to settle the estate and turn her share of the proceeds over to her. The young attorney wrote some forthright letters to his Uncle James who, blundering from one unsuccessful business venture to another, took umbrage at the tone of one of them. If indeed he nursed any long-lasting resentment—and as we read the evidence he did not—surely it would have been at Woodrow Wilson and his mother rather than at Joseph Wilson, who had no connection with the matter. It seems to us futile to rely on this episode, as Weinstein, Anderson, and Link do,[57] for support of the notion that it prejudiced the elder Bones's against *Joseph* Wilson and inspired them to tell groundless stories of the pain he had sometimes inflicted upon his son when his son was a child.

In any case, the close familial ties amongst the elders obviously endured: when Mrs. Bones died in the midst of this contretemps, little Helen Bones was sent to live with Dr. and Mrs. Joseph Wilson. Helen Bones, therefore, personally experienced Dr. Wilson as a surrogate father and had impressions deriving from first-hand knowledge of his manner. Surely had her parents calumniated Joseph Wilson, she would have been able to revise their judgment. Following, more fully than thus far quoted, is her response to Ray Stannard Baker when, years later, the biographer was searching for early letters Wilson may have written his father:

> . . . I very much doubt that a shy and extremely sensitive boy would ever have poured his heart out orally or on paper to Dr. Wilson. WW loved and revered his father and perhaps as a grown man talked to him with freedom, but Uncle Joseph was a cruel tease, with a caustic wit and a sharp tongue, and I remember hearing my own family tell indignantly of how Cousin Woodrow suffered under his teasing. He was proud of WW, especially after his son began to show how unusual he was, but only a man as sweet as Cousin Woodrow could have forgotten the severity of the criticism to the value of which he so often paid tribute, in after life.[58]

There is yet another witness to the forbidding side of Dr. Wilson's nature—one who, surely Weinstein, Anderson, and Link must agree, is unimpeachable. He is Stockton Axson, one of Ellen Axson's younger brothers. An orphan when Ellen Axson married Woodrow Wilson, Stockton Axson came north to live with the young couple. Thus began a lifelong association between Axson and the Woodrow Wilsons which lasted beyond Ellen Wilson's death, encompassed even the second Mrs. Wilson and was characterized throughout by deep affection. From the first, Wilson was solicitous of the well-being of his sensitive, excessively shy young brother-in-law and spent a great deal of time in his company. Old Dr. Wilson too was fond of genial "Stock," perceptive, ever-interested in the verities, full of humor but so ineffably sad.[59]

The two, often simultaneously members of the Wilson household, became fast friends. After the death of his beloved brother-in-law, who he believed would live through the ages, Stockton Axson undertook as a sort of holy obligation the task of making his recollections available to Ray Stannard Baker (Wilson's biographer) and also of writing them down in a series of essays that are in the possession of Professor Link at Princeton University. It was his wish, he wrote, that the truth about Woodrow Wilson, the man, as he knew him through forty years of devoted association, be preserved for posterity. Axson's account of Dr. Joseph R. Wilson and of Woodrow Wilson therefore has unique value. What, then, do we learn from his writings?

Stockton Axson tells us that the key to Wilson's whole character was his love for his father. He loved his mother too but the "daily communion" was with his father and that communion continued even after Dr. Wilson's death: his memory dwelled within his son and permeated all his activities. Axson expressed the opinion that the memory of Dr. Wilson exerted more influence upon Wilson throughout his presidency than that of any living man, that when the President lay down in his bed each night, the thought that would bring him most satisfaction would be that his father might approve his actions that day.

In Axson's opinion, Joseph Ruggles Wilson was a great man who lived out his life in a comparatively obscure environment. He was strikingly handsome, his flowing white mane, strong regular features and large size contributing to his distinguished, dominating appearance. He was erudite, a keen observer, a speaker of distinction, a writer who gloried in the precise, skilled use of the English language. He was a marvellous conversationalist, deliberate and learned without being pedantic, interested in large and serious subjects and possessed of a keen wit as well as an immense fund of stories: books, men, events of the day—all passed within his purview. He was also, however, Axson says, a forbidding man, strong in everything—strong in his affections, strong in his dislikes. When a person pleased him, his humor bubbled genially; but when displeased, his humor bubbled hot, in what Axson termed scalding sarcasms which he said could be really withering. He had in him a certain savage humor, Axson tells us, which caused him to say sometimes cruel things even to those who loved him and whom he loved. Axson does not think he meant to be cruel, but it hurt. Notwithstanding Dr. Wilson's qualities of greatness, Axson wrote, he was a ruthless sort of a man, a man with a distinct streak of perversity in him. In his sarcasm, Dr. Wilson reminded Axson of Jonathan Swift. Axson thought his congregation feared him a little bit even while loving him, for they never knew just exactly where that keen satiric wit might fall. A teacher at various times in his life, Dr. Wilson had what Axson described as strict and sometimes strenuous ideas of discipline. As a young professor of chemistry in Hampden-Sydney College, he once dealt with a student he deemed recalcitrant and impertinent by knocking him down. He then taught the boy some chemistry.[60]

The foregoing account of one facet of Joseph Wilson's personality obviously gives a distorted picture of the whole man. We do not for a moment deny—nor did we in *Woodrow Wilson and Colonel House*[61]— that there is rich and persuasive evidence of the comradeship between Wilson and his father, of abiding love and of the transmission from father to son of moral values and of a range of skills and perceptions that fostered the greatness of Woodrow Wilson. Recognizing and giving full weight to this evidence, however, does not necessitate refusing to recognize, as we think our critics refuse to do, that *all* facets of Joseph Wilson entered into his interaction with his son and that the syndrome we are tracing also had important consequences. Let us sift through the evidence a little further:

There is nothing to indicate that Dr. Wilson ever visited physical punishment upon his son, but his manner was clearly not that of a man whose authority a child would dare overtly defy. And what is known of "Tommy" Wilson seems to us to bespeak a spirit in some measure subdued and discouraged.

By the time "Tommy" was four, Dr. Wilson's pedagogical skills were trained upon him. Wilson himself later recalled:

> When I was a boy, my father would not permit me to blurt things out, or stammer a half-way job of telling whatever I had to tell. If I became excited in explaining some boyish activity he always said, "Steady, now Thomas; wait a minute. Think! Think what it is you wish to say, and then choose your words to say it." As a young boy, therefore, even at the age of four or five, I was taught to think about what I was going to say, and then I was required to say it correctly. Before I was grown, it became a habit.[62]

Wilson's superb verbal skills, which indeed he owed to his father's training, contributed heavily to his later success. But how did four and five year old "Tommy" feel while his father's lessons were being imparted? His daughter Eleanor has left an account based, she states in the preface of her book, on what her parents or other close relatives who had been eyewitnesses told her:

> It was not only his father's voice but the words he used that fascinated Tommy, and he was not so much hurt as ashamed when Joseph corrected him sternly. When he used the wrong word or muddled a sentence, Joseph always demanded, "What do you mean by that?" Tommy would explain and Joseph would bark, "Well, why didn't you say so?"[63]

Sundays, Tommy attended church services and listened, awestruck, as his father, in beautifully wrought language and impressive tones, expounded the austere Calvinist doctrine of the sinful nature of man, election and predestination. He preached orthodox, fundamental theology, dismissing as "the watery gushings of a weak philanthropy" the movement to temper some of the harsh doctrines of the church.[64] Sometimes, when certain sad hymns were played, "Tommy" would cry.

Since the educational system had been disrupted by the Civil War, "Tommy" did not attend school until he was about ten. Instead, efforts were made to teach him at home not only by his father who, according to Stockton Axson, "systematically drilled" him, but also by his mother, his two older sisters and his sympathetic Aunt Marion Bones. By all accounts he was a "slow" pupil. When finally "Tommy" was enrolled in Professor Derry's newly-opened school, he took his place at the foot of his class and remained there. He fared no better in Sunday school with his struggle to learn the catechism: even the shorter was a painful challenge.[65]

A friend from those early days in Augusta, Pleasant Stovall, remembers Wilson as a boy of good character and attainment, precise, slow-spoken, dignified and very orderly. He never, like the rest of the boys, went barefoot. When they went riding, "Tommy" preferred a reliable nag to the more spirited ponies Stovall enjoyed.[66]

In 1870, when "Tommy" was fourteen, the Wilsons moved to Columbia, South Carolina. Dr. Wilson joined his distinguished brother-in-law, Dr. James Woodrow, on the faculty of the Columbia Theological Seminary. "Tommy" became a pupil in a school run by Charles H. Barnwell. His academic progress continued to fail to measure up to his father's standards and now Uncle James Woodrow, too, joined in the attempt to spur the boy to greater effort. There was a third elder disappointed with his performance—his maternal grandfather, Dr. Thomas

Woodrow, also an erudite Presbyterian minister and sometime visitor to Columbia. Of this period Baker wrote:

> There are evidences both in reminiscences and in old letters that in those years Tommy was a subject of serious concern to his elders. The scion of an intellectual race, eager students to the last man of them, surrounded moreover by the best of influences, he makes only a mediocre record in his school work. He should be at the head of his class! Were not his father and his grandfather, was not his famous uncle?[67]

Dr. James Woodrow's daughter told Baker she remembered her father's concern and Dr. Wilson's about "Tommy": "There were family conferences, in which the old Scotch grandfather also joined, as to what should be done with a boy who could not do better than 'Tommy' was doing in his school."[68]

The record is silent as to what was "done" about him, but it is known that whereas the other boys were grouped together in a large class at school, "Tommy" was taught alone.[69] At home, Dr. Wilson continued to train his son. His technique: "severe drill . . . in the use of the English language."[70] His philosophy: "his idea was that if a lad was of fine tempered steel, the more he was beaten the better he was."[71]

In time, the boy's learning problem became less acute: Uncle James Woodrow, giving family news in a letter to his son when "Tommy" was just over sixteen, wrote: "Tommy Wilson still attends Dr. Barnwell's school opposite their house, and is said to be studying well. He seems to have improved."[72] Not that he was yet a good student or regarded as "promising": he did not distinguish himself academically either at Dr. Barnwell's school or at Davidson College, where he spent the year 1873–1874. Not until he was a sophomore at Princeton did he "come to himself" intellectually. Triumphantly, he wrote his father that he had found he had a mind. Dr. Wilson was overjoyed.

How did "Tommy" feel through all those early years when he disappointed his elders? Years later, at the zenith of his career as President of the United States, Wilson visited the church in Carlisle, England, over which his grandfather Woodrow had presided before emigrating to the United States. Asked to speak, the President, with tears in his eyes, recalled his grandfather: "I remember how much he required. I remember the stern lessons of duty he spoke to me. I remember also painfully the things which be expected me to know which I did not know."[73]

In later years Wilson also remembered—gratefully, be it noted, for the training no doubt honed his skills and was motivated by loving concern—how his uncle James Woodrow used to reprove him for inexactitude of expression:

> . . . I learned a certain discretion in his presence which I otherwise would never have learned, and it occurred to me on several occasions I ought to be informed before I expressed an opinion; and the discipline did not come with any painfulness because he was an extremely affable man, kind old gentleman, very fond of me, but I got what was coming to me, and there was no abatement of the process, notwithstanding its joviality and the interesting manner in which he flayed me . . . [74]

Years later too, Wilson (then the distinguished President of Princeton) expressed concern for the son of a friend whose illness necessitated absence from school: "I . . . hope most sincerely that he will not find that he is embarrassed in keeping up with his class. *I know how mortifying that is to a boy.*" [italics added][75]

And there seems poignant autobiographical significance to a passage of a speech Wilson delivered in 1904:

> Those who have read that delightful book of Kenneth Graham's entitled "The Golden Age," the age of childhood, will recall the indictment which he brings against the Olympians, as he calls them,—the grown-up people,—who do not understand the feelings of little folks not only, but do not seem to understand anything very clearly; who do not seem to live in the same world, who are constantly forcing upon the young ones standards and notions which they cannot understand, which they instinctively reject. They live in a world of delightful imagination; they pursue persons and objects that never existed; they make an Argosy laden with gold out of a floating butterfly,—and these stupid Olympians try to translate these things into uninteresting facts.
>
> I suppose that nothing is more painful in the recollections of some of us than the efforts that were made to make us like grown-up people. The delightful follies that we had to eschew, the delicious nonsense that we had to disbelieve, the number of odious prudences that we had to learn. . . .[76]

"Little folks" respond in myriad ways to the particular "Olympians" to whom fate consigns them. "Tommy" never openly rebelled. Instead he became an extravagantly devoted son, ever dutiful and respectful, ever eager to credit his success to "my incomparable

father," ever disposed to compare himself unfavorably with his father
as to appearance and intellect. Surely all these attitudes of Wilson toward his father were heartfelt—we are in agreement with Weinstein,
Anderson, and Link on that. We, as they, think the affectionate dedication of his first book, *Congressional Government*, to his father was a
valid representation of his feelings or, more exactly, of *some* of his feelings. Do Weinstein, Anderson, and Link really consider it beyond the
realm of possibility, however, that notwithstanding this great, positive
and amply documented attachment, the demanding father may have
generated in this sensitive son feelings of inadequacy and also of unconscious resentment? Is it likely that the boy never inwardly rebelled
at the stern religious teachings graven into his soul? Did Woodrow
Wilson enjoy some divine dispensation from experiencing conflicting
emotions about a beloved parent? Is it really unthinkable to Weinstein,
Anderson, and Link that Wilson may have had to deal with ambivalence?

There is the briefest intimation—half a sentence—that such questions crossed our critics' minds. "Dr. Wilson had a tremendous influence on his son," they write, "and *probably no boy grows up without some
resentment toward his father*" (italics supplied). [77] Weinstein, Anderson,
and Link write as though any unconscious resentment Wilson felt toward his father was of minor dimensions and without significant
repercussions for the understanding of his political behavior. They
write as though his early learning difficulties neither resulted from nor
led to psychological problems that importantly affected his development. They leave unmentioned and show no sign of having considered the implications of many self-revealing statements Wilson made
in private conversations or of dozens of self-characterizations to be
found in his letters, in his diaries and sometimes even in his public utterances which bespeak great inner turmoil, to the nature of which, it
seems to us, he furnishes abundant clues. As we read the evidence,
Wilson documents that he suffered poignantly from low self-estimates, enduring feelings of inferiority vis à vis his father, from the
feeling of having been overwhelmed as a child and from bottled-up
rage. He himself reveals how, step by step, he attempted to cope with
these painful feelings first through passive resistance to his father's
demands (as exemplified by the delayed learning), then by identifying
with his father and internalizing his demands and, finally, by working
unremittingly to fashion a sphere of competence within which he

could not only demonstrate his worth, thus countering low self-esti-mates, but also legitimize the assertion of his will and the discharge of aggressive impulses.

Let us look at some of the evidence:

That throughout his life Wilson felt inferior to his father in appear-ance and ability has been abundantly documented in secondary sources: he often ruefully denigrated his own plain face, and extolled his father's distinguished mien and brilliance. "If I had my father's face and figure, it wouldn't make any difference what I said," he once remarked. Even when he was a rising scholar at Princeton, recalls a visitor to the Wilson household, in his father's "majestic presence the professor was a pupil; the parent of three children was an obedient boy."

Weinstein, Anderson, and Link attempt to counter the point that Wilson felt dependent upon his father by marshalling evidence to show that in fact Joseph R. Wilson encountered disappointments in his work, was frequently discouraged and depressed and in later life was in many ways dependent upon his son.[78] The facts they cite are correct but, as we see it, almost beside the point: for psychological reality and objective reality are frequently very different. Children typically per-ceive their parents as all-powerful and, in varying degrees, many adults remain bound to unrealistic assessments of them.

Cary Grayson, Wilson's physician and friend, has written that one of the frequent themes of the President's conversations with him over the years was his reverence for his father, "whom he had loved devot-edly, and whom, to the day of his own death, he regarded as a greater man than himself . . ." From Stockton Axson we learn of a poignant scene at Wilson's Christmas table in 1922 at his home on "S" Street, where the ex-President sat an old and broken man. During dinner, ref-erence was made to someone else and his father. "I wish I were like my father," Wilson said. Mrs. Wilson's sister undertook to suggest that Wilson had surpassed his father. "That is where you are wrong," this great man flashed back.[79]

If the memory of his father remained so vivid—indeed, according to Stockton Axson, it will be recalled, so *controlling* an influence through-out Wilson's life—it is easy enough to imagine Dr. Wilson's over-whelming impact upon young "Tommy." Overt rebellion was obvi-ously unthinkable to the boy faced as he was by so all-powerful an authority. Yet all children have strivings for autonomy. What expression for these could "Tommy" find? In our book, we advanced the hypothesis that his failure to learn to read at the usual time and his poor performance at school indicated resistance to his father's demands or discouragement at his inability to perform well enough. We construe as tending to confirm the former interpretation the fact that as an adult one of Wilson's habitual responses to pressure was *unresponsiveness* calculated to frustrate his opponent. One of his secretaries later wrote:

> Criticism of any kind rarely influenced him. He had a defense for any kind of attack, the simple defense of silence, which none succeeded in breaking down . . . The more abusive, the more vindictive it was, the less force it possessed to penetrate his armor . . .
> "I will not reply," he said. "That is what they want. Nothing is so effective as silence. The thing that hurts worst when you are attacking is to have no attention paid to you."[80]

Stockton Axson remarked the same characteristic and labelled it a kind of "perversity" which would show itself particularly with very importunate people—those who insisted and kept insisting that Wilson do this or that before he was good and ready to do it. In Axson's view, the silence of Woodrow Wilson was worse than the oaths of some men—more withering.[81] Passive resistance in his adulthood to attempts to pressure him, we suggest, may have been the continued use of a coping device learned early in life in response to his father's demands.

Another way for "Tommy" to escape his "Olympians" was to create an inner world in which he was absolute master. It seems to us significant that he described this fantasy world in a letter written during the summer of 1909, a time when Wilson felt his authority as President of Princeton University threatened by Dean Andrew Fleming West who, if our theory is correct, reawakened Wilson's childhood conflict with his father. Locked in bitter battle with West, Wilson wrote:

> I always feel younger in the summer than in any other season, because I then more nearly than at any other time return to the habit of my childhood, when I lived, not in the world actually about me, but in the world of my own thoughts . . . For the world of my thoughts is absolutely my own. No man governs me, and no man's opinion; and everything is as I wish it, as it was when I was a dreaming boy.[82]

At a later time of personal unhappiness and denial—this time over an impossible longing for another woman (Mary Hulbert Peck)—Wilson described himself to her as feeling rebellious at heart, "like a wild bird in its cage" and again spoke of his imagined world in childhood:

> Sometimes (as I must have told you more than once) my whole life seems to me rooted in dreams ... I lived a dream life (almost too exclusively, perhaps) when I was a lad and even now my thought goes back for refreshment to those days when all the world seemed to me a place of heroic adventure, in which one's heart must keep its own counsel while one's hands worked at big things.[83]

Why did his boy's heart have to "keep its own counsel"? Were his feelings such that he could confide them to no one—not even to "my incomparable father," or perhaps *especially* not to his father? Was he unhappy? Available data yield some clues, such as a letter Wilson wrote his wife when he was forty-four years old:

> I wish I "carried an atmosphere," as you do! ... Your presence is so *individual;* mine is so naked and subject to be dominated by what surrounds it. It must be an inestimable protection to be thoroughly individual—to influence instead of being influenced. I have often seen you, serenely and without effort or consciousness, keep your individuality when I was painfully aware that my own had gone hopelessly and ridiculously to pieces. I am defencelessly impressionable; you keep your poise and choose what to be impressed by. I record a mere breath, like a mirror; you receive only those impressions which your nature welcomes.[84]

To us, these seem the words of a person who fears being overwhelmed by an intrusive environment and who, in psychological self-defense, might well feel it imperative not to yield an inch to masterful opponents bent on obliging him to give way. Such feelings, of course, would have a history and we submit that a very likely one can be constructed to accommodate all the known facts of Wilson's childhood. Our theory is that Wilson felt overwhelmed as a child, that his brave attempts to preserve his selfhood through such coping strategies as refusing to learn and taking refuge in the world of his imagination did not suffice. Further, we believe the facts suggest that "Tommy" harbored perfectly natural resentments the very existence of which he was too fearful to admit even to himself let alone express to his formidable father or his sympathetic but very proper and very vulnerable mother who early became inordinately dependent upon him.

This hypothesis is supported by the data indicating that in later life Wilson felt beset by a painful access of explosive emotion the nature of which he recoiled from examining, notwithstanding his remarkable— but very selective—gift for introspection. He once wrote his fiancee:

> It isn't pleasant or convenient to have strong passions: and it is particu- larly hard in my case to have to deal with unamiable feelings; because the only whip with which I can subdue them is the whip of hard study and that lascerates *me* as often as it conquers my crooked dispositions. I hope that none of my friends—and much more none of my enemies!—will ever find out how much it costs me to give up my own way. I have the uncomfortable feeling that I am carrying a volcano about with me.[85]

It is interesting, by the way, to note the early date—1884—of Wilson's prescient allusion to the trouble-making potential of the very trait—the need to have his own way—that later proved his undoing both at Princeton and as President of the United States when he sought Senate approval of the League of Nations Covenant without reservations. For this letter antedates by over a decade the first of Dr. Weinstein's alleged brain damaging "strokes" on which Weinstein, Anderson and Link rely to explain Wilson's self-defeating obduracy in both great battles.

To a newsman, Wilson once said:

> You may not believe it but I sometimes feel like a fire from a far from ex- tinct volcano, and if the lava does not seem to spill over it is because you are not high enough to see into the basin and see the caldron boil.[86]

Obviously, this is a man in turmoil—caused by what? To us it seems a fair assumption that a man who feels he is carrying about a volcano is *angry*. Wilson did not wish to probe the sources of his distress: "I have always had an almost unconquerable disinclination to talk about deep things that underlie motives and conduct," he once wrote a would-be interviewer. To another, whose request he also denied, he explained that his training in writing was superintended by "a very wonderful father" but "I have always made a terrible fist of . . . talking about myself or analyzing any process of my own development." He shrank from having his portrait painted by the noted artist John Sar- gent because, he confessed to Col. House, "he was afraid . . . of Sar- gent's alleged faculty of bringing out the latent soul of his sitter." He- len Bones once heard him say that "he never dared let himself go because he did not know where he would stop."[87] For fearless intro-spection about his own development he substituted an iron self-disci-pline and self-control—these according to people who knew him best were among his most prominent characteristics.

"Cousin Mary, it is possible to control your thoughts, you know," he once said to Mary Hoyt. "Anybody can get nervous prostration, you know. I could have it myself, at the present moment, with the greatest ease."[88]

Indeed "nervous prostration" seems to have been an ever-present threat (and often a reality, as well!) in Wilson's family circle, from his childhood on: his mother was invalided intermittently by obscure ail-ments that his father termed "too sacred for recital."[89] She suffered not only physical pain but also, she confided to "Tom," then a Princeton sophomore, from "weakness and despondency."[90] The record also con-tains intimations of tension in the household arising from what Janet Wilson termed her husband's "constitutional restlessness,"[91] "dark moods"[92] and whatever other behavior it was which led her to write that she firmly believed Joseph R. Wilson had been "out of his mind" before he left home during the summer of 1883 for his usual vacation alone.[93] All members of the household suffered variously from "sav-age" colds, "sick headaches," indigestion and anxious preoccupation with all of these, which were endlessly described and complained of in the family correspondence. And, of course, there was an ever-present sense of the need to expiate one's inevitable sins, to view life as an op-portunity not for pleasure but for earnest work and endeavor. In one of his earliest known religious essays, "Thomas W. Wilson," as he signed himself in his twentieth year, warned that every act must be performed "as an act of which we shall some day be made to render a strict account, as an act done either in the service of God or in that of the Devil."[94] In another religious essay written a few weeks later, Wil-son wrote of the daily battle between soldiers in Christ's army and the hosts of "the Evil One." Those who would enlist under the glorious standards of Christ must know their enemies, the young zealot warned:

> They are evil thoughts, evil desires, evil associations. To avoid evil
> thoughts altogether is, of course, impossible. But whenever one of these
> subtle warriors of evil attacks you, do not fear to test your breastplate;
> wield with power the sword of the Spirit and with skill the shield of faith.
> Overcome evil desires, those powerful and ever present enemies, by con-

stant watchfulness and with the strong weapon of prayer, and by cultivating those heavenly desires which are sure to root out the evil one.[95]

He felt, as he wrote in his diary, that God's "every command is to be
obeyed in every particular," that "in every instance of disobedience
which the Bible has given for our warning and instruction, the of-
fender has been punished for not obeying God's commands *to the very
letter* . . . "[96]

On September 23, 1876, Thomas W. Wilson, a Princeton sophomore,
not quite twenty, read in preparation for writing an essay on Macaulay's
use of language. His diary shows that he approached this assignment,
given by his professor of Rhetoric and English, in some trepidation.

> . . . it has been very hard to think that young men such as we have critical
> judgment enough to criticize such great writers as he has given us a
> choice from. The very name of the author is apt to awe us. I myself
> though have little reverence for the author—no great *name* appalls me,
> though *great writing* does when I think how hopeless the task of trying to
> write as well as the great author I may read has done. But one can but *try*.
> "Genius is divine *perseverance*." Divine *patience* I believe he originally
> used, perseverance is better in my opinion. Genius I cannot claim nor
> even extra brightness but perseverance *all* can have. Before going to bed I
> prayed out loud and found that I enjoyed my prayer much more than
> usual . . . I prayed last night as I have seldom done in the last few
> months. Oh that God would give me more of His Holy Spirit and make
> me something more than the cold Christian I have been of late! I bless His
> holy name for the health and strength of all my past life. During all my
> life I have had nothing but blessings from His hand but He has had noth-
> ing but a slight cold love from me. I shall henceforth endeavor to make
> Him some slightly better return for His many mercies.[97]

The next day—Sabbath—he commenced work on an essay for a Presbyterian publication on the duties of sons to their parents but the
words would not come:

> . . . My thoughts come hard this evening and I have no pleasure in *think-
> ing* so I must not think any more. No one ought to try to write when it re-
> quires such an immense effort as it does from me this evening. My heart
> feels full and yet my thoughts will not clothe themselves in any suitable
> words and will not even put themselves into tangible form. Striving thus
> to express my thoughts which will not come and yet on the subject of
> which I am full is one of the most painful things I know of.[98]

Why did this earnest young man find it such an "immense effort" to write his exhortation to filial piety? To us it seems plausible that his pen was stayed and his pleasure in *thinking* impeded by the welling up of countermanding sentiments. He continued to have difficulty with the piece, in which he adjured his readers to be courteous to their parents, to refrain from impertinence and to heed their commands and advice. He completed it two weeks later.[99]

Years later, Woodrow Wilson—then President of Princeton University, a man already talked of as Presidential timber, a man still yearning to be a statesman—characterized that "man of the people" whose leadership America needed: it is as though he were conjuring up the Princeton sophomore when he said,

> ... A man of the people is a man who has felt that unspoken, that intense, that almost terrifying struggle of humanity, that struggle whose object is, not to get forms of government, not to realize particular formulas or make for any definite goal, but simply to live and be free. He has participated in that struggle; he has felt the blood stream against the tissue; he has known anxiety; he has felt that life contained for him nothing but effort, effort from the rising of the sun to the going down of it. He has, therefore, felt beat in him, if he had any heart, a universal sympathy for those who struggle, a universal understanding of the unutterable things that were in their hearts and the unbearable burdens that were upon their backs ... Such a man with such a consciousness, such a universal human sympathy, such a universal comprehension of what life means, is your man of the people, and no one else can be.[100]

Our critics may say that our description of the Wilson household and of "Tommy's" state of mind is one-sided and therefore inaccurate. It *is* one-sided: for surely there also dwelled in that house love and camaraderie, concern one for the other, learning, wit and wonderful, wide-ranging conversation between father and son. Yet the dour side was real and coexisted with these and had consequences. It is a legitimate enterprise—indeed, an essential one to any who would understand Woodrow Wilson—to try to trace this thread as it was woven into the fabric of his life.

When "Tommy" was going on eleven another child was born to his parents: a son whom they named Joseph Ruggles Wilson Jr. ("Josie"). There are those who might suspect that it was this event which galvanized "Tommy" into learning to read out of fear of losing his parents' love. We shall content ourselves merely to note that it is indeed at about this time that "Tommy" did at last begin to "apply himself." And he identified with his father and strove to mold himself in his father's image. As he himself, speaking many years later of his boyhood, put it: ". . . I saw the world and the tasks of the world through his eyes, and because I believed in him I aspired to do and be the thing that he believed in."[101]

He surrendered himself without reserve to his father's influence. "The only person toward whom his relationship might have some of the characteristics of hero worship," wrote Stockton Axson "was his father." Axson quotes Wilson as saying: "'I can find no man in history I should care to be like. I want to be myself.'"[102] In short, exempting only his father, he made an almost wild declaration of independence: he would "submit" to no one else, living or dead. Over the years, Wilson indeed became more and more like his father: "WW's voice and inflection, in conversation, was unusually similar to that of his father, and in later years the resemblance was so remarkable that one could close his eyes and easily imagine that he was listening to the latter."[103]

According to Stockton Axson, Wilson's mental and temperamental resemblance to his father grew stronger and stronger as time went on.[104] Articles about Dr. Wilson's sermons that appeared in the Columbia, S.C. *Daily Union* during the years the Wilson family lived there afford insight into the uncanny precision with which the son tailored his efforts to "*do*" and "*be*" the thing his father believed in:

> There were times, stated this paper, when Dr. Wilson rose above the plane of his ordinary preaching and spoke with an authority and power above and beyond himself. These inspired efforts were conditioned on the speaker's belief that he had discovered some Divine truth which had eluded the grasp of others but the knowledge and utilization of which truth was essential to the harmonious existence and to the supreme happiness of mankind. Such ideas, concluded the reporter, Erastus W. Everson, "may strike some as novel and speculative."[105]

Wilson's very language—the puns he made, the figures of speech he habitually used (e.g. comparing reading to "eating" and "cramming" the mind to "cramming" the stomach, with indigestion the result in either event)—echoed his father's.

Nor was becoming like his father the full measure of Wilson's developmental task: to achieve a viable identity he had to discover a field of endeavor and within it carve out a sphere of competence in which he could simultaneously *do* and *be* what his father believed in and also find morally sanctioned outlets for that self-assertion so completely eclipsed in his relationship with his parents—in short he had to struggle toward means for overcoming the humiliation of his early incompetence. It was a task to which he lashed himself with every ounce of his strength, and with a sober assessment of his natural talents, the gist of which appears again and again:

> I have come to the conclusion that my friends have no doubt come to long ago and that is that my mind is a very ordinary one indeed. I am nothing as far as intellect goes. But I can plod and work. Thank God for health and strength.[106]

The Princeton student sent his every essay to his father and received in return marvellously incisive critiques, detailed, precise, with a modicum of praise and a full measure of admonition to further effort. When one of "Tommy's" compositions failed to win a hoped-for honor, his father wrote:

> I am hardly sorry that you failed in the "Lit." prize. It is well to learn that you have need of still greater and greater exertion. That you came so near to success is enough for *encouragement*.[107]

"Tommy" spared himself no exertion. Bit by bit, the father's skills were transmitted, practiced and absorbed. Wilson stretched and exercised his faculties until—it took years, of course—he could rely on "that good old hack, my mind" to "do my bidding." That is how he habitually referred to his mind—as "the old nag," a "steady mare," "a most reliable beast," one that could be "counted on to do its task whenever bidden." He trained himself to go to his desk "like a cart horse to the shaft."[108] He toiled like a beast driven, "*flayed*," all the while in the grip of what he later called "my morbid habit of thinking about myself, of examining and chastising my own short-comings and defects!"[109] He was also growing masterful in ways that helped him become a giant among men and gave him great pleasure, though not for any length of time. His burgeoning attainments gave his father great pleasure too. The time came, after Wilson had begun to prove his mettle, that Dr. Wilson referred to his son and himself as "one person." Then the old minister indeed glowed with pride as his "precious son"—"to me the earth's loveliest," "in whose large love I trust so implicitly and in the wealth of whose gem-furnished mind I take such delight"—fulfilled his fondest hopes.[110]

As Wilson struggled to doff the mantle of his childhood incompetence it passed to little "Josie," and "Josie" never succeeded in getting rid of it. While "Tommy" earned his parents' plaudits for one accomplishment after another, "Josie" became the family scapegoat. He did not wish to study. To his parents' distress, he was eager to play. When he was ten, his mother described how "sweet little Josie" was "out-of-doors nearly all the time. I find it very difficult to keep him out of the street— he is so eager after company . . ." A few months later this mother who had discouraged "Tommy" from learning to swim and, when he was eighteen and over, fretted at his interest in watching the activities around the ships anchored at the Wilmington docks and warned him to wear his winter clothing at the end of May—this mother wrote that Josie had a bad cold:

> The other evening he came in with his face all aflame and in a frightful state of heat . . . I wish the child were not quite so excitable—but when he gets with a lot of little girls,—he seems quite beside himself with excitement—I don't know what to do with him sometimes.[111]

References to "Josie" in his parents' letters to Wilson are a chronicle of condescension. Thus, Dr. Wilson to "Tommy" when "Josie" was ten: "Josie, the pet, is hard at his labors of ship-building, the sitting room being his ship-yard. He becomes fatigued only when geography & spelling are urged upon him."[112]

Again, when "Josie" (or "Dode," as he was also nicknamed) was about twelve: "Your dear Mother & Dode are quite well. The former is always busy—the latter always lazy." Wilson, it will be recalled, also had been considered a "lazy" boy, even according to Weinstein, Anderson and Link.[113]

By the time he was sixteen his mother reported that "Dear Josie is studying a little. We are very anxious about his education. Everything seems against his progress." A few weeks later, Janet Wilson appealed for help to the now scholarly and industrious "Woodrow":

> I want you, dear, to write to Josie—and use all your influence with him to induce him to study. He will *have* to study hard the coming months—or he will be mortified when he goes to school—as he will have to do next year—to find himself so far behind hand. I have plead with him—and tried to *insist* upon his studying in earnest—and he makes fair promises—but the result is not very encouraging.[114]

Shortly thereafter, Joseph Wilson reported to his "precious son" that "Dode" was greatly pleased to receive a letter from his big brother:

> I dare say he will take yr. advices—or, at any rate, resolve to do so. He is, as yet, however—although the sweetest of sons—an undetermined problem, causing his dear mother & me much thought.[115]

When he was seventeen, his mother described "Josie" as "quite well and doing wonderfully well considering his disadvantages."[116] For a time when he was about eighteen and a student at South-Western Presbyterian University, Dr. Wilson seemed to have some hope that "Josie" too might discover that he "had a mind." On November 4, 1885, he wrote his beloved "Woodrow," now married and teaching at Bryn Mawr:

> Josie is moving through his studies at an even pace, which will get faster and surer when his mind is fairly awake to their importance[.] Meanwhile he is doing well and ever well-er. Every body likes him, besides, and he seems to like every body (almost)[.] Last month he achieved "excellent" from every professor save one . . . [117]

The following month, "Josie" had to give his first speech at College and was dreading it. However, Janet Wilson wrote in a letter to her "darling Son" in Bryn Mawr, two professors later said "that he had done 'splendidly'—surprised everybody!"[118]

It is hard to discern exactly how long this pleasant "surprise" lasted: "Josie" was still making "quite promising" progress in March 1886, his father wrote. Even in early 1887—Josie was then going on twenty—Janet Wilson reported that he was "studying well and getting on splendidly," although this favorable evaluation was coupled with the usual disparagement: "It strikes me with a sort of gratified amusement to see how he is looked up to—the position he has gained in the estimation of both the college & the town."[119]

By then, too, Dr. Wilson had resumed his derisive tone about his hapless younger son: "Josie is studying as best he knows how, and is I believe making progress in the long road his already wearied steps are travelling."[120]

In the following year (1888) Janet Wilson died. "Josie" continued to live with his father. He also continued to disappoint him, as Dr. Wilson made clear in a letter to his now idolized "Woodrow," at this time a rising professor at Wesleyan:

... You are hour by hour in my thoughts and upon my heart:—and what is just as certain is, that you deserve the place which you occupy within the house of my soul, and even a bigger place were it a bigger soul ... I feel *very* proud of you when I think of what you are doing and doing so well ...

Josie studies a little, goes about a great deal, and is a member of every possible company—even is a "drum-major." I see not a great deal of him, really—and have grave apprehensions as to his future—he is so easily led by others who are not so good as himself. He does nothing wrong—only he will not apply himself to duty when duty is a little hard ... Advise.[121]

The same dichotomy of attitude continued to fill his letters and he finally declared outright that "Woodrow" was his favorite child:

Ah, my son, this old heart—you fill it, and with a charm that is quite unspeakable ... Of course I am not forgetting—and do always remember—the other children, who are very close to my sympathies. But you were my companion more entirely than they; and are now not merely my child to whom consanguinity attaches by a tie of natural regard, but my *friend* to whom community of thought binds by ligatures which are thicker than blood. I am sure that we are the two who thoroughly—most thoroughly—comprehend each other. You satisfy my intellect as I believe I am able to content yours. You gratify my pride also, and I feel assured that your corresponding emotion has its demands measurably met in me, to whom you have long been accustomed to look up with an eye that perceives in me far more than there really is of goodness and of largeness—(for which I parenthetically take this occasion to thank you).
    ... I am looking with expectant interest for a copy of your new book ... I shall want to purchase a number of copies ... for sending to our relatives and others in Buffalo and Cleveland.
    ... Josie is looking (in vain so far) for a business in which to engage. He is a source of real trouble to me on this account: and I am utterly at a loss as to what to do with him.[122]

It is worth recalling that some years before, Dr. Wilson had been in a similar dilemma about the then unstudious "Tommy," i.e., "what should be done" about such a boy, and had conferred with Dr. James Woodrow and "Tommy's" grandfather Woodrow on the subject. Now (in fact he had been doing it for some years) Dr. Wilson solicited his so wonderfully changed older son's advice and help in dealing with the laggard "Josie."

In April 1890, "Josie" found a job as a reporter for the Clarksville, Tennessee *Daily Progress*. Dr. Wilson wrote "My beloved Woodrow" (who had by now won a long-coveted teaching post at Princeton and was just beginning his career there) that "Josie promises well in the discharge of his new duties." However: "He has not time for close study or large reading; and unhappily he does not as yet see the necessity for great application in such directions." A year later, his father pronounced "Josie" "doing well in his small way."[123]

Wilson adopted his father's patronizing attitude. He attended "Josie's" wedding and described "our new sister" in letters to his own wife as "really lovely," possessing "plenty of spirit and sweetness and beauty." She would "hardly satisfy an *intellectual* man . . . Fortunately (though quite inexplicably) 'Dode' is not an intellectual or literary man, but simply a fine sensible fellow, needing just such a wife—and no more."[124] When "Josie" was editor of a small newspaper in Clarksville, Wilson used to laugh and say that his writing was always recognizable by his misuse of the words "principal" and "principle."[125] (Dr. Wilson referred to "Josie's" weekly newspaper as the "Weakly.")

Why, the reader may ask, do we spend so much time on "Josie" who, after all, never "came to himself" and left no imprint on human affairs to claim the attention of later generations? The answer is that the interaction between Dr. and Mrs. Wilson and "Josie," a good deal about which is now known because so many of their letters to Woodrow Wilson in which they give news of the younger brother have become available, provides a "window" through which one can view their parental style.

In *Woodrow Wilson and Colonel House*, we attempted to demonstrate that in certain crucial situations in his public career, Woodrow Wilson's self-defeating stubbornness and unwillingness to defer (or at least make expedient gestures of deference) to men whose cooperation was essential to the accomplishment of his goals were irrational behaviors that arose from underlying low self-estimates against which he had constantly to struggle. We tried to show that for Wilson, carving out a sphere of competence in public life and striving for high achievement were a means of overcoming feelings of unimportance, of moral inferiority, of weakness, of mediocrity, of intellectual inadequacy.[126]

That he had to contend with such feelings a survey of even then-available data seemed readily to indicate. The indications lay upon the surface, some in self-revelations in letters and conversations that were later recollected by those who knew him, others in the very facts of his observable behavior. To fathom the *origins* of such feelings is necessarily a more speculative and difficult enterprise than to demonstrate their mere existence. For example, if a man writes his fiancee, as Wilson did on April 4, 1885, that "communion with my anxieties . . . fills my life when I am alone,"[127] students of that man's life are alerted to the fact that their subject is somehow troubled. Further data are likely to indicate how his anxieties manifest themselves, how he handles them, etc., and these matters are relatively amenable to description. They constitute the *what* of the subject's behavior. The *why* is necessarily a far more complex and speculative matter. Because the data seemed to permit, we allowed ourselves in *Woodrow Wilson and Colonel House* to speculate about the origins of Wilson's low self-estimates and fierce stubbornness, clearly identifying our hypothesis as exactly that—a hypothesis, not susceptible of conclusive proof. Having equipped our readers with appropriate caveats, we offered for their consideration the hypothesis that Wilson's low self-estimates derived from his relationship with his extraordinary father. Weinstein, Anderson, and Link obviously find this theory unpersuasive. Very well. What do they make of the fact that years later, information has become available that tends to confirm the ego-damaging atmosphere of the household in which "Tommy" Wilson was raised, and that indeed Dr. Wilson and even Mrs. Wilson—of this we had been unaware—were given to cruel disparagement and mockery of a child's failure to measure up to their aspirations?

Suppose they acknowledge that Dr. and Mrs. Wilson were indeed hard on "Josie" but argue that their manner toward their older son had been different. We believe such a line of reasoning would founder upon the following extraordinary coincidence: that on the basis of what they contend is practically no evidence concerning Woodrow Wilson, we were able a quarter of a century ago to describe the child-raising techniques that subsequently available information reveals to have been employed by these parents upon *another* of their sons.

It is possible, of course, that Weinstein, Anderson, and Link will regard the evidence we have presented about "Josie's" childhood as inconsequential. That, in any case, would appear to be Professor Link's view since he left so much of the relevant material out of the *Papers of Woodrow Wilson*, the volumes of which are supposed to place at the researcher's disposal "all the materials essential to understanding Wilson's personality, his intellectual, religious, and political development, and his careers as educator, writer, orator, and statesman."[128]

Or perhaps they will concede, as they did in their article in *Political Science Quarterly*, that there exists some small support for our interpretation but, weighed against contrary evidence of the warm familial relationship, it fades into insignificance. No doubt Dr. and Mrs. Wilson loved "Josie" as surely as they had loved "Tommy." No doubt they tried their best, according to their lights, to stimulate his intellectual growth as they had, with such spectacular success, finally, their older son's. Perhaps Weinstein, Anderson, and Link would say of Dr. Wilson's relationship with "Josie" as they did of his relationship with "Tommy" that it was not handicapping, that Dr. Wilson's "teasing" "does not sound harsh or excessive," that, after all, he was "a great wit and punster and used his family as an audience, but there is no indication that he was malicious."[129] Of course he was not malicious: he was the best-meaning of men, with understandable aspirations for his sons. But how, in fact, did the tactics these conscientious parents employed to "encourage" the intellectual and moral development of their sons affect their self-image as human beings?

Wilson himself, it seems to us, offers a clue in a speech he made years later in which he described the household (a household also headed by a minister) from which emerged another great leader—John Wesley:

> The children of that vicarage, swarming a little host about its hearth, were bred in love and fear, love of rectitude and fear of sin, their imagination filled with the ancient sanctions of the religion of the prophets and the martyrs, their lives drilled to right action and the studious service of God. Some things in the intercourse and discipline of that household strike us with a sort of awe, some with repulsion. Those children lived too much in the presence of things unseen; the inflexible consciences of the parents who ruled them brought them under a rigid discipline which disturbed their spirits as much as it enlightened them. But, though gaiety and lightness of heart were there shut out, love was not nor sweetness. No one can read Susanna Wesley's rules for the instruction and development of her children without seeing the tender heart of the true woman whose children were the light of her eyes. This mother was a true counsellor and her children resorted to her as to a sort of providence, feeling safe when she approved. For the stronger spirits among them the regime of that household was a keen and wholesome tonic.
>
> And John Wesley was certainly one of the stronger spirits. He came out of the hands of his mother with the temper of a piece of fine steel.[130]

If there was some parallel between Wilson's own household and the one from which John Wesley emerged, perhaps Wilson regarded himself as one of the "stronger spirits," "with the temper of a piece of fine steel"—the very phrase, indeed, that Joseph R. Wilson used in characterizing him. Were the repellent aspects of the Wesley household also features of his own? Had his spirit and "Josie's" been "disturbed"?

Certain it is that the dozens of surviving letters from "Josie" to Woodrow Wilson, spanning over forty years, testify to his pathetic preoccupation with establishing that he, too, was a worthwhile, successful person, of some importance. As for Wilson, in letters to his beloved "Eileen" (his private name for Ellen Axson Wilson) he referred to himself as "a man of a sensitive, restless, overwrought disposition." He spoke of his "sombre, morbid nature," his "fears," "anxieties," "morose moods," of "my poor, mixed, inexplicable nature." "Deep perturbations are natural to me, deep disturbances of spirit." He spoke of "my natural self-distrust," of having "never been sanguine," of often falling when irritated into "the stern, indignant, defiant humour, the scarcely suppressed belligerent temper, for which there are abundant materials in my disposition." "I have to . . . guard my emotions from painful overflow . . ." he exclaims.[131]

If Wilson felt intellectually incompetent through his childhood, there is evidence also that he felt *unlovable*. A letter from his mother when he was eighteen and the family was moving from Columbia, S.C., to Wilmington, N.C., sheds light, however indirectly, on his self doubts. It also typifies the flavor of her stifling concern:

> My darling Boy,
>   I am so anxious about that cold of yours. How did you take it? Surely you have not laid aside your winter-clothing? Another danger is in sitting without fire these cool nights. Do be careful, my dear boy, for my sake. You seem depressed—but that is because you are not well. You need not imagine that you are not a favorite. *Everybody* here likes and admires you. I could not begin to tell you the kind and flattering things that are said about you, by everybody that knows you . . . Why my darling, nobody could *help* loving you, if they were to try!
>   I have a bad head-ache this morning dear—and won't attempt to write you a letter.[132]

Wilson told his wife, according to her younger sister, that he had been an "awkward and ungainly" youth, shy with girls and too ill at ease to engage in mild flirtations. He did not dance and at social gatherings "the young ladies of the seminary turned aside from this solemn-faced youth . . . Woodrow often told her [i.e. his wife] that the first thing to give him confidence in himself was the fact that *she* loved him."[133] Indeed, Wilson deemed it "one of my chief pleasures . . . to go over again and again the delightful recollections of our first acquaintance and drawing together" and he did so in scores of letters to Ellen Axson Wilson. In the particular one just quoted, written in the fourteenth year of their marriage, he spoke of the "crowning joy" of discovering that so lovely a maiden, redolent "of all the sweet flavours of some old garden of the mind borne about by one herself fresh and of the sunshine . . . could *love me*, who had deemed myself unlovable: and it is that love that has transformed my life, transfusing me with some touch of the sweet savour that was hers. I am like something common and stale that had been lain away in a sweet place and has come out brightened in texture and scented like a garment of state."[134]

After almost a quarter of a century of marriage, he wrote:

> I am naturally a lonely spirit. It was the spirit of isolation and loneliness in me that was exorcised by the blessing of my marriage to you . . . Whenever I am away from you for any length of time it comes back upon me. When I am actually *with* other persons whom I enjoy, the *consciousness* of it often leaves me; to come back again when I am alone. But, thank God, it no longer rules, or can rule, my life.[135]

Ellen Axson Wilson taught Wilson that he was lovable and gave him the sweetest relief from his self-doubts and feelings of inadequacy. Quite simply, she accepted him as he was, thought him wonderful, and told him so. Anyone who has read the hundreds of letters he wrote her during their courtship and marriage will know the desperate intensity of his hunger for her reassurances. To her, he could open his heart without reserve:

> *All* its secrets, its sensitive pride, its morbid self-consciousness, both its strivings after things that are noble and worthy and its inclinations towards things that are unworthy . . . *all* its secrets are yielded up to you— they *will* tell themselves *to you*—and with the rest there run out to you those of which I am a bit ashamed, the things which prove me little, petty, weak; small irritations, transient doubts and discontents which ought never to be spoken—ought, indeed, ignominiously to be driven out, suffered to speak not even to me, much less to you. If I can but write long

enough, I can generally write myself *out* of a dark mood when I write to you, my sweet confessor . . . [136]

He recognized that he had "an insatiable desire to be loved," "to be loved and believed in with that unbounded, unquestioning love and belief which only a woman can give . . ." If, especially when alone, he had "days of self-examination and self-distrust—days of weakness when I do not feel equal to the tasks set for me . . . what a source of steadying and of strength it is to me . . . to have one fixed point of confidence and certainty—the even, unbroken, excellent perfection of my little wife . . ." In another letter, he spoke of the "delightful periods in my day when I can go to you as a tired boy would go to his mother, to be loved and petted. The close, unargued sympathy of these dear intervals is unspeakably soothing and refreshing to me."[137]

If we quote at length, it is because the correspondence is monumental, both in size and in self-revelation, and the theme of Wilson's dependence on his wife to bolster his self-esteem is so prominent throughout. "My one antidote against all ills and discouragements is my love for you," he wrote. "I should feel so absolutely *naught* without you—so without weight or significance!" When he was already President of Princeton and had a circle of close friends he wrote once when she was abroad of "the total inadequacy of *any* substitute companionship," sweet and tender as his friends were: "You are *part of me*[;] they are outside of me."[138] And what message was this treasured *"part of me"* constantly feeding him? One can almost quote at random from the hundreds of letters available, so many expressions are there of Ellen's unconditional love and admiration and confidence in the great destiny of Woodrow Wilson. For example:

> Dearest it is my deliberate conviction—nay I do not *believe* it, I *know*—that the combination of qualities found in you is the rarest, finest, noblest, *grandest* of which human nature is capable. It is a combination which if put in a book in all its naked truth would be censured by every critic as impossible . . . Strength and nobility of character combined with . . . *all* those gifts which go to make a born leader of men, combined with powers of thought of such a kind that he must undoubtedly rank as a *genius*, no less than Burke himself; and added to all this a strength of purpose and of will and powers of application which result in achievements so great that while yet in his earliest manhood his rank is now among the foremost thinkers of his age![139]

Or again:

> ... You are a *genius* ... You satisfy every possible need of my nature; my heart and mind are both filled ... And then, darling, how you satisfy *my* pride and ambition. You don't know how I *glory* in your splendid gifts, your noble, beautiful character, that rare charm of manner and "presence,"—indeed *every*thing about you ... Oh, it is a great thing to be the wife of such a man![140]

Few men would fail to find such letters irresistible. Expressions of delight abound in Wilson's replies. For example: "I am filled with the sweet wonder *of being dear to you,* of being followed everywhere by your loving, and as it were *guardian,* thoughts. It gives me a strange new *elation* and self-confidence." Again: "It is as if my heart were a harp which loves its mistress more for every touch she gives it."[141] His enchantment would not be remarkable—except for the virtuosity of his language—were it not for an added aspect: he not only basked in her approval, he *craved* it. "I *need* you, darling," he wrote her on October 7, 1887—and literally scores of similar expressions are at hand. "... Without you I am morose and beyond healthfulness strenuous ... I always wanted a *sun-beam* of a wife—and I have one! She cures my morbidness by being herself incapable of it. She looks my ugly moods out of countenance with her sweet placid eyes."[142]

To say that he pleaded with her for daily letters when they were apart would be an understatement. He *demanded* them, portrayed himself as in a piteous state, mentally and physically, if he did not receive his daily dose of reassurance from her. "I must write to Woodrow every day," Ellen Axson, then his fiancee, wrote her cousin. "If my letter does not come, he gets a bad headache." Fourteen years after their marriage, she wrote a girlhood friend:

> He is almost terribly dependent on me to keep up his spirits and to "rest" him as he says. So I dare not have "the blues." If I am just a little sky blue he immediately becomes blue black![143]

Wilson himself once put it as follows:

> You are *the* indispensable thing in my life. I wish you knew how often and with what feelings I read the dear words of tenderness and love in your letters! They seem to put life and hope into me. There is a sense in which it may be said that I keep alive on them when I am away from you.

There are times when I am *with* you, as I am sure you know, when I grow faint and all life and hope seem to go out of me because you seem to grow a bit distant, to draw off a bit in feeling, and to look at me as I am—not as the man whom you uncritically love and who loves you, his dear wife and sweet companion, with passionate devotion,—but as a fellow full of unlovable faults and grievous weaknesses whom you are yet bound by some blind compulsion of your heart to love and endure—and revive only when your heart breaks bounds again and comes running back to me! In just the same way, the intervals between your letters, between their words of love, are for me like periods of suspended animation, and I live again only when I read the sweet words of love once more.[144]

It is interesting to note that one of the Wilsons' daughters, Eleanor Wilson McAdoo, writing long years later, connected her father's need of her mother's admiration with a deprivation in his childhood and, in effect, his low self-estimates. She said: "Ellen knew that Woodrow's family, while very proud of him, seldom praised him . . . And because self-depreciation was Woodrow's chief liability, he needed her admiration, as a man needs water in a desert."[145]

It is also interesting to note that a prominent characteristic of all his close personal relationships—with his second wife, with his friends (men and women both)—was the other's disposition to serve as an ever-overflowing reservoir of admiration and approval. He drank deeply from many sources but seemed ever to feel the parched man in the desert. Such intense dependence on constant external reassurance as to his worth suggests, to us at any rate, that here was a man whose inner resources for maintaining his self-esteem had been so damaged that he was obliged all through his life to seek outside supplies with that desperation for them that he himself so often and so eloquently described in his letters. Of this needy side of Woodrow Wilson, the outside world knew nothing. The public man seemed reserved, strong, self-sufficient.

We shall save for future presentation further evidence concerning Wilson's father as his relentlessly driving critic. We also hope to write further about Wilson's longing to do—as he put it—"immortal work," work of such noble service to humanity that to further it he felt morally justified—even *required*—to give full rein to the expression of his aggressions against those who stood in his way. Of interest too and, in our judgment not mere happenstance, is the fact that Wilson's chief adversaries—Dean West at Princeton and Henry Cabot Lodge in the U.S. Senate—resembled Wilson's father in important respects: Lodge had a mordant wit. Both men were strong, erudite, of notable facility with the English language and of patrician (not to say condescending) bearing.

III. Woodrow Wilson's Medical Problems

The third "principal failing" of *Woodrow Wilson and Colonel House*, according to Weinstein, Anderson, and Link is that we "ignore Wilson's neurological disorders as conditions affecting his behavior." They assert unequivocally that he suffered strokes in 1896, 1900, 1904, 1906 and 1907 and that "by the end of World War I, Wilson was showing signs of generalized cerebral involvement." They state further that an episode of illness in April 1919, while he was negotiating the Versailles Peace Treaty in Paris, was not only influenza but

> probably a virus encephalopathy, which, superimposed on pre-existing brain damage, produced changes in behavior which may have influenced the outcome of the peace negotiations. In October 1919 he had a massive stroke that completely paralyzed the left side of his body and produced mental attitudes and personality changes which were important factors in his failure to obtain ratification of the Treaty of Versailles.[146]

We acknowledge that we did not think of Wilson as brain damaged until the stroke he suffered on October 2, 1919. While doing our research for *Woodrow Wilson and Colonel House*, we indeed were alert to the possibility of personality changes following that catastrophe which might have affected his handling of the controversy then raging with the Senate over ratification of the Treaty. It was our conclusion then, as we sifted through the data, and it is our conclusion now, that whatever the nature of the brain damage Wilson sustained in his paralyzing stroke of October, 1919, it did not alter his stance vis à vis the Senate: he had struck his unyielding position long before October 1919—a position that anguished practically everyone who cared personally about him and/or supported U.S. entry into the League of Nations. Indeed, even before the Peace Conference began, he was breathing defiance of Senators whose votes he needed to obtain ratification of the Treaty. Wilson's behavior in this respect after the stroke of October 1919 was entirely consistent with his behavior before it. Both before and after, ample warnings were conveyed to him of the all but inevitable consequences of his refusal at every turn to compromise. Both before and after the stroke he rejected these warnings. Friend and foe alike watched, fascinated, throughout a period beginning months before the October 1919 stroke and ending months after it (when the Treaty met its second and final defeat in the Senate on March 19, 1920) the awesome spectacle of Wilson's step by step repulsion of every opportunity—and there were many—to save the Treaty. The stroke seemed not to modify his behavior one whit.

To those who knew and loved him best, his refusal to compromise was a source of sorrow rather than of surprise. A sense of some terrible inner logic to his self-defeating behavior, in terms of stable, persistent characteristics that they had long since recognized, pervades their narratives.

To quote one reaction to the tragedy of Wilson's defeat is to convey the essence of a score of others that might be cited:

> Woodrow *couldn't* conciliate . . . Speculations as to what might have been are as futile as they are tragic. Woodrow just wasn't built that way.[147]

This was the judgment of Margaret Axson Elliott, Wilson's young sister-in-law who had lived with the Wilsons in Princeton when she was a child, had been a member of the household before, during and after the alleged "strokes" of that period, and therefore was well acquainted with Wilson's "pre-morbid" personality.

Some of Wilson's enemies, too, had insight into the fact that he was somehow propelled into his self-defeating course and held to it by some invincible inner compulsion. Perhaps the keenest student of his personality was his implacable enemy, Henry Cabot Lodge, who, following the Republican victory in the 1918 elections, became chairman of the Senate Foreign Relations Committee. Lodge was determined to engineer Senate rejection of the Peace Treaty (which included the League of Nations Covenant). This was no easy matter, for public opinion favored the Treaty and the necessary two-thirds vote in the Senate to ratify it was clearly available if only Wilson would consent to minor changes.

Lodge hit upon a strategy based upon a shrewd analysis of Wilson's *modus operandi:* Wilson, Lodge later wrote, "was simply an element to be calmly and coolly considered in a great problem of international politics." It was "of vital moment to me" to make "a correct analysis of Mr. Wilson's probable attitude . . ." What emerged from this analysis was Lodge's conviction that Wilson would never agree to accept even minor reservations to the Treaty, that rather than compromise with the Senate and particularly with him (Lodge), Wilson would allow the Treaty with his beloved League in it to be defeated. All he had to do, Lodge calculated, was tack reservations onto the Treaty, particularly onto the League Covenant that Wilson held so dear. Then, if his theory was correct, Wilson would refuse to accept them—however innocuous they were made—and could be counted on himself to destroy what he had invested his lifeblood to create.[148]

The drama unfolded quite as Lodge had foreseen. His tactical finesse in maneuvering Wilson from one excruciating refusal to compromise to another testifies to his deadly insight into the tragic flaw in Wilson's character. This insight was based upon years of hostile but astute observation stretching back to the beginning of Wilson's administration—a period during which, if we understand Weinstein, Anderson, and Link correctly, they believe Wilson to have been relatively free of the effects of the intermittent cerebral vascular disease from which they say he suffered. Lodge was able to perceive certain motivational patterns in Wilson that afforded him awesome manipulative power which endured through all the vicissitudes of Wilson's health. He was not confounded by any perplexing "changes" in Wilson's behavior toward the end of World War I because of the "generalized cerebral involvement" that Weinstein, Anderson, and Link postulate, or the "changes" they allege occurred after his illness in Paris in April 1919 or after the serious stroke that unquestionably occurred in October 1919. His strategy to defeat Wilson remained constant and constantly effective despite the fluctuations in Wilson's health. Indeed, Lodge preyed upon and counted upon the ruinous consistencies of Wilson's self-defeating political behavior. His success at predicting Wilson's reactions suggest the persistence of the characteristic patterns that Lodge had so cunningly discerned.

Weinstein, Anderson, and Link make repeated references to physiologically induced behavior and personality changes in Wilson without delineating the characteristic behavior patterns, the underlying personality, upon which the alleged changes impinged. Changes, after all, are comprehensible only in terms of that which pre-exists. Did the postulated brain damage accentuate certain aspects of a well-established behavior system or did they, in these authors' view, cause quite alien behavior to become manifest?

There was a time when Professor Link recognized the relationship between Wilson's character and the recurrent defeats he suffered. In his book, *Wilson: The Road to the White House,* he wrote:

> The Princeton period was the microcosm of a later macrocosm, and a po-
> litical observer, had he studied carefully Wilson's career as president of
> Princeton University, might have forecast accurately the shape of things
> to come during the period when Wilson was president of the United
> States. What striking similarities there are between the Princeton and the
> national periods! During the first years of both administrations, Wilson
> drove forward with terrific energy and momentum to carry through a
> magnificent reform program, and his accomplishments both at Princeton
> and Washington were great and enduring. Yet in both cases he drove so
> hard, so flatly refused to delegate authority, and broke with so many
> friends that when the inevitable reaction set in he was unable to cope
> with the new situation.[149]

At that time Professor Link thought Wilson's behavior during the quad and graduate college controversies at Princeton unreasonable. "The vagaries of his mind during this period are unfathomable," he wrote.

Professor Link found the most striking fact about the whole Princeton controversy "the absence of any clear-cut issue" and that Wilson had shifted from one issue to another so that "it was almost impossible to tell where he really stood."[150] He attributed Wilson's difficulties at Princeton and later in his career explicitly to his *character* rather than to the logic of the situations he confronted:

> Wilson was a headstrong and determined man who was usually able to
> rationalize his actions in terms of the moral law and to identify his posi-
> tion with the divine will. This combination of strong, almost imperious
> will and intense conviction operated to great advantage when Wilson
> had support among the trustees at Princeton, the legislators at Trenton,
> or the congressmen in Washington, because it gave him great power and
> an impelling drive. The time came at Princeton, Trenton, and Washington
> when Wilson did not command the support of the groups to whom he
> was responsible. Naturally, he was not able to change his character even
> had he wanted to change it, with the result that controversy and disas-
> trous defeat occurred in varying degrees in all three cases.[151]

Professor Link now holds a different view of the Princeton imbroglio, as he indicates in a footnote:

Arthur S. Link wishes to state that much new evidence discovered since the publication of his *Wilson: The Road to the White House* in 1947 has convinced him that his treatment of Wilson and West and the graduate college controversy is inadequate and unbalanced.[152]

The account of the Princeton controversy given by Weinstein, Anderson and Link implies that Wilson's actions in fact derived from a reasonable assessment of the situation rather than from characterological idiosyncrasies. For example Wilson detested West "because West was the condensed symbol of so many of the social, educational, economic, and political problems that Wilson faced at Princeton."

It is easy enough to grant that Wilson's ideals for the University were commendable and that there was some substance to a good many of his objections to Dean West's plans for the graduate college. However, several questions remain. Why, when a compromise was accepted which he himself had suggested as to the site of the graduate school, did he turn away from it? Why, when his supporters had succeeded, by dint of an enormous effort, in stripping West of most of his authority in the administration of the graduate school, did he reject their plan of compromise, claiming that "very deep principles" were involved which "seem to express themselves in every detail of administration"?[153] Why, for the sake of getting his way "in every detail," did he create a ruinous confrontation with West (and later with Lodge) instead of making the substantial progress toward excellent goals that it was practicable to make?

The same question may be asked concerning the earlier quad fight, which rent the Princeton community: his own leadership had created an opportunity to achieve substantial reform of the eating clubs. He spurned it. Why?

Professor Link's repudiation of the interpretation he offered in *Wilson: The Road to the White House* and the treatment of the Princeton controversy in the article by Weinstein, Anderson, and Link suggest that the circumstances justified Wilson's behavior and that his adherence to "very deep principles" explains his stand—in other words that he responded rationally to the situation. At the same time, they argue that "changes" in Wilson's behavior due to brain damage from the alleged strokes of 1896, 1900, 1904, 1906 and 1907 impaired his performance and played a critical role in his defeat. To the extent that they consider Wilson's refusal to compromise in the quad and graduate college battles a reasonable defense of his principles, they reduce the grounds for arguing the significance of the alleged personality and behavioral changes in consequence of the alleged strokes.

If in the article by Weinstein, Anderson, and Link, Professor Link repudiates the interpretive structure of *Wilson: The Road to the White House*, Dr. Weinstein also discloses a change in one of his key diagnoses: that of Wilson's illness in Paris in April, 1919. In his widely read and widely quoted earlier article, "Woodrow Wilson's Neurological Illness" published in 1970, Dr. Weinstein stated that the most likely cause of Wilson's illness during the Peace Conference was a "cerebral vascular occlusion (blood clot in the brain)"—in short, a stroke. He construed certain aspects of Wilson's behavior during and after his illness (e.g. his order that his staff use official automobiles only for official business and his concern that the French servants in his house were spies) as irrational and delusional—evidence of the kind of behavioral change that would confirm brain damage caused by a stroke. Weinstein described the "cerebral vascular occlusion" as

> a lesion in the right cerebral hemisphere extending to include deeper structures in the limbic-reticular system. With the history of lesions of the left side of the brain, indicated by the attacks of right-sided paresthesia and left monocular blindness from 1896 to 1908, he now had evidence of bilateral damage, a condition affecting emotional and social behavior more severely than a unilateral lesion.[154]

This medical description was so precise and authoritative in tone that few laymen would dare to take issue with it. The problem is that the major evidence on which it relied—the allegedly strange changes in Wilson's behavior—is tittle-tattle that has gained momentum and grown in absurdity in its passage from one source to another. The historical record, as we shall shortly attempt to show, provides a background against which Wilson's "strange behavior," viewed in context, seems reasonable and rational. In any case, in the article by Weinstein, Anderson, and Link readers learn that Wilson did not have a stroke in Paris after all: it was influenza, as most historians had thought all along. However, it was not only influenza: according to these authors, it was "probably a virus encephalopathy." As for the minutely described stroke of Dr. Weinstein's earlier article, a footnote states that new evidence indicates that it is not likely to have occurred.[155] It must be noted that one crucial aspect of Dr. Weinstein's diagnosis remains constant: that in April 1919 Woodrow Wilson sustained brain damage that significantly affected his behavior. In both articles readers hear of the aforementioned "strange" changes of behavior that signify altered brain function.

Let us examine them: one manifestation of Wilson's "irrational behavior" cited by Weinstein in his earlier article (which presumably constitutes part of the documentation of the "changes in behavior" alleged by Weinstein, Anderson, and Link) was Wilson's instruction to his personal staff in Paris that they use official limousines only for official business. Irwin "Ike" Hoover, White House Head Usher who served as chief of Wilson's household staff in Paris, is the source of this tale, which he recorded in his book, *42 Years in the White House*. This gentleman, as his letters to his wife indicate, had grown accustomed to taking joyrides practically every day—sometimes two and three times a day. ("It is fine to order up a big limousine, say 'to the hotel' and off it goes," he wrote his wife. "Come out, say 'home' and you are on the way back." Of the scores of letters he wrote home, there is scarcely a handful—except when he was at sea en route to or from the Conference—in which he did not articulate his use or non-use of the limousines for the particular day covered. "Ike" missed his family—and also his Dodge automobile to which he referred affectionately in several letters.)[156] Other staff members fell into the same habit of rushing for the cars the moment the President and Mrs. Wilson went out.

One day during his illness in April 1919 the President sent for one member of his staff after the other and found that they were all out in the cars. This angered him and he ordered the staff to curtail use of the cars for personal pleasure.[157] We see nothing "strange" or "irrational" in Wilson's crackdown. The only strange element, it seems to us, is that he did not sooner lose his temper at Hoover's profligate abuse of privilege.

On the basis of "Ike" Hoover's account, Weinstein also accepted as "markedly irrational behavior" after Wilson's April 1919, illness that he was concerned that the French servants in the house the French government had placed at his disposal were spies. The fact is that many Americans at the Conference were worried about spies. Joseph Grew, Secretary of the American Commission, issued directives warning of the need for the secure handling of confidential papers, for burning trash, for being alert to the possibility that telephones were being tapped, and that French employees might be spying for their government. During the very week of Wilson's illness, Dr. Grayson wrote in his diary that one of the servants who claimed not to speak English had been found to know English fluently and that the French government was engaged in spying on the President. Mrs. Wilson's secretary, Edith Benham, noted in her diary on March 29, 1919 that conversations at meals had to be restrained because "Colonel House says there are spies here in the house who report everything to the Foreign Office." Colonel House noted in his diary at the beginning of the Conference that the private wire between his study and Wilson's "is constantly 'covered' to see that it is not tapped."[158]

It seems to us grotesque that Wilson's concern for security at the Conference should be interpreted by Weinstein and others as evidence of brain damage. Was Joseph Grew also brain damaged? And Dr. Grayson, Colonel House and Miss Benham too?

Of course the question to which all the foregoing discussion leads is: how would competent, independent medical authority evaluate Woodrow Wilson's illnesses throughout his career and Dr. Weinstein's diagnoses of them? For a response to this question, we turned to Dr. Michael F. Marmor, Associate Professor of Ophthalmology at the Stanford University School of Medicine. We placed at Dr. Marmor's disposal all the data in our possession relating to Wilson's health[159] and made available to him the relevant volumes of *The Papers of Woodrow Wilson* as well as the source materials cited by Dr. Weinstein in his various articles.

Dr. Marmor embodied the results of his review in a letter to us dated May 18, 1981. A copy of this letter is attached. It speaks for itself and we need only note here Dr. Marmor's main conclusions: that in the absence of documented findings or medical records, Dr. Weinstein's analysis is necessarily speculative; that his own reading of the evidence leads him to question both the medical interpretations of Dr. Weinstein and the propriety of presenting such views as historical fact.

In conclusion, we should like to say a few words about *The Papers of Woodrow Wilson,* of which Professor Link is editor. The preparation of *The Papers of Woodrow Wilson* is one of the major projects in historiography in our time. These volumes are meant to preserve for posterity a true and unbiased record concerning Woodrow Wilson. Scholars today consult *The Papers* on the assumption—an assumption upon which they ought to be able to rely—that the facts stated in the informational notes to various documents are true and accurate. Scholars will continue to consult *The Papers* on this assumption for many generations to come—for as long, indeed, as humankind is interested in the life and strivings of Woodrow Wilson. As we noted at the beginning of this paper, the editorial matter of several of these volumes contains unqualified allusions to Wilson's so-called "strokes" between the years 1896 and 1907. (The volumes covering the period of the Paris Peace Conference into which Wilson's illness of April 1919 falls have not yet been published.) We believe that these allusions have prejudiced the objectivity of *The Papers of Woodrow Wilson* and have already misled a number of writers.[160] We also believe that those in charge of the project have a reverence for the truth and a fidelity to their scholarly duties. We suggest that a review of these editorial notes, which elevate Dr. Weinstein's controversial medical hypotheses to the status of historical fact, is in order.

Letter of Medical Opinion from Michael F. Marmor, M. D.

 STANFORD UNIVERSITY MEDICAL CENTER

STANFORD, CALIFORNIA 94305 • (415) 497-5517

STANFORD UNIVERSITY SCHOOL OF MEDICINE
Department of Surgery
Division of Ophthalmology

May 18, 1981

Dr. and Mrs. Alexander George
Department of Political Science
Stanford University
Stanford, California 94305

Dear Dr. and Mrs. George:

I have reviewed at length the medical and historical source material which bears upon the possibility that Woodrow Wilson had neurologic disease. I am preparing a comprehensive analysis of this material for publication and this letter represents a summary of my impressions and conclusions. You have my permission to quote from this letter, with the proviso that statements should not be taken out of context or used without sufficient material to provide a balanced picture of my views.

Let me say at the outset that the medical analysis of historical figures is by nature a speculative process. In the absence of documented findings or medical records, one must rely upon guesswork and judgment to analyze lay descriptions of disease. Physicians are trained to consider all of the rare and unlikely disease which might afflict their patients, lest one be missed. However, in looking back over history, the approach should probably be the opposite: given the symptoms, search for the most common and likely causes. Under these constraints, historical diagnoses will rarely have the certainty of scientific fact, and should in general be considered hypothesis.

In a series of articles, psychiatrist Edwin Weinstein has argued that Wilson suffered from serious cerebrovascular disease over a period of nearly thirty years, and that discrete strokes accounted for behavioral changes at several critical junctures in Wilson's professional life. This view has been accepted by the eminent historian Arthur Link, who has referred to these "strokes" without qualification in the current edition of *The Papers of Woodrow Wilson*. My own reading of the evidence leads me to question both the medical interpretations of Dr. Weinstein, and the propriety of presenting such views as historical fact.

Weinstein's thesis is that Wilson suffered for many years from cerebrovascular disease, primarily carotid artery insufficiency, and had discrete strokes which influenced his professional behavior. Weinstein contends cerebrovascular disease first became manifest as disability of the right arm, resulting from one or more small strokes in 1896. The strongest and most direct evidence for stroke is considered to be Wilson's episode of left visual loss in 1906, which Weinstein describes as diagnostic of left carotid occlusive disease. Finally the illness which Wilson suffered during the 1919 Peace Conference is viewed as viral encephalopathy superimposed on preexisting brain damage. Each of these points merits careful analysis.

Wilson had difficulty with his right hand and arm for more than twenty years, and referred on numerous occasions to "writer's cramp" which was apparently diagnosed as a "neuritis." The precise symptoms are not spelled out, but the hand and arm were often painful, especially while writing. These symptoms began long before the alleged stroke of 1896, and references to this complaint can be found in the Wilson papers as far back as 1884. There are no references to suggest a sudden onset of symptoms (as from a stroke) in either 1884 or 1896, and the symptoms are too chronic to call them a result of transient ischemic attacks. Furthermore, Wilson also had occasional discomfort and pain in his *left* arm.

"Writer's cramp" is poorly understood as a clinical entity. Some cases may have an organic basis from pathology such as arthritic joint damage or inflammation of the nerves, but many are thought to represent an occupational neurosis. Characteristically, the patient has difficulty writing more than a few words, but lacks any major disability for other activities. This fits the descriptions of Wilson's disorder, and there is evidence that even during his severe periods of disability he was able to write brief ledger entries with his right hand which rules out any serious paralysis or limitation of movement. To accept this condition as writer's cramp (even without a precise definition of that term) seems perfectly reasonable in view of the nature and duration of the symptoms, whereas to fit these symptoms into a stroke syndrome places them in the category of unusual manifestations.

The 1906 episode is interpreted by Weinstein as direct evidence for cerebrovascular disease, since right-sided weakness and left-sided blindness are often associated with insufficiency or occlusion of the left carotid artery. However, the ocular findings in Wilson's case argue *against* a diagnosis of carotid occlusion. Wilson awoke one morning aware of poor vision in his left eye, which numerous sources indicate was found to result from bursting of a blood vessel and hemorrhage inside the eye. The fact of the matter is that retinal hemorrhage is *not* a sign of carotid occlusive disease. Carotid disease most characteristically leads to occlusion of the retinal arteries which causes a loss of vision but produces a very different picture (without hemorrhage) inside the eye. Arterial occlusion would not have been described in the language used by Wilson and his family members.

Wilson's doctors noted signs of arteriosclerosis and mild hypertension, and there seems little doubt that he had systemic vascular disease. The most likely cause for Wilson's eye disease would be a retinal vein occlusion, which is often associated with hypertensive vascular disease, and which produces diffuse hemorrhages in the retina. Other possibilities include hemorrhagic macular degeneration. The point to emphasize is that these ocular hemorrhages occur frequently as isolated events; they give evidence of generalized vascular pathology but they do not constitute strokes or carry any direct implication of cerebral ischemia or symptomatology.

There are other reasons to doubt a stroke in 1906. The stroke would have affected the left cerebral hemisphere which has major control over language and speech, yet Wilson clearly suffered no impairment in these areas. Weinstein implies that a stroke caused personality changes that affected Wilson's subsequent activities, but the literature on strokes is quite clear in emphasizing that personality changes are not a characteristic of the stroke syndrome in the absence of cognitive changes or dementia. Weinstein carefully qualifies his argument to state that Wilson's behavioral changes in 1906 were an adaptation to his illness and could result from stress as well as brain damage. Considering that Wilson had indeed suffered an ocular hemorrhage, and that he was working with intensity as president of Princeton University, why should it be necessary to invoke strokes or cerebral pathology to account for his actions?

Similar problems arise in analyzing the illness that began on April 3, 1919, during the Peace Conference. Weinstein initially concluded that Wilson had suffered a stroke to explain his behavior during the conference, but the tenuousness of the stroke hypothesis is shown by Weinstein's shift to a diagnosis of viral encephalopathy when new evidence made it clear that Wilson had had respiratory disease. I fail to see the need for postulating any diagnoses beyond severe influenza to account for Wilson's behavior. Wilson was ill with respiratory symptoms and high fever, and there are surely few of us who cannot attest to the debilitating effect of severe flu. Wilson was confined to bed for five days but was incapacitated only on the first day, after which he resumed conferring and decision making from his bedroom. The term "viral encephalopathy" may apply to a broad range of symptoms, from minimal headache and irritability, to severe somnolence, convulsions, and death. Wilson clearly did not have the latter, and some would argue that the former are in fact a routine component of the flu syndrome. Wilson's activities for the remainder of April 1919 seem quite consistent with a history of severe but uncomplicated influenza, and I should think the burden of proof would be to show otherwise.

Wilson probably had systemic vascular disease for a good part of his life, and there is no question that he ultimately suffered a severe stroke in the fall of 1919. Neither of these observations, however, can be construed as evidence for multiple strokes or for significant neurologic dysfunction during the earlier years of his career. Chronic vascular disease may cause subtle changes in mentation, ultimately resulting in dementia. Could Wilson have had very mild degrees of change accumulating over the years? Certainly this is possible, but how does one distinguish this type of subtle degeneration from other aspects of maturation and aging which are evident in everyone? This man actively ran one of the major universities in the United States, campaigned articulately for the presidency, and was clearly a lucid and powerful thinker in political affairs up to the moment of his serious stroke in 1919.

The interpretations which I have chosen to emphasize focus upon common and ordinary conditions, rather than the unusual or the extreme. I think the odds favor such an interpretation, but these views are admittedly hypothetical and open to review or criticism by others. I hope that my arguments will, at the least, raise reasonable doubts about the stroke theory and return it to a position of hypothesis rather than fact in historical source material.

With warm regards,

(Signed) Michael F. Marmor, M.D.
Associate Professor
Division of Ophthalmology
Chief, Ophthalmology Section
Veterans Administration Medical Center
Palo Alto, California

Notes

We wish to express our cordial thanks to the staff of the Manuscript Division, The Library of Congress, for facilitating our research there and especially to Dr. David Wigdor, Specialist, 20th Century Political History.

At the Yale University Library, Arthur Walworth took precious time from his own work on Woodrow Wilson and the Paris Peace Conference to direct our attention to documents of particular interest from his own files and in the papers of Colonel House.

Professor Link and Dr. David W. Hirst accorded us many courtesies, for which we thank them, at the Firestone Library, Princeton University.

At all stages of our work on this project we have benefited from the expert knowledge and wisdom of Margaret M. Stuart, M.D.

Four staunch friends—Joseph M. Goldsen, A. E. Hanson, Elise F. Kendrick and Lee R. Lombard (who has been trying for over half a century to improve Juliette George's diction)—read and reacted to the first version of this manuscript. We are grateful anew to each of them.

We thank Ellen Friedenthal for being an eagle-eyed proofreader.

1. See Weinstein, Edwin A., Anderson, James William, and Arthur S. Link, "Woodrow Wilson's Political Personality: A Reappraisal," *Political Science Quarterly* vol. 94, no. 4 (Winter, 1978) pp. 585–598.

2. George, Alexander L. and George, Juliette L. *Woodrow Wilson and Colonel House: A Personality Study* (New York: John Day, 1956; Dover Publications, 1964).

3. Weinstein, Anderson, and Link, *op. cit.*, p. 586. We are exiled in good company. Some years ago Professor Link wrote of Ray Stannard Baker that his eight-volume *Woodrow Wilson: Life and Letters* suffered from Baker's having "to a large degree imposed his own personality profile upon Wilson." Moreover, claims Link (without justification, in our opinion), Baker portrayed Wilson "as being mainly feminine in personality, if not virtually a sexual neuter." This of the man in whose early volumes Woodrow Wilson fairly springs to life. Baker's prodigious research resulted in the collection of that rich raw data upon which Link's own work—and that of every other Wilson scholar—heavily rests. (See Link, A. S. [ed.], *Woodrow Wilson: A Profile* [New York: Hill and Wang, 1968], pp. vii–viii.)

4. We shall here cite two of the more than dozen instances we have thus far collected: of Wilson's illness in May, 1906, it is stated in the Introduction to vol. 16 of *The Papers of Woodrow Wilson*, p. vii: "Years of excessive work take their toll in late May 1906, when Wilson suffers a major stroke that seems for a moment to threaten his life . . ." In December 1907, Moses Taylor Pyne, a Princeton trustee, wrote Wilson saying he was sorry to learn "that you were suffering from an attack of Neuritis." (*Ibid.*, vol. 17, p. 549.) Link's editorial footnote to the word "Neuritis" (*Ibid.*, p. 550) reads: "In fact, Wilson had unquestionably suffered a slight stroke."

5. Weinstein, Anderson, and Link, *op. cit.*, p. 587.

6. *Ibid.*, p. 598.

7. George and George, *op. cit.*, p. 323.

8. In this instance, Juliette L. George. Generally, we shall not try to indicate which of us did particular portions of the research or writing of *Woodrow Wilson and Colonel House.*

9. Floto's book was published by Universitetforlaget I Aarhus in 1973.

10. Weinstein, Anderson, and Link, *op. cit.*, p. 597.

11. Floto, *op. cit.*, pp. 13, 20, 21. We cite Floto solely on the question of our research and do not mean to suggest that she endorses our interpretation of the House-Wilson relationship. To be sure, she credits us with "elucidating the 'mechanism'" of the friendship in an "unassailable" fashion, but she is critical of our analysis of the "break." Her book is an important contribution to a continuing discussion among historians. We think, however, that the assertion by Weinstein, Anderson, and Link (*op. cit.*, p. 597) that Floto "proves conclusively that the cause of the so-called break between the two men was House's failure to follow Wilson's explicit instructions while the latter was in the United States" is an overstatement.

12. Weinstein, Anderson, and Link, *op. cit.*, p. 592.

13. George and George, *op. cit.*, p. 5.

14. Arthur S. Link, ed., *The Papers of Woodrow Wilson* (Princeton, NJ: Princeton University Press, 1966) vol. 1, p. xxii. (We shall hereafter refer to this series of books as *Papers.*)

15. Weinstein, Anderson, and Link, *op. cit.*, p. 587.

16. George and George, *op. cit.*, p. 12.

17. George and George, *op. cit.*, p. 7.

18. Weinstein, Anderson, and Link, *op. cit.*, pp. 588–89.

19. Arthur S. Link, *Wilson: The Road to the White House* (Princeton, NJ: Princeton University Press, 1947), p. 2.

20. Ray Stannard Baker, *Woodrow Wilson: Life & Letters* (New York: Doubleday, Page, 1927), vol. I, pp. 36–37.

21. George and George, *op. cit.*, p. 7.

22. Arthur S. Link, "The Case for Woodrow Wilson," *Harper's Magazine,* (April 1967), p. 91. In anticipation of the argument that Wilson did poorly because his schooling was disrupted in consequence of the disrupted times, let us point out that "Tommy" was a *conspicuously* poor student compared to his peers. According to Baker, "'Tommy' Wilson's school work was decidedly below average" and his teacher complained to Dr. Joseph Wilson that "Tommy" was at the foot of his class not for want of ability but because he wouldn't study. (Ray Stannard Baker, *op. cit.*, vol. I, p. 42; also the papers of Ray Stannard Baker, Library of Congress, Series IB, Box 3, "Memo for the Augusta Period," p. 10.) Link had referred to Wilson as a "late starter" in *Woodrow Wilson: A Brief Biography* (Cleveland, OH: The World Publishing Co., 1963), p. 18.

23. Arthur S. Link, ed., *Woodrow Wilson: A Profile* (New York: Hill & Wang, 1968), p. xiv–xv.

24. Weinstein, Anderson, and Link, *op. cit.*, p. 588.

25. M. Rutter, "Prevalence and Types of Dyslexia," in A. L. Benton and D. Pearl, eds., *Dyslexia: An Appraisal of Current Knowledge* (New York: Oxford University Press, 1978), pp. 5, 24. The chapters in this book were written for the NIMH conference.

26. A. L. Benton, "Some Conclusions About Dyslexia," *Ibid.*, p. 453.

27. M. Rutter, *op. cit.*, p. 9.

28. J. R. Hughes, "Electroencephalographic and Neurophysiological Studies in Dyslexia," *Ibid.*, p. 234.

29. Leon Eisenberg, "Psychiatric Aspects of Language Disability," in D. D. Duane and M. B. Rawson, eds., *Reading, Perception and Language: Papers from the World Congress on Dyslexia* (Baltimore, MD: York Press, 1975), p. 225. See also O. Spreen, "The Dyslexias: A Discussion of Neurobehavioral Research," in Benton and Pearl, *op. cit.*, pp. 178–179.

30. M. Rutter, *op. cit.*, p. 24.

31. Weinstein, Anderson, and Link, *op. cit.*, p. 588.

32. Wilson to Ellen Axson, Dec. 22, 1883. *Papers,* vol. 2, p. 596.

33. Wilson to Ellen Axson, Nov. 8, 1884. *Papers,* vol. 3, p. 415.

34. Wilson to Ellen Axson, Jan. 21, 1885. *Papers,* vol. 3, p. 627.

35. Wilson to Ellen Axson, Jan. 20, 1885, and Feb. 13, 1885. *Papers,* vol. 3, p. 623; vol. 4, pp. 244–45.

36. Wilson to Albert Shaw, Jan. 28, 1885, *Ibid.*, p. 195.

37. Wilson to Heath Dabney, Feb. 14, 1885, *Papers,* vol. 4, pp. 248–249

38. Wilson to Ellen Axson, Feb. 17, 1885. *Ibid.*, p. 263.

39. Wilson to Ellen Axson, Feb. 19, 1885. *Ibid.*, p. 269.

40. See *Papers,* vol. 1, pp. 83–128, p. 132 ff. See also p. 128 for Wilson to his sister Annie Howe April 19, 1876, in which he reports "employing most of the last week in reading" and finding "a great deal of enjoyment" in it.

41. See *Papers,* vol. 13, pp. 267–297.

42. Weinstein, Anderson, and Link, *op. cit.*, p. 588.

43. Harriet Woodrow Welles to Ray Stannard Baker, Aug. 14, 1925; Papers of Ray Stannard Baker, Series IB, Box 40.

44. "Material on Woodrow Wilson Prepared by Dr. Stockton Axson with Occasional Assistance of Admiral Cary T. Grayson," a memoir owned personally by Professor Link. Chapter entitled "Health and Recreations," p. 15. We wish to thank Professor Link for granting us access to this manuscript.

45. Wilson to Dr. Azel W. Hazen, March 29, 1897, *Papers,* vol. 10, p. 201. Wilson to Ellen Axson Wilson, June 17, 21, 23, 1896, and July 3, Aug. 18, 1896, *Papers,* vol. 9, pp. 519, 523, 527, 532, 573. Also see Wilson to Ellen Axson Wilson, June 29, 1908, *Papers,* vol. 18, p. 345.

46. Macdonald Critchley, *The Dyslexic Child* (Springfield, IL: Charles C. Thomas, 1970), pp. 36–40.

47. M. Rutter, *op. cit.*, p. 18.

48. M. Critchley, "Topics Worthy of Research," in A. H. Keeney and V. T. Keeney, *Dyslexia: Diagnosis and Treatment of Reading Disorders,* (St. Louis, MO: C. V. Mosby Company, 1968), pp. 171–172.

49. L. Eisenberg, *op. cit.*, p. 220.

50. D. Duane, "Summary of the World Congress on Dyslexia," in Duane and Rawson, *op. cit.*, p. 5. See also Critchley, *op. cit.*, p. 97.

51. Weinstein, Anderson, and Link, *op. cit.*, p. 588–589.

52. Papers of Ray Stannard Baker, Box 109, "Memorandum of Interviews with Dr. Cary T. Grayson on February 18, 19, 1926 at Washington."

53. Weinstein, Anderson, and Link, *op. cit.*, p. 588–589.

54. Stockton Axson, *op. cit.* (see footnote 44), chapter entitled "Woodrow Wilson and his Father," p. 20; Eleanor Wilson McAdoo, *The Woodrow Wilsons* (New York: The Macmillan Company, 1937), p. 43; *The Priceless Gift* (New York: McGraw-Hill Book Company, 1962), p. 217; "Memorandum of Conversation with Jessie Wilson Sayre and Eleanor Wilson McAdoo," May 30, 1926, papers of Ray Stannard Baker, Series IB, Box 28; "Memorandum of Conversation with Stockton Axson and Professor George Howe," February 24, 1925, papers of Ray Stannard Baker, Box 99, Stockton Axson folder.

55. Helen Bones to Ray Stannard Baker, Oct. 16, 1926, papers of Ray Stannard Baker, Box 102, Helen Bones folder.

56. James Wilson Woodrow to Ray Stannard Baker, Jan. 27, 1926, papers of Ray Stannard Baker, Box 124, James Wilson Woodrow folder.

57. Arthur S. Link to Alexander L. George and Juliette L. George, Dec. 10, 1979, confirmed that Weinstein, Anderson, and Link had indeed based their statement that there was "bad blood" between the Boneses and the Wilsons on material concerning James Bones's handling of Mrs. Wilson's share of the estate of William Woodrow.

58. Helen Bones to Ray Stannard Baker, July 2, 1925, papers of Ray Stannard Baker, Box 102, Helen Bones folder.

59. From an early age, Stockton Axson suffered from periodic severe depressions. He was frequently treated for this but apparently never cured.

60. Stockton Axson, *op. cit.* (see footnote 44), chapter entitled "Woodrow Wilson and his Father, pp. 5, 8, 15–16; chapter entitled "Dr. Joseph R. Wilson," pp. 1, 2, 9, 12–13; chapter entitled "The Personality of Woodrow Wilson," pp. 32–34; chapter entitled "Personality of Wilson," Part II, p. 24; untitled chapter, pp. 4–5.

61. George and George, *op. cit.*, see pp. 3, 12–13.

62. David Lawrence, *The True Story of Woodrow Wilson* (New York: George H. Doran, 1924), p. 18.

63. Eleanor Wilson McAdoo, *The Priceless Gift* (New York: McGraw-Hill, 1962), pp. x, 121.

64. See Wilson papers, Series XI, Reel 524 for some of Dr. Wilson's sermons and for his address at Southwest Presbyterian University in June, 1885. Also see George Osborn, "The Influence of Joseph R. Wilson on his Son Woodrow Wilson," *North Carolina Historical Review*, vol. XXXII, Oct. 1955, pp. 519–543.

65. Jessie Bones Brower to Ray Stannard Baker, Nov. 5, 1925, papers of Ray Stannard Baker, Box 102, Jessie B. Brower folder; Stockton Axson, *op. cit.* (see footnote 44), "Woodrow Wilson and his Father," p. 5; Ray Stannard Baker, *op. cit.*, vol. I, pp. 42, 46–48.

66. Pleasant Stovall to Ray Stannard Baker, June 1, 1925, papers of Ray Stannard Baker, Box 122, Pleasant Stovall folder.

67. Ray Stannard Baker, "Memo of a Visit to Columbia, S.C.," p. 14, papers of Ray Stannard Baker, Series IB, Box 3.

68. Ibid. Also see Box 124, Marion Woodrow folder.

69. John H. Pearson to Wilson, June 11, 1902, *Papers,* vol. 12, p. 415.

70. Stockton Axson, *op. cit.* (see footnote 44), chapter entitled "Woodrow Wilson's Educational Career," p. 1.

71. Ray Stannard Baker, "Memorandum of talk with Miss Margaret Wilson, March 12, 1925," papers of Ray Stannard Baker, Series IB, Box 41. Margaret Wilson was the eldest of Wilson's three daughters. See also Edith Bolling Wilson, *My Memoir* (New York: Bobbs-Merrill, 1939), pp. 57–58.

72. James Woodrow to his son James, Feb. 24, 1873, papers of Ray Stannard Baker, Box 124, Marion Woodrow folder.

73. Ray Stannard Baker and William E. Dodd, eds., *The Public Papers of Woodrow Wilson* (Harper and Brothers, 1927), vol. III, p. 347.

74. Wilson's address to Princeton Club in Chicago, March 12, 1908, *Papers,* vol. 18, pp. 32–33.

75. Wilson to Cyrus H. McCormick, Dec. 21, 1908, *Papers,* vol. 18, p. 562.

76. Wilson's address, "The Young People and the Church," Oct. 13, 1904, *Papers,* vol. 15, p. 510.

77. Weinstein, Anderson, and Link, *op. cit.,* p. 592. Italics added.

78. Weinstein, Anderson, and Link, *op. cit.,* p. 591.

79. Ray Stannard Baker, *op. cit.* (see footnote 20), vol. I, pp. 31, 46; Cary Grayson, *Woodrow Wilson: An Intimate Memoir* (Potomac Books, Inc., 1960), p. 37; Stockton Axson, *op. cit.* (see footnote 44), chapter entitled "Two Visits to 'S' Street," p. 6; Harper G. M. in William S. Myers, ed., *Some Princeton Memories* (Princeton, N.J.: Princeton University Press, 1946), p. 2.

80. Unpublished manuscript by Charles Swem, section entitled "Criticism," Box 12, papers of Charles Swem, Princeton University Library.

81. Stockton Axson, *op. cit.* (see footnote 44), chapter entitled "The Personality of Woodrow Wilson," pp. 40–44. Many others had noted Wilson's stubbornness. As one young preceptor who had supported him during the Quad fight at Princeton put it, ". . . criticism made him close as a razor-edged clam, and the more force applied in trying to open it the tighter it closed." J. Duncan Spaeth in *Some Princeton Memories,* (see footnote 79), p. 76.

82. Wilson to Mary Hulbert Peck, June 26, 1909, *Papers,* vol. 19, p. 271.

83. Wilson to Mary Hulbert Peck, July 30, 1911, *Papers,* vol. 23, p. 239–40.

84. Wilson to Ellen Axson Wilson, March 25, 1900, *Papers,* vol. 11, p. 526.

85. Wilson to Ellen Axson, Dec. 7, 1884, *Papers,* vol. 3, p. 522.

86. David Lawrence, *The True Story of Woodrow Wilson* (New York: George H. Doran, 1924), p. 220.

87. Woodrow Wilson to unidentified correspondent, 1911, papers of Ray Stannard Baker, Series III, Box V, collector's item sent by R.D.H. Emerson; Wilson to Hamilton Holt, Feb. 27, 1918 cited in Ray Stannard Baker, *op. cit.,* vol.

VII, p. 571; diary of Edward M. House, entry Nov. 15, 1916, House Collection, Yale University Library; Ray Stannard Baker, "Memorandum of Talk with Helen Bones" (undated), papers of Ray Stannard Baker, Series IB, Box 4.

88. See Stockton Axson, *op. cit.* (footnote 44), chapter entitled "Personality of Wilson," Part I, pp. 21–22; Memorandum by Mary Hoyt, papers of Ray Stannard Baker, Series IB, Box 20, p. 17; Ray Stannard Baker, "Memorandum of Conversations with the Misses Smith, March 12 and 13, 1927," p. 12, papers of Ray Stannard Baker, Box 122.

89. Joseph R. Wilson to Woodrow Wilson, April 17, 1879, Wilson papers, Series 2, Reel 5. Professor Link and his staff edited out of the published version of this letter in *Papers,* vol. 1, p. 477, the portion concerning Janet Wilson's poor health.

90. Janet Wilson to Woodrow Wilson, Dec. 6, 1876, Wilson papers, Series 2, Reel 4. This letter is entirely omitted from *The Papers of Woodrow Wilson.*

91. Janet Wilson to Woodrow Wilson, Sept. 16, 1878, Wilson papers, Series 2, Reel 5. This letter is entirely omitted from *The Papers of Woodrow Wilson.*

92. Janet Wilson to Woodrow Wilson, June 5, 1880, *Papers,* vol. 1, p. 659.

93. Janet Wilson to Woodrow Wilson, Dec. 21, 1883, Wilson papers, Series 2, Reel 6. This passage has been edited out of the letter as printed in *The Papers of Woodrow Wilson,* vol. 2, p. 594.

94. Woodrow Wilson, "A Religious Essay," c. Aug. 11, 1876, *Papers,* vol. 1, p. 177.

95. Woodrow Wilson, "Christ's Army," c. Aug. 17, 1876, *Papers,* vol. 1, p. 181.

96. Woodrow Wilson, "The Positive in Religion," c. Oct. 15, 1876, *Ibid.,* p. 212.

97. Woodrow Wilson, diary entry Sept. 23, 1876, *Papers,* vol. 1, p. 198.

98. Woodrow Wilson, diary entry Sept. 24, 1876, Ibid., p. 199.

99. Woodrow Wilson, diary entry Oct. 8, 1876, *Papers,* vol. 1, p. 205; Essay, "One Duty of a Son to His Parents," Ibid., pp. 205–207.

100. Woodrow Wilson, "Abraham Lincoln: A Man of the People," an address delivered Feb. 12, 1909, *Papers,* vol. 19, p. 44.

101. Woodrow Wilson, "Remarks to the Princeton Alumni Association of the District of Columbia," May 29, 1914, *Papers,* vol. 30, p. 106.

102. Ray Stannard Baker, "Memorandum of Conversations with Stockton Axson, February 8, 10, and 11, 1925," papers of Ray Stannard Baker, Box 99.

103. James Wilson Woodrow to Hattie Woodrow Welles (his sister), Dec. 1925, papers of Ray Stannard Baker, Series 1B, Box 40.

104. Stockton Axson, *op. cit.* (see footnote 44), chapter entitled "The Personality of Woodrow Wilson," pp. 32–34; Stockton Axson's comments on Ray Stannard Baker's mss., papers of Ray Stannard Baker, Box 100, Axson folder no. 2.

105. George C. Osborn, "The Influence of Joseph R. Wilson on His Son Woodrow Wilson," *The North Carolina Historical Review,* vol. XXXII, no. 4, Oct., 1955, pp. 524–525.

106. Woodrow Wilson, diary entry Oct. 27, 1876, *Papers,* vol. 1, p. 217.

107. Joseph R. Wilson to Woodrow Wilson, Nov. 5, 1877, *Papers,* vol. 1, p. 315.

108. Woodrow Wilson to Mary Hulbert Peck, Aug. 8, 1909, Sept. 5, 1909, Feb. 28, 1910, Dec. 17, 1910, *Papers,* vol. 19, pp. 330, 358, vol. 20, p. 186, vol. 22, p. 210; Woodrow Wilson to Ellen Axson (Wilson) Oct. 30, 1883, July 18, 1902, *Papers,* vol. 2, p. 503, vol. 14, p. 24; Stockton Axson, *op. cit.* (see footnote 44), outline for chapter "Wilson the Author."

109. Woodrow Wilson to Ellen Axson, April 25, 1885, *Papers,* vol. 4, p. 527.

110. Joseph R. Wilson to Woodrow Wilson, Sept. 8, 1888, papers of Woodrow Wilson, Series 2, Reel 9 (not printed in *Papers*), March 6, 1889, May 11, 1891, *Papers,* vol. 6, p. 137, vol. 7, p. 206.

111. Janet Wilson to Woodrow Wilson, Feb. 28, June 6, 1877, papers of Woodrow Wilson, Series 2, Reel 4. These passages are omitted from the letters as printed in *Papers,* vol. 1, p. 251 and pp. 272–273. Janet Wilson to Woodrow Wilson, May 20, 1874, *Papers,* vol. 1, p. 50.

112. Joseph R. Wilson to Woodrow Wilson, Nov. 23, 1877, papers of Woodrow Wilson, Series 2, Reel 4. This passage is omitted from the letter as printed in *Papers,* vol. 1, p. 321.

113. Joseph R. Wilson to Woodrow Wilson, c. Jan. 10, 1879, *Papers,* vol. 1, p. 444. Weinstein, Anderson, and Link, *op. cit.,* p. 588.

114. Janet Wilson to Woodrow Wilson, Dec. 4, 1883, papers of Woodrow Wilson, Series 2, Reel 6. This passage is omitted from the letter as printed in *Papers,* vol. 2, p. 563; Janet Wilson to Woodrow Wilson, Dec. 21, 1883, *Papers,* vol. 2, p. 594.

115. Joseph R. Wilson to Woodrow Wilson, Jan. 1, 1884, *Papers,* vol. 2, p. 641.

116. Janet Wilson to Woodrow Wilson, March 28, 1884, papers of Woodrow Wilson, Series 2, Reel 7. This passage is omitted from the letter as printed in *Papers,* vol. 3, p. 102.

117. *Papers,* vol. 5, p. 40.

118. Janet Wilson to Woodrow Wilson, Dec. 16, 1885, papers of Woodrow Wilson, Series 2, Reel 8. This letter is omitted from *The Papers of Woodrow Wilson.*

119. Joseph R. Wilson to Woodrow Wilson, March 27, 1886, *Papers,* vol. 5, p. 145; Janet Wilson to Woodrow Wilson, Feb. 23, 1887, papers of Woodrow Wilson, Series 2, Reel 8. We do not find this letter printed in *The Papers of Woodrow Wilson.*

120. Joseph R. Wilson to Woodrow Wilson, Jan. 12, 1887, papers of Woodrow Wilson, Series 2, Reel 8. This passage is omitted from the letter as printed in *Papers,* vol. 5, pp. 430–431.

121. Joseph R. Wilson to Woodrow Wilson, March 6, 1889, *Papers,* vol. 6, pp. 137–138.

122. Joseph R. Wilson to Woodrow Wilson, Oct. 5, 1889, *Papers,* vol. 6, pp. 400–401.

123. Joseph R. Wilson to Woodrow Wilson, Sept. 15, 1890, Oct. 13, 1891, *Papers,* vol. 7, pp. 11, 312.

124. Woodrow Wilson to Ellen Axson Wilson, June 17, 18, 21, 1892, *Papers,* vol. 8, pp. 4, 6, 13.

125. Memorandum by Stockton Axson, Sept. 6, 1931, pp. 13–14, papers of Ray Stannard Baker, Box 99.

126. See also Alexander L. George, "Power as a Compensatory Value for Political Leaders," *The Journal of Social Issues,* vol. XXIV, no. 3, July 1968, pp. 29–49.

127. *Papers,* vol. 4, p. 451.

128. *Papers,* vol. 1, p. xiv.

129. Weinstein, Anderson, and Link, *op. cit.,* p. 590.

130. "John Wesley's Place in History," an address by Wilson, c. June 30, 1903, *Papers,* vol. 14, p. 506.

131. Wilson to Ellen Axson (Wilson), Feb. 17, 1885, March 13, 1892, July 20, 1908, August 9, 1902, Feb. 23, 1900, Jan. 28, 1895, March 20, 1885, Aug. 29, 1902, *Papers,* vol. 4, p. 263, vol. 7, p. 483, vol. 18, p. 372, vol. 14, p. 68, vol. 11, p. 436, vol. 9, p. 137, vol. 4, p. 389, vol. 14, p. 118.

132. Janet Wilson to Woodrow Wilson, May 20, 1874, *Papers,* vol. 1, p. 50.

133. Margaret Axson Elliott, *My Aunt Louisa and Woodrow Wilson* (The University of North Carolina Press, 1944), p. 157.

134. Woodrow Wilson to Ellen Axson Wilson, Aug. 13, 1899, *Papers,* vol. 11, pp. 226–227.

135. Woodrow Wilson to Ellen Axson Wilson, Aug. 3, 1908, *Papers,* vol. 18, pp. 387–388.

136. Woodrow Wilson to Ellen Axson, April 25, 1885, *Papers,* vol. 4, pp. 527.

137. Woodrow Wilson to Ellen Axson Wilson, Dec. 9, 1884, Aug. 4, 1899, July 18, 1902, August 25, 1902; *Papers,* vol. 3, pp. 528–529; vol. 11, p. 206; vol. 14, p. 24, pp. 105–106. We are not here concerned with the sexual component of his love for Ellen, which was very strong, and the anguish it caused him, or with his revelations to her about (and the actual manifestations of) his indomitable sexual interest in other women. That, however, is another subject.

138. Woodrow Wilson to Ellen Axson Wilson, Feb. 4, 1897, April 14, 1904, *Papers,* vol. 10, p. 144; vol. 15, p. 247.

139. Ellen Axson Wilson to Woodrow Wilson, April 3 [1892], *Papers,* vol. 7, p. 542.

140. Ellen Axson Wilson to Woodrow Wilson, May 18, 1886, *Papers,* vol. 5, pp. 237–238.

141. Woodrow Wilson to Ellen Axson (Wilson), April 25, 1885, May 22, 1886, *Papers,* vol. 4, p. 529; vol. 5, p. 249.

142. Woodrow Wilson to Ellen Axson Wilson, Oct. 7, 1887, *Papers,* vol. 5, p. 611.

143. Memorandum by Mary Hoyt, Oct., 1926, p. 3, papers of Ray Stannard Baker, Box 111; George Osborn, "Letters from Ellen Axson Wilson to Anna Harris of Rome, Georgia 1885–1912," *The Georgia Historical Quarterly,* vol. XXXVIII, Dec. 1954, pp. 369–394.

144. Woodrow Wilson to Ellen Axson Wilson, Aug. 18, 1908, *Papers,* vol. 18, p. 403.

145. Eleanor Wilson McAdoo, *The Priceless Gift* (New York: McGraw-Hill, 1962), p. 180.

146. Weinstein, Anderson, and Link, *op. cit.*, pp. 587, 593–594.

147. Margaret Axson Elliott, *My Aunt Louisa and Woodrow Wilson* (Chapel Hill, NC: The University of North Carolina Press, 1944), p. 224–225.

148. Henry Cabot Lodge, *The Senate and the League of Nations* (Charles Scribner's Sons, 1925), pp. 226, 212–213, 218–219.

149. Arthur S. Link, *The Road to the White House* (Princeton, N.J.: Princeton University Press, 1947), pp. 90–91.

150. Ibid., pp. 76, 78.

151. Ibid., pp. viii–ix.

152. Weinstein, Anderson, and Link, *op. cit.*, p. 596.

153. Woodrow Wilson to Zephaniah Felt, May 17, 1910, *Papers,* vol. 20, p. 459.

154. Edwin A. Weinstein, "Woodrow Wilson's Neurological Illness," *The Journal of American History,* vol. 57 (1970), pp. 341–342.

155. Weinstein, Anderson, and Link, *op. cit.*, p. 594, footnote 26.

156. Papers of Irwin Hoover, Library of Congress, Box 2.

157. Diary of Cary T. Grayson, April 5, 1919; Gilbert Close to Arthur Walworth, May 7, 1951, papers of Arthur Walworth, Yale University Library.

158. Memoranda #29, 32, 47 from Secretary of the American Commission to Negotiate Peace to members of the Commission and their staffs, papers of Tasker H. Bliss, Library of Congress, Container 286; diary of Cary T. Grayson, April 8, 1919; diary of Edith Benham Helm, Library of Congress, March 29, 1919; diary of Edward M. House, Yale University Library, Jan. 7, 1919.

159. This included our correspondence with both Professor Link and Dr. Weinstein concerning the data upon which they relied for the preparation of their article and, most particularly, for Dr. Weinstein's diagnoses of Wilson's illnesses in 1906 and in Paris in April 1919. Professor Link informed us (letter dated March 1, 1979) that he had no medical records concerning Wilson that have not already been published in the *Papers of Woodrow Wilson* or are not available in the Wilson papers at the Library of Congress.

Weinstein, Anderson, and Link claimed in their article (p. 596) that the "stroke" of 1906 was "recognized as such." In response to our inquiry as to when this illness was recognized as a stroke and by whom, Dr. Weinstein (letter dated Sept. 12, 1979) stated that Wilson's doctors may not have told him in so many words that he had had a stroke but they must have known he did. He cited as "evidence" various sources which Dr. Marmor has reviewed. In a subsequent letter (Oct. 3, 1979) Dr. Weinstein said he had no other sources.

We were especially interested to know on the basis of what "new evidence" referred to in the article by Weinstein, Anderson, and Link, Dr. Weinstein changed his diagnosis of Wilson's illness in Paris in April, 1919 from a stroke to flu "probably a virus encephalopathy." This material, which Professor Link initially denied us because of a pledge of confidentiality from which he was subsequently released, was finally made available to us in October 1980. This document was indeed an important one—the diary of Wilson's physician throughout his presidency, Dr. Cary T. Grayson—and it has been reviewed by Dr. Marmor. We wish to record our thanks to Professor Link for allowing us to use it.

160. See, e.g., John Mulder, *Woodrow Wilson: The Years of Preparation* (Princeton, N.J.: Princeton University Press, 1978), pp. 145, 147 for unequivocal references to Wilson's "stroke" of 1896 and its supposed effect on his thinking; see also pp. 185–186 for an account of Wilson's 1906 illness in which the "stroke" hypothesis also appears. There are numerous other references to the effects of Wilson's alleged strokes on his thinking and behavior.

* * *

Postscript from *Political Science Quarterly*

As noted on pp. 7 and 77, a condensed version of the foregoing paper appeared in the Winter 1981–1982 issue of *Political Science Quarterly*. Shortly before the condensation went to press, Dr. Weinstein's book, *Woodrow Wilson: A Medical and Psychological Biography* was published. *PSQ* printed our immediate reaction to Weinstein's book as a "Postscript" to our article as follows:

Postscript

A book by Edwin A. Weinstein, *Woodrow Wilson: A Medical and Psychological Biography*, has appeared since this article was completed. We can only note here that Weinstein persists in presenting, as if it were indisputable fact, his theory that Wilson suffered a series of disabling strokes dating back to 1896. The book contains numerous statements implying the existence of medical data and opinion which, so far as we know, simply are not available in the historical record.[1] An even more serious concern is that Weinstein has omitted data of critical diagnostic significance, thus precluding an objective evaluation of his hypotheses by his medical peers. His account of Wilson's episode of visual loss in 1906 is an important case in point.

In describing the 1906 episode, Weinstein writes that Mrs. Wilson "searched for evidence that would bear out the Doctor's opinion that her husband's stroke had been brought on by strain and overwork." He also writes that the Princeton trustees "agreed that the stroke had been caused by overwork." However, we know of no evidence (and Weinstein offers none) that Wilson's doctors, Mrs. Wilson, or the Princeton trustees stated, implied, or even believed that Wilson had suffered a stroke.

Weinstein titles his chapter about the 1906 episode "A Major Stroke and Its Consequences," and he begins with a general description of carotid occlusive disease. In this disorder, blood clots or arteriosclerotic plaques in the neck may fragment and form emboli that lodge in smaller arteries such as those within the eye. He then writes that Wilson's ophthalmologist (Dr. George E. de Schweinitz) "told him that he had sustained a blood clot in the eye," the obvious implication being the "clot" refers to an embolus from the carotid. We believe this is a misleading description because important evidence has been omitted. What de Schweinitz actually told Wilson is not known. It can only be inferred from letters written by Wilson and Mrs. Wilson at the time, and from the later recollection of such knowledgeable people as John Grier Hibben (who had accompanied Wilson to Dr. de Schweinitz's office), Stockton Axson, Drs. Cary Grayson and E.P. Davis, and Eleanor Wilson McAdoo. *All* of these sources say that Wilson's loss of vision was caused by a hemorrhage or burst blood vessel within his eye. Yet Weinstein omits any mention of hemorrhage in his book, even though the distinction between hemorrhage and embolic clot is critical, because bleeding within the eye is *not* characteristic of carotid occlusive disease and indeed militates against that diagnosis. Weinstein's only cited source for the word "clot" is a letter from Ellen Axson Wilson to a cousin in which she says: "Two weeks ago yesterday Woodrow waked up perfectly blind in one eye!—it turned out from the bursting of a blood vessel in it. . . . The clot in the eye is being absorbed with extraordinary rapidity." The world "clot" in the context of Mrs. Wilson's letter seems clearly to refer to a coagulum from the burst blood vessel rather than to a embolus.

We (Michael F. Marmor, Juliette L. George, and Alexander L. George) hope to comment more fully on Weinstein's book elsewhere.

Notes

1. Edwin A. Weinstein, *Woodrow Wilson: A Medical and Psychological Biography* (Princeton, N.J.: Princeton University Press, 1981), pp. 165-167. See also Ellen Axson Wilson to Mary Hoyt, 12 June (1906), *Papers of Woodrow Wilson,* vol. 16, p. 423; Wilson to Nicholas Murray Butler, 1 June 1906, ibid., p. 413; "Memorandum of Interviews with Grayson," Papers of Ray Stannard Baker, Box 109, p. 3; ibid., Box 5, Notebook XXII, pp. 56–57; Cary T. Grayson, *Woodrow Wilson: An Intimate Memoir* (New York: Holt, Rinehart and Winston, 1960 and 1977), p. 81; Stockton Axson, "Material on Woodrow Wilson," chapter entitled "Health and Recreations," p. 23, and chapter entitled "The Physical Man," p. 10. In the Papers of Ray Stannard Baker, see conversation with John Grier Hibben, 18 June 1925, Box 111; conversation with E. P. Davis, M.D., 12 November 1925, Box 106; E. P. Davis, "Memoranda Concerning Woodrow Wilson"; and Gilbert Close to Ray Stannard Baker, 26 September 1925, Box 103. See also Eleanor Wilson McAdoo, *The Priceless Gift* (New York: McGraw-Hill Book Company, 1962), p. 241. It is interesting to note that Weinstein himself, in his article "Woodrow Wilson's Neurological Illness," stated: "De Schweinitz found that the blindness had been caused by the bursting of a blood vessel in the eye" (p. 334). De Schweinitz's finding of a burst blood vessel is also reported in a footnote in *The Papers of Woodrow Wilson,* vol. 16, p. 412, n. 1.

Additional References

Following the appearance in *Political Science Quarterly* of a condensed version of the foregoing paper, a number of articles discussing some of the issues raised in both versions, were published. Since the appearance of those early articles, which are listed below, several additional volumes of *The Papers of Woodrow Wilson* have been published containing essays and editorial matter directly relevant to these issues.

We hope in a future publication to comment on this later material in *The Papers* as well as on Dr. Weinstein's book. Meanwhile, readers may be interested in a chapter by Dewey W. Grantham, *"The Papers of Woodrow Wilson:* A Preliminary Appraisal," in John Milton Cooper, Jr., and Charles E. Neu, eds., *The Wilson Era: Essays in Honor of Arthur S. Link* (Arlington Heights, Ill.: Harlan Davidson, 1991), pp. 281–301. Grantham reports (see pp. 290–291) that even among historians admiring of Link's splendid accomplishment as Editor of *The Papers of Woodrow Wilson,* there is considerable criticism, some of it extremely sharp, of his having included essays and editorial notes in *The Papers* that present what Grantham characterizes as "a particular interpretation" of Wilson's medical history.

For earlier articles following publication in *Political Science Quarterly* of the condensed version of our reply to Weinstein, Anderson, and Link, see:

George, Juliette L., and Alexander L., *"Woodrow Wilson and Colonel House:* A Reply to Weinstein, Anderson, and Link," *Political Science Quarterly,* vol. 96, no. 4 (Winter 1981–82), pp. 641–665. (Includes Marmor, M. F., letter of medical opinion, pp. 663–665.)

George, Juliette L., and Alexander L., "Comments on 'Woodrow Wilson Re-examined: The Mind-Body Controversy Redux and Other Disputations,'" *Political Psychology,* vol. 4, no. 2 (June 1983), pp. 307–312.

George, Juliette L., Marmor, Michael F., and George, Alexander L., "Research Note/Issues in Wilson Scholarship: References to Early 'Strokes' in the *Papers of Woodrow Wilson, Journal of American History,* vol. 70, no. 4 (March 1984), pp. 845–853, 955–956.

George, Juliette L., Marmor, Michael F., and George, Alexander L., Letter to the Editor, *Journal of American History,* vol. 71, no. 1 (June 1984), pp. 198–212.

Link, Arthur S., Hirst, David W., Davidson, John Wells, Little, John E., Letter to the Editor, *Journal of American History,* vol. 70, no. 4 (March 1984), pp. 945–955.

Marmor, Michael F., "Wilson, Strokes, and Zebras," *New England Journal of Medicine,* vol. 307 (August 26, 1982), pp. 528–534. (Ensuing correspondence between Marmor and Weinstein, E. A., ibid., vol. 308 (1983), p. 164.)

Marmor, Michael F., "A Bad Case of History: *Woodrow Wilson: A Medical and Psychological Biography,"* The Sciences, vol. 23 (January/February 1983), pp. 36–38. See Marmor and Weinstein's ensuing correspondence in ibid. (September/October 1983), pp. 2, 4, 6.

Marmor, Michael F., "Comments on 'Woodrow Wilson Re-examined: The Mind-Body Controversy Redux and Other Disputations,'" *Political Psychology,* vol. 4, no. 2 (June 1983), pp. 325–327.

Marmor, Michael F., "The Eyes of Woodrow Wilson: Retinal Vascular Disease and George de Schweinitz," *Ophthalmology,* vol. 92, no. 3 (March 1985), pp. 454–465.

Post, Jerrold M., "Woodrow Wilson Re-examined: The Mind-Body Controversy Redux and Other Disputations," *Political Psychology,* vol. 4, no. 2 (June 1983), pp. 289–306.

Post, Jerrold M., "Reply to the Three Comments on 'Woodrow Wilson Re-examined: The Mind-Body Controversy Redux and Other Disputations,'" *Political Psychology,* vol. 4, no. 2 (June 1983), pp. 329–331.

Ross, Dorthy, "Woodrow Wilson and the Case for Psychohistory," *Journal of American History,* vol. 69 (December 1982), pp. 659–668.

Weinstein, Edwin A., *Woodrow Wilson: A Medical and Psychological Biography* (Princeton, N.J.: Princeton University Press 1981).

Weinstein, Edwin A., Letter to the Editor, *New England Journal of Medicine,* vol. 308, no. 3 (January 20, 1983), p. 164.

Weinstein, Edwin A., "Comments on 'Woodrow Wilson Re-examined: The Mind-Body Controversy Redux and Other Disputations,'" *Political Psychology,* vol. 4, no. 2 (June 1983), pp. 313–324.

Weinstein, Edwin A., Letter to the Editor, *The Sciences,* vol. 23 (September/October 1983), p. 4.

5

Assessing Presidential Character

Alexander L. George

I

Shortly after James Forrestal resigned as Secretary of Defense in late March 1949, the nation was shocked to learn that he was under treatment for a severe mental illness. Within a few months Forrestal committed suicide. This tragic occurrence, coming after Forrestal's highly successful career in government, directly challenged the long-standing mental-health mythology prevalent in Washington. The essence of the myth, as noted by Albert Deutsch at the time,[1] was the belief that "no Very Important Person, under any circumstances, can possibly suffer from a psychosis." The denial of this possibility in official Washington was of a piece with widely shared beliefs that to suffer a mental illness was a disgrace that automatically and permanently rendered one unfit for public office.

It would go much too far to say that a new set of attitudes has replaced the mental-health mythology prevalent twenty-five years ago. Nonetheless, there has been some change in this respect, partly as a result of a better understanding of the nature of mental illness and mental health, and wider acceptance of modern preventive and therapeu-

---

For extensive and helpful comments on an earlier draft of this review I am indebted to Fred Greenstein. I remain solely responsible, of course, for the contents. In addition, James David Barber kindly offered an extensive and useful critique which enabled me to clarify many points and to avoid inadvertent misrepresentations. However, on a number of important issues we have not been able to reach agreement.

tic approaches. In addition, the disposition to challenge the mental-health mythology has been strengthened by concern over the possibility that an unbalanced political or military leader might trigger thermonuclear war.[2]

The possibility that major psychiatric impairment in an important official may not be detected or controlled in time to prevent a policy disaster is a matter for legitimate concern; nonetheless it identifies only a part—some would say only a small part—of the problem. There remains the broader and murkier question of the adverse effects that the personalities of leaders who are not ill may exert on public policy and the conduct of the affairs of state. Thus, paradoxically, the conventional wisdom that "every man has his breaking point" serves to obscure from view the fact that few political leaders actually break down under the stress of making difficult decisions or under the even greater stress of having to cope with the adverse consequences of decisions already made.

Certainly we need to know more about psychological and institutional coping mechanisms that help political leaders to remain emotionally intact, enabling them to continue functioning despite acute or persistent stress of various kinds. Narrowly construed, an individual who copes with stress without breaking down can be said to enjoy adequate mental health. But since we are concerned here with individuals who occupy high political office, we cannot limit attention to the consequences of a leader's performance under stress solely for his own emotional well-being. We must be at least equally concerned with the consequences for others of the ways in which he copes with latent or actual personal stresses of policy making and other tasks. Coping devices that are functional for the individual may sometimes have a dysfunctional impact on policy and political outcomes.

For this reason, broader criteria are needed than those traditionally applied by psychologists and psychiatrists in judging whether an individual copes adequately with stress. But to develop and apply broader criteria is not, as we shall see, an easy task. For one thing, the investigator's own political values can easily color his judgment as to whether a leader copes successfully with stressful tasks *from the standpoint of the polity*. Thus, for example, when the investigator disagrees with the policy a leader continues to pursue despite evidence of its mounting costs, he is more likely to judge that leader as rigid and stubborn than when he supports that policy. Similarly, a leader who takes a firm stand and draws the line in disputes with political opponents may be judged to be engaged in highly adaptive behavior by an investigator who believes that such behavior is required by the situation; but the same behavior may be judged to be irrationally aggressive by a different investigator whose system of values leads to a different perception of the requirements and dangers implicit in the same situation.

The intrusion of the investigator's own political values can distort both the validity and reliability of his judgments regarding a political leader's psychological fitness for office. This was all too evident in the responses psychiatrists made to a poll by FACT magazine during the presidential campaign of 1964. Among the questions asked was the following: "Do you believe Barry Goldwater is psychologically fit to serve as President of the United States?" The questionnaire, sent to all 12,356 psychiatrists in the United States, as listed in the current directory of the American Medical Association, was returned by 2,417 (about 19.5 per cent). Of these, 1,189 said he was not fit and 657 said he was fit. On the other hand, almost 600 indicated they were unable to answer because they did not know enough about Goldwater.

In addition, comments were volunteered by some 162 of the psychiatrists who responded to the mail survey. In his analysis of these comments (as reproduced in FACT magazine), David Ray notes that there was virtually no agreement among the psychiatrists in question about what qualities would make a leader psychologically fit or psychologically unfit. Moreover, there was evidence in the comments that evaluations of Goldwater's fitness were influenced by the diagnosticians' own political values. In quite a few cases, psychiatrists explicitly or implicitly linked their judgments about Goldwater's psychological fitness to endorsements or repudiations of the political values they attributed to Goldwater.[3] It is sobering to recall, as Ray reminds us, that almost 2,000 psychiatrists were willing on this occasion to claim and express professional expertise in a situation in which they were clearly unjustified in doing so. It should be noted that FACT's survey was repudiated by both the American Medical Association, which referred to it as "an example of yellow journalism," and the American Psychiatric Association, which dismissed it as "a hodge-podge of personal political opinion rather than professional diagnosis."[4]

We are confronted, therefore, with the question whether it is feasible to assess the personalities of candidates for political office and to predict their performance in ways that will satisfy the criteria of objectivity, reliability, and validity. Consideration of this question must deal with both the *scope* of such evaluations and the adequacy of *procedures* for making such judgments. In discussing the scope of psychological assessments, a useful distinction can be made between detection of major mental illness on the one hand and assessment of psychological fitness for a particular office on the other. To focus evaluation exclusively on detection of a current mental illness makes the task of diagnosis more manageable, but it leaves the door open to lesser personality disturbances or characteristics that may entail high political risks. Although it is increasingly questioned whether mental illness can be regarded as an entity, the manifestations of at least some severe illnesses are relatively clearcut and more easily identifiable than the wider range of personality characteristics that may make a person unfit for high political office.

The distinction between *screening* candidates for office and *monitoring* the health of officials is also one to keep in mind. If an official suffered a disabling mental illness, the problem would be to obtain a competent medical certification and either to persuade the official to resign or to put into effect provisions for removing him from his official duties, either temporarily or permanently. So far as a President is concerned, such a procedure would be much more difficult than for a lesser official, and it is problematical whether the 25th amendment offers a satisfactory solution for such a contingency.

The screening of candidates for elected office encounters special difficulties. The question to be asked about candidates is not merely whether they currently suffer major mental illness, but also whether they are likely to develop one later in office. But prediction of a major mental illness is not only more difficult and more uncertain than its diagnosis; it also raises very difficult "decision rule" problems: what *degree of risk* of a future mental breakdown should be regarded as unacceptable and as grounds for disqualifying a candidate, and *who* should make this judgment? Since very few persons are likely to be certified as altogether invulnerable to the risk of future mental illness, a conservative decision rule would eliminate most candidates, whereas a more permissive one would accept many candidates for whom some risk of a future mental breakdown could not be excluded. Where should the line be drawn? And by whom? Because of these several difficulties, few observers go further than to suggest that candidates should voluntarily subject themselves to appropriate medical examinations and release the results to the public so that it can vote in whatever way it deems appropriate.[5]

The task of designing valid and acceptable procedures for screening candidates becomes appreciably more complicated if the scope of the evaluation is broadened to cover psychological fitness and detection of character flaws. It would be extremely difficult to judge whether motivational structures and coping patterns imbedded in the personality of a candidate will turn out to be acutely dysfunctional in performing the duties of an office. Whether given personality characteristics will be disruptive of rational decision making or affect performance adversely in other ways is likely to be a matter of degree as well as of circumstance. For a leader's performance, the disruptive potential of certain personality patterns is likely to be highly situation-specific, and a coping strategy that tends to produce adverse political consequences in certain situations may be quite functional in other situations. It would be all the more difficult, therefore, to draw a line as to the level of risk judged to be acceptable (the problem of decision rule already alluded to).[6] Additional observations on problems of screening and monitoring will be presented in the concluding section of this review.

II

With these considerations in mind, we turn to James David Barber's effort to devise means for predicting performance in the Presidency well enough to assist in the evaluation and selection of candidates to that office. Barber acknowledges that "this kind of prediction is not easy" and recognizes that "predicting with even approximate accuracy is going to require some sharp tools and close attention in their use" (p. 6). Barber does not claim to have produced a finely honed theory for this purpose. Nonetheless, he published his book, which contains a hundred-page analysis of Richard Nixon entitled "The Nixon Prediction," early in 1972 for possible use in the presidential election; and he followed it up, after Senator McGovern's nomination by the Democratic Party, with a brief analysis of his personality and expected performance in the Presidency.[7] Barber justified his decision to do so not only on practical grounds, but also with reference to the possibility that attempts at prediction can serve to sharpen the theory (p. 6; also p. vii).

Barber has been criticized for introducing the unfinished, as yet untested results of his scholarship into the political arena. This is a criticism with which I happen to sympathize, and which I will discuss further in the concluding section. At the same time, however, Barber's critics must come to grips with the serious intellectual effort and considerable research that has gone into the construction of his theory. For, in marked contrast to the pseudo-scientific, indeed antiscientific character of FACT's muckraking approach to assessing Goldwater's psychological fitness in 1964, Barber's book reflects the many years of intensive research he has devoted to developing a rich and complex theory of the ways in which the personality of political leaders can express itself in their political behavior.

Besides, it is possible that Barber's theory, its limitations notwithstanding, enabled him—or at least encouraged him—to make a prediction in his book regarding the likelihood of a major political catastrophe if Richard Nixon were reelected which may turn out in some respects to be a correct prediction. Certainly the Watergate scandal and the other illegal activities undertaken by members of the Administration, which have come to light since March, 1973, constitute a political catastrophe of the first magnitude. The question remains, however, whether this was the kind of catastrophe Barber predicted; additionally, whether and to what extent the events in question can be explained in terms of Nixon's character; and, if so, whether in terms of Barber's theory of character, some modification of it, or some other personality theory. These are likely to be difficult questions for qualified, objective psychohistorians to answer even at some point in the future, when the crisis engendered by Watergate has run its course and the historical record is fuller and more accessible.[8] We must also keep in mind that Barber's prediction of a character-induced tragedy for Nixon is an open-ended one, and that it may receive confirmation in the remainder of the President's second term.

I shall attempt to provide as coherent an exposition of Barber's work as possible and to strike a balanced appraisal. If I focus on the weaknesses of his theory as I see them, it is in order to try to show how this kind of research can be put on a more solid, cumulative footing. It must be said at the outset that the task of evaluating Barber's theory is rendered more difficult by the way in which he has chosen to present it in this book. In order to reach a broader public during the election year, Barber apparently decided to popularize the presentation of his theory somewhat. In any case, the book is not as tightly argued and certainly not as adequately documented as it would have to be in order to persuade a specialized professional audience of the merits of his theory. Rather, the book reflects an effort to combine sensitive clinical-literary insights with strong normative impulses toward finding a rather immediate handle—the process of selecting a President—for dealing with some of the dilemmas of our era.

Barber's study is better understood and more fairly judged when viewed in the context of his earlier work, to which he calls the attention of the reader (p. 455). Barber is among those scholars who have demonstrated that attempts to absorb all political leaders into a single personality type—which followed from a misreading of Harold Lasswell's earlier writings—were unjustified and should be abandoned. In *The Lawmakers* (1965), to which we shall return later, Barber skillfully differentiated a variety of motivational patterns that led a diverse group of individuals to enter the Connecticut state legislature. He identified four types of legislators—"Lawmaker," "Spectator," "Advertiser," and "Reluctant"—and offered insightful speculative analyses of the way in which the distinctive personality configurations associated with each type affected their orientation to and activity in the role of legislator. This set of hypotheses, with important adaptations to be noted later, was carried over and applied in Barber's work on presidential leadership, in which he has been engaged for almost a decade. The origins, development, and empirical-theoretical foundations of Barber's study of presidential character are more amply reported in his earlier publications; these should be consulted by readers who wish to understand better, and to evaluate, the scholarly base on which the present book rests.

This is not to say that the difficult problems of theory and methodology, on which Barber has relatively little to say in *Presidential Character*, have been adequately dealt with in his earlier publications, enabling him to move easily and comfortably to the task of making his findings available for a more general audience. Indeed, *Presidential Character* is entirely explicit in acknowledging the tentative, uncertain nature of the theory. Barber recognizes that the ambitious task he has set for himself carries with it a most complex and difficult set of requirements. Let us turn, therefore, to the way in which he attempts to define and meet these requirements.

In keeping with the emphasis in modern theories of personality, Barber avoids a narrow preoccupation with unconscious needs and ego defenses, and instead opts for a broader ego-psychological view of personality. In his Preface, Barber indicates that he has eschewed "psychoanalytic interpretations at the symbolic level" and has employed an approach that is "much closer to the psychology of adaptation" (p. vi). He defines personality in terms of three components: "character," "world view," and "style." All three of these components of personality—especially "world view" and "style"—highlight the developmental and adaptive facets of personality. In addition, for Barber (and others), "character" provides at least a link to, and a reflection of, unconscious needs, ego defenses, and psychodynamics.

To employ personality variables for explaining or predicting a President's political behavior requires *situational analysis*—or, more specifically, some way of analyzing or anticipating the complex, two-way interplay between personality and situational factors. But situational factors affecting presidential performance are numerous and complex, and they include variables as well as constants; so the task of assessing the interaction between personality and situation cannot be easily accomplished. The investigator must assess not only the ways in which situational factors constrain the behavior of a President, but also the ways in which the President's personality and behavior shape the situation over time. Barber does make at least general provision for situational factors in his theoretical framework. He postulates that a President's personality interacts with (a) *"the power situation"* (i.e., "the support he has from the public and interest groups, the party balance in Congress, the thrust of Supreme Court opinion" [p. 8]), and also with (b) *"the climate of expectations"* (i.e., "the predominant needs thrust up to him by the people," focusing around needs such as the demand for reassurance, a sense of progress and action, and a sense of legitimacy from, and in, the Presidency [p. 9]).

However suggestive and rich in its implications, this conceptualization of situational constraints on presidential performance is, as Barber recognizes (p. vii), only a starting point for developing the kind of rich typology of the variety of situations within which presidential performance takes place.[9] And, indeed, the description of both power situation and climate of expectations is elaborated in the individual profiles of the Presidents.

The way in which Barber defines and operationalizes each of the three components of personality must be discussed further. The most visible part of a political leader's personality is his "style," which Barber defines as his "habitual way of performing three political roles: rhetoric, personal relations, and homework" (p. 7). A clearer explication of this important facet of personality is provided in Barber's earlier publications. An individual's style is a creative adaptation that emerges from a confluence in late adolescence or early adulthood of his *motives* (or needs), the *resources* (skills and competences) he possesses, and the *opportunities* the unfolding situation offers him, somewhat fortuitously, to make something of himself, to find something that "works" for himself and infuses self-confidence and a sense of competence. The discovery of a style provides the individual with a way of relating selectively and productively to the environment in a manner that is expected to yield satisfaction. Thus understood, Barber's notion of style and his related notion of "first independent political success" is reminiscent, as he has noted earlier,[10] of parts of Erik Erikson's conception of identity crisis and of what I have called the process of defining, carving out, or discovering a sphere of competence for performance as an adult.

Barber's concept of style provides a particularly useful way of bridging role and personality variables in studying a leader's behavior in *any* position. One of the limitations of traditional role theory from this standpoint has been that typologies of role orientations (and/or role definitions) have been couched with reference to the tasks or functions of a particular position.[11] Thus the various functions, or role tasks, of a President have been traditionally described in terms of chief-of-state, commander-in-chief, party leader, etc. Much more useful for studying the interaction between personality and role is Barber's ingenious way of identifying role functions in more general terms, independent of the idiosyncratic features of any particular position. The three general role demands or functions that Barber identifies—*rhetoric* (words), *business* (work), and *personal relations* (people)—arise, as he notes, in some way in any political position.

By defining style as the personality's acquisition of a characteristic way of utilizing words, work, and/or people for adapting to environmental demands and opportunities, Barber provides us with an incisive but flexible starting point for assessing the "fit" between one aspect of personality (i.e., style) and the specific role demands of a given position. Since different political positions generate different role demands, it is possible for the investigator to note whether a leader's style, which has been highly adaptive in one position, is likely to be equally adaptive—or perhaps even maladaptive—in a different position.

Collective biographical analyses employing a theoretical framework are rare. Barber's trenchant analysis of the styles of the eleven Presidents discussed in his book (and, in an earlier essay,[12] of Andrew Johnson's style) contributes much to an understanding of their different approaches to the Presidency and their behavior in that office. Clearly, the analysis of style is also relevant for assessing some aspects of the expected performance of candidates for the Presidency. A style such as Lyndon B. Johnson's, which was highly adaptive to the role of Senate Majority Leader and resulted in a brilliant performance by him in that position, was predictably less suited to the different role demands of the Presidency. The resulting strain, or lack of fit, helps to account for serious deficiencies in LBJ's performance in the Presidency.[13]

The possible lack of fit between an individual's personality and the demands of his role has long been recognized as one of the sources of "role strain," but it has not been easy to find satisfactory ways of studying it and assessing its actual or expected impact on performance and political outcomes.[14] Barber's conceptualization of style is therefore an important theoretical contribution. Even though the notion of style remains simple and undeveloped, each of the three modes of adaptative activity—toward words, work, and people—is capable of elaboration. (I shall defer, for the moment, discussion of the need for a substantial elaboration of Barber's concept of style.)

"World view," another component of personality in Barber's theory, consists of the individual's "primary, politically relevant beliefs, particularly his conceptions of social causality, human nature, and the central moral conflicts of the time" (pp. 7–8). World view refers to the fundamental philosophical and ideological beliefs and premises held by political leaders that shape their behavior. But only a few of these are listed and employed by Barber.

For Barber, the core of personality lies in "character." He defines it as "the way the President orients himself toward life—not for the moment, but enduringly" (p. 8). Character has its main development in childhood (whereas world view emerges in adolescence, and style in early adulthood) and remains relatively stable thereafter. "The stance toward life I call character," Barber explains, "grows out of the child's experiments in relating to parents, brothers and sisters, and peers at play and in school, as well as to his own body and the objects around it" (p. 10). Further, of the three components of personality, "character provides the main thrust and broad direction—but it does not *determine,* in any fixed sense, world view and style" (p. 11; Barber's emphasis). What Barber appears to be saying—and certainly it is justified—is that one's character will *constrain* the world view and style he will adopt later, but that there is still room for variation in the world view and style that will emerge as *congruent* with a given type of character.

Barber's theory requires an understanding of the interplay between these three components of a leader's personality in shaping his behavior. Although he emphasizes this and disavows reductionist explanations in terms of character, the core of his theory and its use in explanation and prediction of the most important aspects of presidential performance come to rest upon the special significance he attributes to the role of character. Thus, as he announces at the beginning of the book, "the core of the argument (which organizes the structure of the book) is that Presidential character . . . comes in four varieties. The most important thing to know about a President or candidate is where he fits among these types. . . . " (p. 6).

The concepts of style and world view, as they stand in Barber's theory, provide only the most general indications of the propensities of choice an individual brings into decision-making situations. It would be particularly useful from this standpoint to enrich Barber's concept of style by linking it with those developments in cognitive psychology which view personality as, among other things, an information-processing system. It would also be useful to replace "world view" with the broader concept of "belief system" (to include cognitive maps of politics and operational codes as well as ideology). The resulting enrichment of Barber's concept of personality would enable the investigator to undertake more refined and more specific analyses of a President's decision-making behavior.

A President's belief system influences both his diagnosis of situations and the way in which he responds to them. A President's cognitive style, on the other hand, influences the way in which he attempts to provide for his cognitive *and* emotional needs as a decisionmaker. Decision making can be stressful in a variety of ways. In addition to noting how a President provides for his cognitive needs, the investigator will want to note how the executive provides for the emotional needs generated by his decision-making activity. Both will influence the way in which he organizes and uses channels of information,

analysis, and advice, and the kinds of persons he relies upon for satisfying cognitive and emotional needs. The concept of cognitive style is
particularly germane for understanding the role of personality variables in the performance of Presidents and, indeed, of executives generally. It is by employing the concept of cognitive style, and by working within the framework of the particular cognitive style displayed
by the subject, that the investigator can identify and assess the interaction among the psychodynamic patterns, ego defenses, and constructive coping resources available to the individual.

Working with the variable of cognitive style will facilitate the important task of moving from the study of the executive *qua* individual
to a study of his interactions with other individuals in small-group
contexts, and with representatives of the larger organization over
which he presides. In the most general sense, a President's cognitive
style constrains the nature of his participation with others in small-
group decision making and shapes his orientation to the organizational processes of search, evaluation, and choice, and to the phenomenon of bureaucratic politics within the organization. Use of the
concept of cognitive style will facilitate what Harold Lasswell referred
to many years ago as "impact analysis"—the technique of studying
the kinds of men with whom a leader surrounds himself and the ways
in which they serve his various needs.[15]

In sum, both belief system and cognitive style are aspects of personality that play an important role in determining performance in the Presidency. These variables and their influence are not ignored in the biographical profiles of Presidents that comprise the bulk of Barber's book,
but they are dealt with in an impressionistic and fragmentary way.
Moreover, there is no explicit provision for dealing with such important
personality variables in Barber's framework. His conceptualization of
personality, therefore, in terms of character, world view, and style, remains incomplete. The emphasis on "character" in his theory does not
make up for the neglect of belief system under "world view" and the additional neglect of cognitive style in his otherwise admirable and highly
useful notion of "style." Instead of amplifying and elaborating his concept in these directions, however, Barber began several years ago to shift
from his earlier emphasis on style to stress on the importance of character as a basis for explaining and predicting Presidential performance.[16]

In shifting emphasis from style to character, Barber does not have
the advantage of inheriting from the work of personality theorists a

firm, well-established handle on character. The concept is not at all well defined or consistently defined within the realm of personality theory. Although intended to refer to a fundamental or core component of personality, the term "character" in practice is applied loosely and means many different things.

It is not surprising, therefore, that though apparently influenced by Karen Horney's writings in particular, Barber avoids leaning too heavily or explicitly on any of the extant character theories.[17] Rather, he formulates an eclectic conceptualization of character that is ostensibly quite parsimonious. Barber chooses to settle for four character types of his own which he evolves from two dimensions—*"activity-passivity"* and *"positive-negative affect toward one's activity."* These two dimensions (which he sometimes refers to as variables or "baselines") refer to how much energy an individual invests in his activity and how he feels about what he does (p. 11). I shall return later to some of the ambiguity and other difficulties associated with the two dimensions.

Barber defends his conceptualization of character by asserting that his two dimensions tap what is essential and common to most theories of personality.[18] But neither in *Presidential Character* nor in his earlier writings does he attempt to show how his two dimensions are grounded in the specialized literature on personality.[19] Moreover, it is very much to the point that as his work has progressed, Barber has modified the definition of one of his two dimensions,[20] and also has moved from an initially modest employment of the two dimensions in *The Lawmakers* for describing merely the phenomenological layer of behavior to the present, much more ambitious use of them for tapping underlying facets of character.

In *Presidential Character*, Barber acknowledges that his two dimensions "are crude clues to character." Nonetheless, he asserts that "they are leads into four basic character patterns long familiar in psychological research" (p. 12). Not only does the statement lack documentation; no effort is made to argue that the familiarity of the character patterns in the literature vouchsafes for their validity and the use to which he will put them.

By crossing and combining the two dichotomous dimensions, Barber obtains four character types: the *active-positive*, the *active-negative*, the *passive-positive*, and the *passive-negative*. At first glance, therefore, whatever else may be said about its simplicity, this four-fold character typology seems at least to be derived quite systematically from the two explicit dimensions. But, in fact, the four types are much richer in content and far more complex than this would indicate. For, as the reader quickly finds out, to each of the four character-type labels Barber adds a great deal of additional personality theory that goes well beyond the initial meanings given to the active-passive and the positive-negative dimensions. He inserts a distinctive *psychodynamic* and *developmental* pattern into his description of each character type. Thus, briefly paraphrasing and quoting from pp. 12–13, the results are as follows:

> The *"active-positive"* character is *"adaptive."* He displays a congruence between much of his activity and the enjoyment of it, thereby "indicating relatively high self-esteem and relative success in relating to the environment." He shows "an orientation toward productiveness as a value and an ability to use his styles flexibly, adaptively. . . . He sees himself as developing over time relatively well defined personal goals," and emphasizes "rational mastery."
>
> The *"active-negative"* character is *"compulsive."* He experiences a "contradiction . . . between relatively intense effort and relatively low emotional reward for that effort." His activity has a "compulsive," compensatory character; "he seems ambitious, striving upward, power-seeking . . . he has a persistent problem in managing his aggressive feelings. His self-image is vague and discontinuous. . . . "
>
> The *"passive-positive"* character is *"compliant."* He is "receptive" and "other-directed," a personality "whose life is a search for affection as a reward for being agreeable and cooperative rather than personally assertive." He experiences a "contradiction . . . between low self-esteem (on grounds of being unlovable, unattractive) and a superficial optimism."
>
> The *"passive-negative"* character is *"withdrawn."* He is oriented "toward doing dutiful service; this compensates for low self-esteem based on a sense of uselessness." His tendency is "to withdraw, to escape from the conflict and uncertainty of politics by emphasizing vague principles (especially prohibitions) and procedural arrangements. . . . "

Given the richness and implications of these character types, we shall want to keep in mind the problems of *constructing* such typologies and the problems of *using* them for purposes of explanation and prediction of presidential performance.[21]

III

Prediction of the expected performance of a candidate who exemplifies one of these character types requires the investigator to envisage how the candidate would interact with the *major role demands* of the Presidency as these, in turn, are shaped by the constraints of the many *situational configurations* he can be expected to encounter in that position. How, then, does Barber arrive at and justify his judgments regarding the expected performance of facets of the presidential role by the four different character types? He adopts an inductive procedure of somewhat complex proportions. The reviewer must proceed with caution in attempting to grasp Barber's research strategy and to reconstruct the often implicit logic of inquiry imbedded in the study.

The inductive component of his procedure consists in first explaining some important aspects of the performance of past Presidents in terms of their character types, and then extrapolating from the results of these historical explanations some general hypotheses to the effect that candidates with similar character types can be expected to perform those aspects of the role similarly, at least in a general way, under comparable circumstances. From this inductive procedure emerge general predictions for each of his four character types.

Thus, the *active-positives* (FDR, Truman, Kennedy) "display personal strengths specially attuned to the Presidency, strengths which enabled them to make of that office an engine of progress" (p. 210). While emphasizing the virtues of the active-positive type in general, Barber does note in passing certain dangers or risks for this type. Although Barber evidently does not consider the risks associated with active-positive Presidents to be equal to those to which active-negative characters are prone, the historical example he cites of FDR's effort to pack the Supreme Court is hardly reassuring in this respect. Indeed, commenting on this event, Barber observes that active-positives, "in their haste to make things happen, may too quickly and easily knock down the 'formalities' that hold the democratic order in place" (p. 246).

The *active-negatives* (Wilson, Hoover, LBJ) have character-rooted needs that "invade and dominate, to an unusual degree, their political habits and perceptions" (p. 141). They tend to "persevere rigidly in a disastrous policy" (p. 95).

Passive-negatives (Coolidge, Eisenhower) "pose a different danger . . . the danger of drift" (p. 145). They leave "vacant the energizing, initiating, stimulating possibilities of the role" (p. 173). Yet in certain historical circumstances this type can provide a needed "breathing spell" for recovery after a period of frantic politics (p. 145).

Passive-positives (Taft, Harding) are, like the passive-negatives, "responders, not initiators or pushers . . . " (p. 174). Yet, "for a people in search of community, they provide a refreshing hopefulness and at least some sense of sharing and caring" (p. 206).

We now turn to some of the problems and issues raised by Barber's inductive research strategy, not all of which I can assess with confidence. In order to discuss these matters in the necessary detail, I will focus on only one of Barber's four types, the active-negative, and forego attention to the interesting chapters he presents on the other three.

A. Using the Character Typology for Diagnosing Presidents

Quite obviously, the inductive procedure depends, among other things, on the correctness of the diagnosis of each President's character. Some of Barber's diagnoses seem more apt than others. There are several reasons for this. While the four types are sharply drawn at the outset and are stated as if they were mutually exclusive, in fact every person is, as Barber recognizes, some mixture of all four. This complicates the task of using the typology to diagnose a President and leads Barber to look for the dominant type-tendency displayed by each. Even that is difficult to establish on occasion. (We shall return to this problem later.) Still another source of difficulty stems from the fact that the historical data available for the diagnoses vary in quantity and quality. It appears to me that on occasion Barber interprets the available data rather heavily to reach some of his diagnoses. More to the point, the diagnostic procedure is not operationalized to the extent that it is objective enough *in all respects* to offer assurance that acceptable levels of reliability—not to speak of validity—can be achieved in scoring judgments. (Scholars specializing on one or another of these Presidents may disagree with Barber's character diagnosis of that individual.)

Some components or attributes of each character type are more easily applied than others. It must be remembered in this connection that Barber's conceptualization of character is very complex; it deals not merely with surface manifestations of activity-passivity and positive-negative effect, but also with underlying psychodynamic patterns, basic self-esteem, and personality needs for power, affection, respect, and so forth. The two dimensions are easiest to use for purposes of diagnosis since they tap the surface or phenomenological layer of behavior. The data are not always as good for lending strong support to Barber's additional contention that a President who is, for example, an active-positive or a passive-negative *on the surface* also displays the psychodynamic patterns, needs, etc. *said to be associated with that type in Barber's character theory.*

Barber's diagnoses of past Presidents may help to establish the validity of each of his character types. What is particularly in need of validation is the critical premise that in each of Barber's character types the various features attributed to that type do indeed go together, and only with each other. Each of his types is presented as a highly distinctive composite or cluster of characteristics. The theoretical and empirical basis for this important assumption remains obscure, notwithstanding Barber's assurance that his four character patterns have been "long familiar in psychological research" (p. 12). When Barber turns to the task of diagnosing the Presidents, therefore, the reader who is concerned about the validity of the character typology is interested to see whether Barber will be able to show that all components of a character type are clearly present in the biography of each President diagnosed as exemplifying that type. Indeed, one may speculate that Barber found himself under some pressure to find such evidence. If each President clearly displayed all of the behavioral components of one type or another, then the historical profiles of the Presidents will serve to test and support the validity of Barber's type constructs;[22] if not, the entire typology will need to be modified or discarded.[23]

B. Explaining a President's Actions in Terms of His Character

The inductive strategy employed in the study is also sensitive, of course, to Barber's efforts to explain various facets of a President's actions in terms of personality or character variables. The methodological problem in such explanations is acute. It is not difficult to find evidence that a subject's character-rooted needs or motives, or other aspects of his personality, are *expressed* in his behavior in a particular situation. Such evidence is a necessary *but insufficient* condition for establishing the *critical causal importance* of those personality factors in the explanation of that behavior. The fact that an individual strives for or achieves gratification of personal needs or motives in his performance of a political role does not automatically bestow decisive causal importance to this variable. Performance in executive positions such as the Presidency is sensitive to a variety of constraints. Faced with the play of multiple, complexly interacting causal variables, the investigator is bound to have great difficulty in assessing the weight of any given factor. Much behavior is over-determined, and often the most that can be said is that personality needs or other personality characteristics were among the many contributing factors. When the behavior of the executive is subject to cross-pressures, the critical role of personality factors in his decisions may emerge more clearly; but even in such situations the causal weight or decisiveness of the personality factor may be low.[24]

An understanding of the many facets, the complexities, and the apparent inconsistencies of an individual's personality (not merely the dominant patterns of the type he most closely resembles), and a familiarity with his behavior in a variety of past situations is necessary in order to make more discriminating explanations of past behavior and to deal with the treacherous problem of prediction. Of considerable importance in this respect are the strength and operation of the individual's ego controls—that is, his ability to control and regulate the expression of personal needs, anxieties, and defenses in order to prevent them from distorting his effort to appraise situations realistically and deal with them effectively. The effectiveness of ego controls is not to be gauged by success in denying any expression at all to personal needs in one's political functioning. This would be impossible in any case. Rather, ego controls that are well developed include the capacity for harnessing in more constructive directions the expression of one's personal needs in political behavior.[25]

Thus, personal motives and needs aroused by a particular situation may serve to alert the individual to perceive the opportunities presented by that situation. The possibility of gratifying these personal needs may also help to energize the individual to meet difficult role and situational requirements. As a result, personality factors may facilitate and improve performance of role requirements. At the same time, an individual's ego controls may be strong enough to curb the expression of personal needs unless the behavior that would gratify them is also required by the situation and the role demands. In other words, an individual's personality needs may be subjected to effective reality-testing and disciplined by awareness of role and situational requirements *before* they are allowed expression in his performance. Personality can be said to have a dysfunctional, adverse effect on the individual's performance only when there is reason to believe that it has led him to a distorted or inadequate perception of role and situational requirements, or to a choice of inferior ways of meeting them.[26]Given the difficulties of making the type of complex historical explanation that Barber attempts, it would not be reasonable to hold up unusually high standards in evaluating the plausibility of his explanations. Many of them are indeed plausible as well as insightful. I would have difficulty assessing others without immersing myself in the relevant but vast historical materials on each of the Presidents. Nonetheless, even a sympathetic and reasonably careful reading of the historical chapters left me with the impression that Barber's explanations are sometimes strained and bent in the direction of his theory. Alternative explanations for a given behavior are not always recognized or adequately discussed.

Barber's theory indeed sensitizes him—and through him the reader—to see unexpected facets of the way in which personality *expresses* itself in political behavior. That is fascinating and richly rewarding so far as it goes. But, faced with the play of multiple causal variables, Barber tends to give greater weight to the personality variable; and, faced with the choice of three components of his personality construct, he is quicker to attribute critical events to the impact of a President's character than to that of his world view. For example, one might suppose that it was Hoover's deeply ingrained political philosophy of individualism that stood in the way of his accepting the novel idea of a federal dole as a response to unemployment. For Barber, however, Hoover's continued opposition to the public dole is clearly to be explained in terms of his character—i.e., the peculiar psychodynamics of "rigidification" that the active-negative is disposed to when ego-involvement is triggered by opposition and criticism. Similarly, the key to Johnson's policy of escalation against North Vietnam and his persistence in that policy despite rising costs and public criticism is all too clearly and decisively attributed by Barber to Johnson's character rather than to world view, domestic politics, or other factors.

Thus, although Barber is fully aware of and warns against the kind of psychological reductionism that has long plagued psychobiography, the difficulty of the task places him in jeopardy of committing this cardinal sin himself. At the same time, it is only fair to recognize that the requirements of his inductive strategy push Barber into attempting an unusually large number of difficult historical explanations within the span of a single book. It has simply not been possible, as Barber acknowledges in his Preface, for one investigator to discharge so heavy a burden of scholarship.

C. Validating the Hypothesis of the "Tragedy-Prone" Active-Negative Character

Let us take a closer look now at Barber's explanatory thesis that all three active-negative Presidents (Wilson, Hoover, LBJ) suffered political "tragedies" that were "rooted" in their distinctive type of character, which pressed each of them to "persevere rigidly in a disastrous policy" (p. 95; similar formulations elsewhere). This explanation is crucial to Barber's inductive strategy. From it he concludes that active-negatives are particularly disposed to disastrous performance if elected to the Presidency.

As I noted earlier, it is the interaction of personality with situational variables that shapes presidential performance. For the active-negative type, the situational factor that creates the possibility of a catastrophic performance has to do with the special nature of political power in our government. Recalling Richard Neustadt's analysis of presidential power as being highly dependent upon the power to persuade, Barber sees the active-negative type as having particular difficulty in adjusting to the requirements implicit in this situational constraint. He observes at the outset of Chapter 2, "Three Tragic Tales," that it is about "three Presidents who seem to have forgotten that power means persuasion." Continuing, Barber states the inductive generalization he has drawn from his three case studies: "Different as they were in other ways, Woodrow Wilson, Herbert Hoover, and Lyndon B. Johnson came to share in their Presidencies *a common pattern: a process of rigidification*, a movement from political dexterity to narrow insistence on a failing course of action despite abundant evidence of the failure. *Each of these three helped arrange his own defeat*, and in the course of doing that, left the nation worse off then it might have been" (p. 18; emphasis added).

Three questions are relevant to an evaluation of this inductive generalization. (1) Are the tragedies comparable enough to support the generalization? (2) Is the critical role which Barber assigns to character in his explanation of each tragedy adequately demonstrated? (3) Does a similar psychodynamic pattern ("rigidification") underlie each man's behavior during the events leading to his disaster?

The three tragedies refer to completely different kinds of political events: Wilson's failure to get Senate ratification of the League of Nations; Hoover's dissipation of the public's confidence in him, as a result of which he failed in his bid for reelection in 1932; Johnson's increasingly costly and unpopular Vietnam policy, which led to his decision not to stand for reelection. What is critical for evaluating Barber's generalization is whether *the structure of the situation* in each of these three tragic episodes brought to the fore that peculiar problem of presidential power described by Neustadt which, as we noted, Barber considers critical in explaining and predicting tragedies for active-negative Presidents. A situational constraint of this kind was certainly present in Wilson's tragedy; indeed, it plays a very visible and important role in descriptions and explanations of Wilson's astonishingly inept handling of the Senate. Wilson's aggressive stubbornness in that struggle can be plausibly explained with reference to latent psychodynamic patterns imbedded in his personality which were activated by this situation (and which, Barber fails to recall, had been activated on several earlier occasions in similarly structured situations).

Since the kind of tragedy predicted by Barber for active-negative Presidents can occur only via an interaction between core elements of the active-negative character and a particular kind of situational configuration, an equally careful delineation of the structure of the situation that faced Hoover and Johnson would be necessary in order to judge whether the tragedies they suffered have explanations similar to Wilson's. Barber's descriptions of the situational configurations facing Hoover and Johnson are inadequate in this respect; they do not enable him to display with equal visibility or plausibility that their tragedies developed out of an interaction between character and situation.

Wilson's effort to bring the United States into the League of Nations was widely acknowledged to be a worthwhile goal and enjoyed more than sufficient support both in the Senate and in the country to bring it to fruition. Wilson's tragedy developed from the fact that his own behavior was instrumental in preventing the imminent and expected realization of this goal. Barber fails to note that, of the three Presidents, only Wilson snatched defeat from the jaws of victory. The nature of Hoover's tragedy is much more diffuse. Barber seems to define it in terms of Hoover's prolonged refusal to authorize a public dole for the unemployed by the Federal Government, which led to a loss of public confidence and Hoover's defeat in the election of 1932. Indeed, the tragedy for the public lay in the prolongation of the misery of the un-employed occasioned by Hoover's attitude towards a public dole. It is not wholly satisfactory, as some of Barber's formulations imply, to re-gard Hoover's defeat in 1932 as the chief component of Hoover's per-sonal tragedy, since he seems not to have been much interested in re-election until after his policies and leadership came under strong attack. The personal side of the tragedy surely lay more in the fact that Hoover, a sincere humanitarian, nonetheless contributed to the contin-ued misery of the unemployed by his opposition to the public dole.

Barber's thesis is that Hoover's continued opposition to the dole is explained by the peculiar psychological rigidification to which active-negative persons are subject when they perceive political opposition as posing fundamental threats to their power and rectitude. This inter-pretation would be more plausible if Barber gave evidence that he had considered alternative explanations and found reason to reject them. Certainly Hoover was stubborn on the matter of a public dole, but he appears to have strongly opposed it from the beginning—*before* at-tacks on his policies posed threats to his power and rectitude—be-cause he found the idea peculiarly antithetical to his political philoso-phy. One might consider, therefore, why the dole played so important a role in Hoover's personal ideology, and what it had come to symbol-ize for him in terms of his own personal development. This is merely a reminder that many different kinds of personality involvements may lie at the root of strongly-held political opinions. It behooves the inves-tigator to consider alternative psychological interpretations and to give evidence that he has resisted the temptation to impose his fa-vored psychological theory on the data simply because it provides a plausible interpretation.

Barber's interpretation of Hoover's character-induced tragedy would also gain in plausibility if he had given evidence of having con-sidered a purely cognitive explanation of it in terms of world view and had found it unsatisfactory. Here (and elsewhere in his study) Barber fails to come to grips with a major theoretical and methodological problem that is central to his theory. "Stubborn" behavior at the mani-fest level can have different underlying causes. Thus, the underlying dynamics of Wilson's stubbornness in the fight over the League appear to me to be quite different from Hoover's in the matter of the public dole. There is strong evidence of an ego-defensive, aggressive psychodynamic pattern in Wilson's stubbornness vis-à-vis his Senate opponents over the form in which their reservations about the League Covenant should be expressed. In Hoover's case, the materials reported by Barber suggest the possibility of a strong *cognitive* basis for Hoover's opposition to the dole, rooted in his political philosophy. Moreover, Barber recognizes (pp. 28–29) that from the beginning of the depression Hoover did everything he could to encourage relief for the unemployed through private and voluntary channels; and, while opposing a public dole from Washington, he stated more than once that if the day came when voluntary agencies were unable to find resources to prevent hunger and suffering, he would employ federal resources. Indeed, however belatedly, he did move in this direction in the summer of 1932. Barber reports this (p. 30), but fails to note that Hoover's policy reversal would seem to contradict the thesis that he was in the grip of a characterological rigidification.[27]

A similar policy reversal took place in LBJ's Vietnam policy when he de-escalated and then suspended the bombing of North Vietnam in 1968. This, too, is noted by Barber (pp. 41–42), but without recognizing that it also apparently contradicts his thesis regarding rigidification. Nor does Barber take into account that, in contrast to Hoover and Johnson, Wilson did *not* reverse course in his battle with the Senate; rather than accept relatively insignificant compromises that would have assured passage of the treaty, Wilson accepted its defeat.

In this and other respects, Barber's analysis of the "tragic tales" of the three active-negative Presidents is marred by a tendency to focus on the similarities and to ignore or downplay the significance of the differences. In his search for generalization, Barber appears to have taken an essentially correct explanation for Wilson's tragedy and imposed it, with much less evidence that it fits, as an explanation for Hoover's and Johnson's tragedies.[28] Curiously, Barber fails to mention the well-known and well-documented fact that the League tragedy was strikingly foreshadowed by Wilson's difficulties as President of Princeton University and as Governor of New Jersey.[29] The repetitive pattern of self-defeating behavior in his career provides strong support for the interpretation of Wilson. Noteworthy is the fact that such repetitive tragic patterns were evidently lacking in the careers of Hoover and Johnson. The question arises whether Wilson, though sharing certain compulsive character traits with Hoover and LBJ, was not also different from them in important respects.

Finally, as already suggested, because Barber does not take into account the strength and operation of ego controls, his theory of the active-negative character does not offer any help in explaining or predicting whether and when the process of rigidification, once underway, gets turned off in persons with this type of character. And yet this possibility is central to the task of using the theory to predict performance.

IV

Barber's analysis of Nixon is by far the longest and most detailed of his presidential profiles, occupying about a hundred pages, almost a quarter of the entire book. It is testimony to Barber's respect for evidence and his recognition of the hazardous nature of the enterprise that he finally comes to question whether Nixon really fits the active-negative character well enough to support the prediction of a tragedy. But one must read to the very end of Barber's long analysis (pp. 441–42) to become aware of the full dimensions of his uncertainty about Nixon. At the outset, Barber appears to be unequivocal and quite confident of his diagnosis of Nixon and of the prediction. "Nixon was—and is—an active-negative type. The danger in his Presidency is the same as the danger Wilson, Hoover, and Johnson succumbed to: rigid adherence to a failing line of policy. . . . In Nixon's case, every one of the elements found in the Wilson, Hoover, and Johnson cases is present and discernible in the history of his public years" (p. 347). "One could hardly be wrong about Nixon's overall placement in the active-negative category" (p. 348).[30] The diagnosis and prediction are repeated along the way (pp. 418, 441).

A note of uncertainty enters, however, when Barber turns to the task of interpreting Nixon's performance during the first term of his Presidency. Barber acknowledges that the kind of tragedy predicted for Nixon had not materialized as of late 1971. Instead, Nixon thus far "appeared to many, including many strong opponents, as a highly flexible expert politician carefully wending his way through a tangle of issues as he approached the 1972 campaign" (p. 418).

Having undertaken the Nixon prediction in 1968–69 in part as an experiment to test his theory (p. 6), Barber was confronted in 1971 by the difficult task of deciding whether events and non-events during the first term served to disconfirm his theory or at least important parts of it.[31] The prior question, however, is whether the prediction of a political tragedy can indeed be taken as a critical experiment to test the theory. Barber appeared to think so at the outset; but the contrary view (which he eventually embraces), is more defensible. It is of some importance for our purposes to understand why his prediction cannot serve the function of a critical test of his theory. Assuming that a *tendency* to political tragedy is present in the active-negative character, whether it develops depends on other variables which may or may not materialize during the course of a man's Presidency. For one thing, it depends on the occurrence of a situation of the kind that will trigger rigidification. What are the characteristics of such a situation, and how likely is it to occur during a President's incumbency? It is difficult for Barber to postulate the objective characteristics of such a situation with any specificity. (It is much easier to identify, as he does, the kind of subjective perception of it by an active-negative President which would lead to or accompany rigidification.)

Not only situational variables but also personality variables that are *not* included in Barber's conceptualization of personality are critical to his prediction. Whether the process of rigidification is triggered in the first place and whether it proceeds unchecked to produce a political catastrophe depends on the person's ability to control such tendencies within himself. The strength of these ego controls under differing circumstances is difficult to foresee. Even if we assume the validity of the theory of the active-negative character, it does not tell us how the critical variable of ego controls will appear in different individuals who exemplify this character type. That can be deduced— only with difficulty—from a careful analysis of the individual himself and the history of his past behavior. One can imagine that some active-negative characters are able to acquire much stronger and more resourceful controls than others over the disruptive tendencies latent in their personalities. Moreover, an individual's ego controls and, more generally, his ability to engage in unimpaired reality-testing can be strengthened or impeded by the small-group and organizational contexts in which he functions. For example, with the help of close advisers and personal staff, an executive may develop considerable resourcefulness in structuring and managing the immediate environment so as to shield himself from stressful experiences that distract, provoke, fatigue, or otherwise intrude upon his preferred way of performing in the role.[32]

For these and perhaps other reasons, the use of such a prediction to test the theory and to permit the investigator to proceed, if necessary, to the laudable objective of "correction by evidence" (p. 6) becomes elusive. So elusive, perhaps, that the theory is in danger of not being subject to falsification, at least by means of the kind of prediction-experiment Barber employs. Barber was indeed justified in deciding not to abandon his theory on the basis of the evidence of Nixon's first term. Instead, he found sufficient indications of the behavioral dynamics associated with the active-negative type in Nixon's first term to justify his continued adherence to both the theory and the prediction. This is unexceptional to be sure; but at the same time we must note that since even the non-occurrence of the prediction cannot be held to invalidate the theory, we are left without a clear indication of what it would take to falsify it.

Chapter 12 of *Presidential Character* is largely given over to "the critical question: has the President already shown signs presaging the kind of tragic freezing Wilson, Hoover, and Johnson fell into?" (p. 419). Throughout most of this chapter (pp. 421–41), Barber answers this question affirmatively, noting that the President indulged in aggressive rhetoric, concentrated power in his office, increasingly isolated himself, and gave unmistakable evidence in the Carswell case and the Cambodian venture that he scored high "on the core active-negative demand—to control and not be controlled . . . " (p. 425). The missing element for a full-blown tragedy, Barber suggests, was that in his first term Nixon had "not yet found a cause comparable to Wilson's crusade for the League, Hoover's stand against the dole, or Johnson's pursuit of military victory . . . " (p. 425).

A closer look at the Carswell case and the Cambodian venture, however, raises questions concerning Barber's thesis. If these examples furnish him with indications "that the underlying Nixon character is still there" (p. 425), as evidenced by the fact that Nixon threw down the gauntlet in the Carswell case and reacted to opposition with "the air of injured pride, the attribution of low motives, and [a] threatening tone . . . " (p. 429),[33] they also furnish evidence that Nixon's *controls* over these tendencies were strong and effective enough to limit and cut short the process of rigidification.[34] At first, Barber ignores the significance of these controls, while attempting to find a basis for saving and reformulating his theory. But in the end he tacitly recognizes them and concedes that Nixon is a "special variant" of the active-negative character in that, *"with his remarkable flexibility regarding issues and ideologies, Nixon can be 'defeated' any number of times on specific questions of policy without feeling personally threatened. His investment is not in values, not in standing fast for some principle. . . . His investment is in himself, and Nixon's self is taken up with its management . . . "* (pp. 441–42; emphasis added).

Nixon's behavior now emerges as so different from what we have been led to expect from active-negative Presidents that one wonders whether Barber has misdiagnosed him or whether the differences among active-negatives are greater after all than the similarities and common patterns that Barber has emphasized throughout his study. These differences may well be crucial to Barber's prediction. Is Nixon another Wilson? I think not. Some of the differences have already been noted; in addition, although they share a compulsive component in their personalities, only Wilson was a compulsive *reformer.* Nixon has lacked Wilson's unquenchable need for serving as the instrument for high moral achievements in the political arena which, when thwarted, could trigger rigidification. (Whether his commitment to certain foreign policy objectives constitutes a change in this respect remains to be seen.)

Another difference is that the power drive that Barber attributes to both men was clearly present only in the underlying need structure and dynamics of Wilson's personality (and was aroused, it should be added, only under special circumstances). The case Barber constructs for Nixon's "power need" (pp. 365–74) is not well-founded and only superficially plausible. (Whether a more convincing case could be made is problematical and must remain an open question.) Much of the behavior that Barber cites as evincing a power need may well turn out, upon close inspection, to be evidence not of that, but rather of Nixon's strong need for *respect.*[35] In certain circumstances it may be quite important to gauge correctly whether a President's behavior is motivated by a need for respect as against a need for power. If his personal stakes in a contested issue have to do with respect rather than power, he may find it easier—if an appropriately deferential face-saving scenario can be improvised or is provided by opponents—to back down.

For Nixon, power appears to be a secondary, *instrumental* value, not a core need of his character. Nixon does show ample interest in power and is often skillful in power maneuvers. But, as is well known, traits displayed at the surface level of behavior can have quite different underlying dynamic patterns. As the history of research on the authoritarian type and much other work on personality indicates, it is risky to infer from the presence of traits at the phenomenological layer of behavior that a deep-seated personality need exists for that kind of behavior.[36] Manifest behavior of the same kind, displayed by different individuals, may serve different functions in the workings of their personality systems. More refined, discriminating indicators and instruments are needed to infer deep-seated characterological needs from behavior. An interest and skill in power may be *learned* and displayed by a person *in response to role and situational requirements*. And it may be employed to facilitate gratification of other kinds of personality needs, such as for respect, achievement, well-being, etc.

Unlike Wilson, who displayed political ambitions from early adolescence, the young Nixon showed little interest in politics. Wilson as an adolescent identified with political statesmen and consciously modeled himself on great political orators; in contrast, political leadership for Nixon, as Barber notes, "just happened" accidentally when he was approaching his mid-thirties (p. 359). This in itself is not decisive, since an individual's power drive need not be directed to the arena of politics but may find an outlet in some other kind of activity in which political conflict and opportunities for expressing power needs are available. But if a power need is imbedded in a person's character, one expects to find some indication in his earlier years that he pursues power as a means of compensation for damaged self-esteem. No evidence of this kind is presented for Nixon's earlier years; rather, his ambition as a youth seems to have been motored by a need for respect and financial security rather than by a power need *per se*. Barber recognizes, moreover, that "ambition is a quality nearly every politician shares" and that "in its broadest sense it means little more than striving itself—for whatever goal" (p. 366).

Ambition *per se*, then, is not evidence of power need or power drive (the two terms are used interchangeably here). Nonetheless, Barber confuses evidence of Nixon's ambition with power drive. Much of the material cited as evidence of a power need is drawn from various events that occurred while Nixon was Vice President under Eisenhower. In reviewing the frustrations and dilemmas Nixon experienced as Vice President, Barber is too quick to regard as power maneuvers and power sensitivity Nixon's efforts to remain on the Republican presidential ticket in 1952, his resentment of slights, and his efforts to survive the Vice Presidency and preserve opportunities for becoming the presidential candidate.

Turning to another aspect of the interpretation, Barber correctly predicts various aspects of Nixon's style in the Presidency and, further, that Nixon would move toward power concentration rather than carry out his stated intention of diluting the historic trend toward centralization of power in the White House—and, within that, in the hands of the President himself (pp. 421–22). That trend, of course, has roots in complex problems of modern government; the fact of further concentration of power in the White House under Nixon cannot be taken *ipso facto* as reliable evidence of a characterological power need. There has indeed been unusual centralization of decision making by the executive branch in the White House. The National Security Council was reorganized by Nixon and Kissinger so as to draw the power to influence major foreign and national security policies away from the departments and into the White House. This NSC model has been replicated to some extent in other policy areas. The result has been a "miniaturization" of the executive branch within the White House.[37]

Attempts to explain developments of this kind solely with reference to a President's presumed power need carry with them the danger of an oversimplified or totally erroneous explanation. To bypass the consideration of other variables that affect such developments in favor of a characterological explanation can only reduce the plausibility of personality interpretations. Besides, to the extent that the personality of the chief executive is a factor, variables other than the postulate of a deep-seated power need may be involved. One can see Nixon's centralization of decision-making power in the White House as a management strategy for coping with the ever-present, stubborn problem of bureaucratic politics within the executive branch (which in various ways reduces a President's ability to engage in policy initiatives), and for obtaining implementation of his policies by the departments and agencies. Such a management strategy may indeed have had particular appeal for one who, like Nixon, has had a pronounced distrust of the bureaucratic departments, wanted to preserve as much power as possible to influence at least the most important policy problems his administration must deal with, hoped to deal with policy crises with as little damage as possible to his personal political position, and whose approach to his work has been influenced by the special cognitive style and conscientiousness engendered by the "compulsive" component in his personal makeup.

Ironically, a coping strategy that is designed to deal with certain clearly perceived problems affecting one's ability to govern may itself entail a new set of dimly perceived risks. As many observers of Nixon's style of management have continually noted, there are real dangers in the extent to which executive-branch decision making has been centralized in the White House, particularly when coupled with the President's well-known preference for solo decision making. Notwithstanding his demand for well-prepared options from his staff and the conscientious homework he engages in before making an important decision, Nixon's tendency to withdraw from direct consultation and from the give-and-take of a system of adversary proceedings or multiple advocacy is worrisome. It increases the likelihood of poor decisions that misjudge salient aspects of the situation. Nonetheless, however seriously flawed such decisions may be on occasion, the personality factor in the explanation is not necessarily a deep-seated characterological power drive; nor does the mere invocation of a presumed need of this kind clarify or illuminate very well those cognitive and psychodynamic variables within the personality system that are interacting with situational and role variables.

I noted earlier that, while Barber concludes his interpretation of Nixon's performance in the first term by acknowledging that Nixon is a special variant of the active-negative type, he continues to assert his prediction of a character-induced tragedy. He emphasizes (not implausibly, but cryptically) that a second term may pose special temptations to the President (pp. 348, 442, 447), and focuses his prediction of rigidification on a more sharply delimited situation: "But let the issue reach his central concern, the concern of self-management, and the fat may go into the fire. Threats to his independence in particular—the sense he is being controlled from without because he cannot be trusted, because he is weak or stupid or unstable—will call forth a strong inner response." (Were not the oppositions to the Carswell appointment and to the Cambodian venture, one may ask, precisely such threats?) Barber continues, "only when . . . he cannot escape [a crisis] by moving on to some alternative crisis, and he experiences a sense of entrapment is he likely to move toward the classic form of rigidification" (p. 442).

Having thus redefined and reasserted his prediction, Barber closes his profile of Nixon with an unexpected hedge. Speaking of heroes for whom Nixon has expressed admiration in the past, Barber observes that "conceivably" Nixon "could come to find an example in another man of independence, unheroic Harry Truman . . . " (p. 442). The significance of this cryptic remark lies in the fact that Harry Truman is diagnosed elsewhere in the book as having an active-*positive* character. It would appear, therefore, that Barber's uncertainty about Nixon, whom he has already conceded to be a special variant of the active-negative type, is such that he cannot exclude the possibility that Nixon may emerge as an active-positive.

In view of the foregoing, it is all the more disappointing that Barber has so little to say about the possible significance of the period following Nixon's "withdrawal" from politics in 1962, after his defeat in the California gubernatorial election. Was there growth and change during this period? Did the realization of the ambition thwarted in his early adulthood to be accepted into a prestigious New York or Washington law firm and the process of staging a successful comeback in politics contribute to the shaping of a "new Nixon," as was widely suggested at the time? Barber passes over this possibility very quickly, stressing instead that evidences of the man's earlier personality can be found during his first term and that these are likely to "overshadow any transformations his moves from New York to Washington may have engendered"[38] (pp. 418–19).

Highlighted here is a major problem in Barber's theory of personality. While he recognizes that character is not firmly fixed in childhood (e.g., p. 10), in effect he operates with a notion of character structure as being generally static for at least three of his four character types, and in particular for the active-negative. The important exception in this respect is the active-positive type who, unburdened by problems of self-esteem, is capable of growth through experience. It may be recalled in this connection that ego psychology and the psychology of adaptation, on which Barber draws effectively in other respects, have muted the earlier notion that character structure retains a timeless fixity once it has been shaped in childhood. This important theoretical development has not found its way adequately into Barber's conceptualization of personality. Admittedly, it would not be an easy matter for Barber to incorporate into his own theory Erik Erikson's notion of identity as a dynamic development with roots in different phases of development and related to changing historical forces, or to modify his approach to personality by drawing upon social-learning theory, with its heavy emphasis on modeling, learning, and situationally determined behavior. But it seems to me that something important contained in these alternative theories is missing in a theory of personality such as Barber's. Without it, his approach is not conducive to grasping possibly important changes in personality.[39] (I shall return to this question in discussing the problems of using personality typologies for diagnosing individuals.)

Before proceeding, I should point out several additional aspects of the analysis of Nixon. The active-negative character, it will be recalled, displays a "compulsive" quality in his activity. This characteristic is indeed evident in some aspects of Nixon's approach to decision making. Barber describes Nixon's classic crisis in fascinating detail, drawing on Nixon's own revealing account (in *Six Crises*) of how he has learned to handle critical events, what he perceives the dangers to be, and the satisfactions he derives from mastering them. Barber offers the interpretation that going through such crises fulfills an important need in Nixon's personality: "he relives each time the agony of self-definition. . . . There in a short space of time Nixon acts out the drama of his life— over and over again" (pp. 417, 421). The implication of Barber's analysis is not only that Nixon maintains self-esteem in this way, but that he relishes (seeks? even provokes?) crises for this reason, and that the effort to satisfy his need for self-esteem by crisis decision-making carries grave risks.[40] After all, even Nixon recognizes and speaks openly of the way in which he must steer himself through such crises in order to control tendencies he perceives within himself—at first to avoid the issue and later to indulge his aggressive feelings or to let down his guard.

Admittedly, Nixon's own description is occasion for concern at first glance. We must remind ourselves, however, that Nixon experienced many such crises in the past and that none of them resulted in the kind of tragedy Barber predicts. While Nixon may have to struggle for self-management, much of it appears at the conscious level; and, in any case, Nixon has thus far been relatively successful in self-management.[41] Viewed from a different perspective, therefore, one may see, in Nixon's classic crises, methods for coping with decisional stresses that he is aware of and attentive to.

Finally, one must distinguish between the *process* and the *substance* of the decisions. The process of the classic crisis may indeed be disruptive at times of rationality and of reality-oriented decision making. But this cannot simply be assumed to be the case; such a determination requires careful analysis and judgment on the investigator's part. The fact that one disapproves of a policy decision that emerges from the process of a classic crisis does not constitute a valid basis for assuming that the substance of the decision was contaminated by the subjective substratum. Moreover, even an objectively bad decision may stem from causes (e.g., inadequate information, bad advice, stupidity) other than the intrusion of disruptive personality dynamics.

It is appropriate in this connection to recall that some years ago, when political scientists were exposed to early developments in ego psychology, they were struck by the fact that arousal of a leader's anxieties and ego defenses could severely impair his ability to deal rationally with a situation. As a result, political scientists—and, indeed, some psychiatrists and psychologists as well—tended to regard any display of ego defenses (such as denial, projection, or rationalization) by a political leader in a stressful situation as a telltale sign that his ability to cope rationally and effectively with that situation had been impaired. Decisions taken in these circumstances were regarded with suspicion, and any inadequacy perceived in the substance of the decision was explained as being the unfortunate by-product of the leader's resort to ego defenses to cope with his anxieties. Explanatory hypotheses of this kind often oversimplified and distorted the role of unconscious emotional factors in decision making.

Recent developments in ego psychology and in studies of the nature of coping processes offer political scientists a much more refined and discriminating understanding of these matters. Many of the classical ego-defense mechanisms can be used constructively by an individual in the total process of coping. Defensive operations such as withdrawal, denial, or projection do not necessarily preclude intelligent and reasonable adaptation to a difficult situation. Rather, these defensive maneuvers may give the individual time to regroup ego resources and provide him with the short-run, tactical ego support that sustains him momentarily until he can return to employing more constructive ego capacities such as information seeking, role rehearsal, or planning in order to deal with the problem.[42]

V

Central to Barber's theory is his typology of character, many aspects of which have already been discussed. Here I shall comment on it more explicitly from the standpoint of some well-known problems that have been encountered in the *construction* of personality typologies and in their *use*. The two sets of problems are, of course, related: the use to which a typology is to be put defines the nature and requirements of the typology to be constructed. Barber's intended use of his typology is, as we have noted, a very ambitious one; accordingly, the requirements that have to be met in constructing it are very demanding. A complex form of psychological analysis is presumed. A reconstruction of the logic by means of which his types are erected identifies three overlapping but analytically separate operations. In Fred Greenstein's terminology,[43] these tasks include (1) a description of the *phenomenology* (or "presenting characteristics") of the individual's behavior; (2) an attempt to establish the *psychological dynamics* underlying these patterns of observed behavior; and (3) an attempt to identify the *developmental experiences* that account for the emergence of the observed patterns and inferred underlying psychodynamics.

This set of distinctions among the phenomenological, psychodynamic, and psychogenetic layers of behavior is useful, indeed necessary, for clarifying theoretical and methodological issues and for identifying the requirements for validating the interrelationships postulated within each of Barber's type constructs. A character type of the kind Barber has postulated is a *composite* of the three levels of analysis. What is more, his typology presumes a causal theory linking stated patterns of behavior at the phenomenological level with underlying dynamics and the developmental experiences that account for them. Validation of the type construct requires empirical analysis that is appropriate to the causal theory imbedded therein. Definitions and concepts cannot do the work of validation.

Typologies of this kind presumably summarize findings from a wide range of studies of individuals. Typologies necessarily abstract common features from individual cases, but abstraction cannot justify ignoring or lowering the requirement for validation of the implicit causal theory linking the three layers of behavior. Putting the causal theory in the form of a typology rather than in a more detailed analysis of a single individual does not get rid of or simplify the requirement of validation. We have already discussed in some detail the problem of validation for Barber's character types. Rather than to repeat or summarize, let us go on to another problem in the construction and use of personality typologies.

In abstracting common features from individual cases for the purpose of a typology, one has to be selective. The full complexity of each individual's personality cannot be easily incorporated into a type; an attempt to do so would proliferate the number of specialized types formulated. At least initially, therefore, relatively few characteristics (e.g., Barber's active-passive and positive-negative dimensions) are singled out from which to construct a relatively small number of basic types. An attempt may be made later to identify clusters or syndromes of still other characteristics that are thought to be associated with these initial nuclear defining characteristics.

The number of basic types in personality typologies is often small, and these few basic types are sharply demarcated and mutually exclusive. Each type, that is, is distinct and separate. As Carl Hempel notes, however, there are dangers in constructing typologies in this way. Drawing precise boundary lines between the dimensions of a typology can easily prove to be an "artificial, theoretically sterile, procedure." The resulting personality types are in the nature of "extreme" or "pure" types, "of which concrete instances are rarely if ever found. . . ."[44]

Barber's four character types are indeed *pure types* in this sense; each type is but one component of the complex structure of any individual's character. As Hempel notes (and as Barber would agree),[45] pure types "cannot be construed as class concepts: individual cases cannot be subsumed under them as instances, but can only be characterized as to the extent to which they approximate them."[46] Consistent with this postulate, Barber notes (p. 449) that every person's character is some mix of all four types, a mix in which one type presumably dominates or is especially prominent. Again, it is a matter of "tendencies, broad directions; no individual man exactly fits a category" (p. 13; see also p. 7).

Enough has been said to make it clear that Barber's four character types can only be *a starting point* for the diagnosis of an individual. Indeed, he does use them as starting points in developing his profiles of the Presidents; but, somewhat inconsistently, he also tends to use his four pure types as labels for them, since he has not developed a more refined set of mixed types to work with. We must recall that the value of a typology of this kind to the biographer—who must attempt to describe and explain the relevant behavior of an individual in its concreteness and complexity—is necessarily limited because of the artificially pure character of each type construct. The biographer cannot be satisfied with labelling his subject as being an instance of, or bearing a certain resemblance to, a pure type. To do so oversimplifies the task of making use of the theories and findings of dynamic psychology and personality studies, and is likely to yield results of a limited and disappointing character. The problem at issue here is not always clearly recognized or properly dealt with. *Classification is often confused with diagnosis.* To tag the subject with a label drawn from a typology, to place him in a pigeonhole of one of its pure types, does not provide what the biographer needs most: namely, a more discriminating, differentiated theory regarding the individual's more complex personality.[47]

The problem of diagnosis versus classification is a familiar one in clinical psychology where a distinction is sometimes made between the "sponge" and the "file-drawer" clinician. The former approaches the subject with a relatively open mind—sensitized, to be sure, by general theory and by available typologies—in order to develop a specific theory about that particular person from an intensive analysis of his behavior and case history. In contrast, the file-drawer clinician is inclined to gain insight into the patient by making an astute classification of him in terms of type characteristics. For present purposes it is important to recognize that the *sophisticated* file-drawer clinician often goes beyond the use of simple pure types to articulate *subtypes* for each of the basic classifications. In this way, a simple typology can be expanded to provide a set of *mixed types,* which is more discriminating and useful for diagnosing the complexity of any individual subject than the use of pure types.

Barber's diagnoses of the Presidents strike me, for the most part, as those of a file-drawer clinician. Although Barber is aware of the limitations of pure types generally, the inadequacies of his approach are accentuated because he has not yet found a way of transforming his four pure types into a larger number of more complex subtypes. As a result, Barber's classificatory scheme does not provide him with a systematic description of what Hempel calls mixed types, which would come closer than his pure types to catching the complexity of character and personality. Lacking subtypes in his theory, Barber tends to squeeze each President into one or another of the four pure types, hoping thereby to catch at least the dominant or most prominent aspects of his character.

This is not to say that Barber reifies his types; to some extent at least, he recognizes the lack of a close fit and attempts to describe it in an *ad hoc* fashion. Thus we learn that Eisenhower, though "best approximated in the passive-negative category" (p. 156) is a "more complicated mix" (p. 146) and "comes as close as any President to being one who strays beyond our crude categories" (p. 157); that there was a strong "compensatory" element in Truman's rhetoric and his decisiveness, and that his aggressiveness requires that he be placed "near the active-negative end" of the active-positive category to which Barber has assigned him (pp. 261–62, 292); that in 1932–33, there was some question whether Roosevelt would "turn out to be a passive-positive type" rather than, as it emerged, "active-positive" (pp. 235, 292); that John F. Kennedy's orientation to activity was not without ambivalence and contradictory themes, and that this "active-positive" President had to cope with the temptation towards detachment and passivity (p. 343); that there was considerable active leadership in the early years of "passive-positive" Harding's Presidency (p. 193); and that, as noted earlier, Nixon is a "special variant" of the "active-negative" type (p. 441).

In the end, therefore, Barber's use of a primitive, undeveloped variant of the file-drawer approach—as against a more sophisticated version employing mixed types—leaves the reader uncertain of the adequacy of his diagnoses of the Presidents for the task at hand. It is clear that Barber has become enmeshed in the familiar and ever treacherous problem of falling between stools: as he plunges into the case studies of the Presidents, he is pulled toward recognition of their individuality, but the strong typological impulse motivating his work and his search for common patterns may well have cut short a fuller consideration of important differences among individuals once they had been assigned to the same character type.

A number of difficult questions emerge which are not taken up by Barber. If every President is some mixture of all four types, what are the implications for the task of explanation and prediction of his performance? How do diverse character trends coexist within the personality, and how does the tension between them manifest itself in behavior under different circumstances? What aspects of the role and situational requirements of the Presidency fit well with each of the diverse character trends to be found within each individual? Can the presidential role bring out or strengthen one particular side of the incumbent's mixed character type?

As these questions imply, although character types can be useful as a starting point for the diagnosis of an individual, they do not offer a substitute for a full-fledged model of that individual's personality or a short-cut method for developing one. Such a limitation is inherent in the nature of character types, for they always abstract and simplify. Accordingly, character types cannot identify the full set of needs, psychodynamic patterns, ego resources, and coping strategies possessed by the individual, all of which are relevant to his performance in the Presidency.

Another problem encountered in Barber's typology concerns the clarity and usefulness of the two dimensions—active-passive and positive-negative—that serve as the starting point and form the ostensible basis for his four character types. I alluded earlier in this review to the ambiguity of these two dimensions. In one usage, they are employed as *descriptive* terms in order to portray behavior at the manifest level— i.e., the "presenting characteristics" at the phenomenological level. So long as this usage of the terms is observed, the only question that arises is whether to regard each dimension as a *dichotomous attribute* (a person is either active or passive, and either positive or negative) or as a *continuum* (whereby each person is placed at some point on each dimension to reflect an averaging-out or overall assessment).[48] Conceivably, such a choice could make a difference in the theory, but the matter is ignored in Barber's treatment.

In any case and perhaps more important, the usage of these two dimensions and their implications in Barber's concept of character is not confined to the descriptive, phenomenological level. Thus, in explaining why "these two simple dimensions" can be expected "to outline the main character types," Barber emphasizes that active-passive and positive-negative "stand for two central features of anyone's orientation toward life . . . " (p. 12). The implication is that these two dimensions tap not merely the phenomenological layer of behavior, but reach into the origins of character which Barber has defined as "what life has marked into a man's being," the way in which he "orients himself toward life" (p. 8).

Be that as it may, the issue of clarity of usage is pushed aside by the even more important fact that the nature of "activity" at the manifest level of behavior and its significance within the personality system can differ strikingly from individual to individual. "Activity" can have different origins and can also reflect quite different underlying psychodynamic patterns. Although Barber may not agree with the interpretation advanced here, some of his materials suggest that high activity and decisiveness (including protestations of decisiveness) at the phenomenological level can be, as in Truman's case, "a defense against its opposite, against the fear that he would lapse into vagueness, wandering, cowardice, dependence . . . " (p. 262); and that the activity of even an active-positive type can be motivated by personal needs that escape the reality-oriented controls of the personality and result in behavior that is counterproductive for the self and the polity (pp. 271–73).

The relationship of activity to passivity at the psychodynamic and psychogenetic levels, therefore, is far more complex than is implied by the description of manifest behavior in these terms.[49] One is driven to conclude that it is not useful—indeed, it may confuse rather than clarify matters—to base a character typology on descriptions of behavior that are couched in terms of an undifferentiated active-passive dimension or variable at the phenomenological level, ignoring the fact that *qualitatively different activity* is displayed at the manifest level by different individuals.

The dimension of positive-negative affect also encounters difficulties. The attempt to deal, as Barber does, with the question of the subject's affect towards his *activity* inherits some of the ambiguities of this concept which we have already noted, and encounters other difficulties as well. A few observations will have to suffice to indicate that the important question of affect that Barber has raised could benefit from more detailed analysis. The phenomenon of the "affectless" person, which has led some theorists of personality to postulate a detached-character type, is not easily encompassed or described in terms of Barber's dimension of positive-negative affect. (To attempt to do so would risk confusing *low* affect of any kind with *negative* affect.) Similarly, *ambivalence* of affect towards one's activity is not easily accommodated by a simple positive-negative scale.[50] The questions raised here cannot be brushed aside since the expression or non-expression of affect towards activity does not stand by itself in Barber's theory, but is part of distinctive configurations in which certain psychodynamic and psychogenetic processes are also postulated.[51]

Given the difficulties Barber's four-fold typology of character encounters, and the questionable assumptions and ambiguities associated with the two dimensions on which it is based, the question arises as to what can be done about them. One possibility, already suggested in our discussion of the need for mixed types, is to develop a more complicated and sophisticated version of the present typology. In my judgment, the dimensions of active-passive and positive-negative affect, as presently defined and operationalized, are unsuitable for the kind of rich developmental and psychodynamic character typology Barber has attempted to formulate; they can be retained only if they are altered to take note of *qualitative* differences in activity and affect displayed at the phenomenological level of behavior. If this differentiation can be accomplished, the more refined version of the two dimensions might be employed in order to develop a richer array of character *subtypes* which will move the typology from pure types into mixed types that reflect the greater complexity of character in real life.

Another possibility would be to simplify the present typology radically in some way. Instead of continuing Barber's ambitious quest for character types that link phenomenological, psychodynamic, and psychogenetic variables in distinctive causal configurations, one might rely on some convenient indicators of phenomenology (i.e., presenting characteristics) to formulate simpler trait/type classifications that deliberately forego the attempt to interconnect the resulting personality types via some deductive format such as Barber's four-fold table.[52]

Still another possibility, probably too difficult to envisage at this time, would be to move the typology away from its present use as a classificatory scheme to an ordering procedure. This move would involve arrangement of individuals along several axes, replacing the four-fold classificatory table by reference spaces of several dimensions, permitting subtler distinctions than the present typology and opening the way toward dealing with each dimension as a quantitative variable rather than a dichotomous attribute.[53]

In any case, none of the three alternatives addresses the question of the *validity* of the typology, which must be accorded priority over the problem of what to do with the pure form in which Barber's character types are presently stated.

VI

Barber's study emerges as the first systematic effort to apply personality theory to the task of assessing candidates for the Presidency. In doing so, Barber moves the discussion away from an exclusive preoccupation with the dangers associated with the possibility that an incumbent may develop a major mental illness. His study adds new support to the thesis that various facets of personality can have an important effect on the performance of presidential duties and the use of presidential powers, and can sometimes make a real difference in terms of political outcomes.

It is not new for political scientists and others to note that variations in performance of the presidential role can occur as a result of differences, among other things, in the personalities of incumbents. In *Presidential Power*, Richard Neustadt offered suggestive but unformalized observations on variations in the personal qualities of past Presidents which affected their ability to deal with some of the difficult role requirements of the office. However, the conceptualization and operationalization of these personal qualities, or facets of personality, have remained a problem. Erwin Hargrove attempted, with a measure of success, to fill this gap by distinguishing between personality needs, mental traits, and values and ideology.[54] Barber has come forward with a more complex conceptualization of personality in terms of character, world view, and style.

Certainly Barber's theory proves itself—as does any good theory—insofar as it sensitizes the investigator to notice many interesting facets of personality that are expressed in a leader's political behavior. The theory also helps to draw sharp contrasts between Presidents with different types of personalities, and it enables the investigator to pull together his observations and interpretations about a President into a set of coherent patterns rather than to settle for a series of interesting but discursive observations. A theory of this kind also assists the investigator to provide an explicit, reasoned basis for making predictions, if he is so inclined. Barber has displayed considerable courage in accepting the challenge of testing a theory by making predictions in the hope that such predictions can then be used to help assess and improve the theory. These are important contributions on which to build in the future.

It is true, as Barber argues, that even an incomplete theory based on crude clues to character can be used to generate relevant assessments and predictions about political candidates. However, if a theory is inadequately validated and if, in addition, the assessments and predictions it generates are likely to be affected by the investigator's own political values, serious questions may arise regarding the confidence that can be attached to the predictions. In my judgment—and leaving aside the elusive question whether his own political values have influenced his assessments of Presidents and candidates—Barber's theory is insufficiently developed and insufficiently validated to carry the burden of prediction. As Barber's forecast regarding Nixon illustrates, predictions of presidential performance generated by the theory are subject to considerable uncertainty. One may question, therefore, whether the theory is ready for practical use in the process of assessment and selection of presidential candidates. As this implies, I believe that the distinction between the scientific and policy arenas must be more sharply drawn in evaluating Barber's theory and the use to which he puts it. The desire to undertake predictions in order to test and improve the theory in the scientific arena is not at issue here; that task can be attempted, of course, without introducing an ongoing study into the political arena. Nor is Barber's right to do so, or his judgment in doing so, in question here. At the same time, however, a reviewer has an obligation to express his own assessment as to whether a theory of this kind is ready for practical application.

Efforts to devise relevant and valid procedures for screening political candidates raise many complex and interlocking questions that will need to be studied by groups of diverse specialists working together over a period of years. It is by no means clear that sufficiently valid procedures can be developed, or that they can then be operationalized and applied adequately, for screening candidates for elective office. And, in any case, the question of how and by whom such procedures would be applied, and how the results would be inserted into the processes of the selection of candidates and electoral choice, remains unanswered.

Barber's effort to bypass some of these questions by offering his results to the general public creates problems of its own and invites new dangers. If individual scholars are to publish personality assessments of candidates in which they set their own criteria and exercise their own judgment regarding the validity of their findings, then we can expect the political arena to be flooded by pseudo-scholarly, politically biased personality analyses of political candidates that fall far short of the standards to which Barber himself subscribes. The desire to make unfinished, inadequately validated scholarly efforts relevant in the extremely difficult enterprise of personality assessment will undoubtedly lead to a lowering of standards and a debasement of objectivity. We are already witnessing efforts to convert psychohistory into a method for evaluating living political actors—a dubious use of the hard-earned and fragile scholarly reputation of psychohistory, which threatens to revive the discredited practice of using psychoanalytic theory to debunk historical figures.[55] If this trend continues, character analysis will degenerate into character assassination, and efforts to develop scholarly and responsible investigation of the role of personality in the behavior of political leaders will be set back a generation.

We are left with dilemmas that will not be easily resolved. Insofar as the focus of concern is psychological fitness for political office, rather than major mental illness, it does indeed appear necessary (although whether it is scientifically or politically feasible is an entirely different matter) to place emphasis on *screening* candidates before an election rather than *monitoring* their performance in office. It is far more difficult to remove from office an elected official who is not mentally ill but, in someone's judgment, performs poorly because of presumed characterological problems than it is to persuade people that a candidate's personality shortcomings make it undesirable to elect him to an important political office.

On the other hand, if the focus of concern is major mental illness, then it appears that greater reliance will have to be placed on monitoring the health of elected officials in office rather than on attempting to screen out candidates on the grounds that they are poor risks insofar as future mental illness is concerned.[56] Screening candidates for the risk of severe mental illness in the future (as against its present actuality) is not likely to achieve levels of political acceptability or predictive validity. Monitoring would still be necessary to identify and treat emergent mental illness in officeholders; and, indeed, monitoring can contribute far more to dealing with the risk of severe mental illness than screening. Moreover, monitoring for mental illness would seem to be more feasible medically and more acceptable politically than screening.

We are left with the prospect that more can be done with the circumscribed problem of major mental illness by reliance on monitoring rather than on screening; the broader, in some ways more important problem of psychological or characterological fitness is likely to prove intractable to efforts to devise either screening or monitoring procedures. Whatever the practical outcome, however, it is important to move forward with efforts to improve knowledge, not merely of the stresses typically encountered by officials with different kinds of personalities, but also of the ways in which they cope with stress and, particularly, of the consequences that their patterns of coping may have for the quality of their performance. Such knowledge, combined with an awareness of variations in the cognitive styles of different kinds of personalities, may be helpful in efforts to make appropriate adjustments in the structure and management of top-level decision-making processes.

Notes

1. Deutsch's remarks, delivered at a meeting of the American Psychiatric Association, are quoted in Arnold A. Rogow, *James Forrestal: A Study of Personality, Politics, and Policy* (New York 1963), p. 44.

2. The possibility that mental illness could strike political or military leaders in the era of push-button warfare has been dramatized in films and novels such as *Dr. Strangelove, Seven Days in May,* and *Night of Camp David.* A sober statement of this stark possibility was also offered by political scientist Arnold Rogow in his perceptive biography of Forrestal (fn. 1), p. 346. In a later publication Rogow noted that the serious consequences of illnesses such as Forrestal's for policy decisions tend to be checked by various built-in safeguards of officeholding in a hierarchical, bureaucratic form of government: "Most key policy decisions are distributed over a number of persons and a variety of agencies," and there is a tendency within the bureaucracy "to remove or reduce the decision-making authority of the sick official while leaving him in office." "Private Illness and Public Policy: The Cases of James Forrestal and John Winant," *American Journal of Psychiatry,* cxxv (February 1969), p. 1096.

3. David Ray, "The Psychiatric Screening of Political Leaders: The Goldwater Case and Beyond," seminar paper, Political Science Department, Stanford University, 1972. See also the brief account in Arnold Rogow, *The Psychiatrists* (New York 1970), pp. 125–27.

4. Despite these admonitions, Ralph Ginzburg (publisher of FACT, which had since expired, and now publisher of *Avant Garde*) announced four years later that more than 2,000 psychiatrists had responded to questions about the psychological fitness of President Johnson. The results, however, were never published, perhaps because of Johnson's announcement that he would not be a candidate for reelection. Rogow (fn. 3), p. 128. Also, in 1968 Senator Goldwater sued the publishers of FACT for libel and was awarded a judgment of $75,000 in punitive damages by a Federal District Court. The judgment was subsequently upheld on appeal.

5. Public discussion of this possibility was triggered by the disclosure, after his nomination as Vice President on the Democratic Party ticket, that Senator Eagleton had been treated for depression on several occasions earlier in his career. See, for example, Michael J. Halberstam, M.D., "Who's Medically Fit for the White House?" *New York Times Magazine,* October 22, 1972, pp. 39ff; James

Reston, "The Need for a System of Health Checks," reprinted in *San Francisco Sunday Herald Examiner and Chronicle,* August 6, 1972.

6. The preceding paragraphs draw in part upon the seminar discussion of David Ray's paper in which Dr. Rudolf Moos, and Dr. John Adams, M.D., of the Psychiatry Department, Stanford Medical Center, participated.

7. "The Question of Presidential Character," *Saturday Review of the Society,* LV (October 1972), pp. 62–66. In this article, Senator McGovern is diagnosed as exemplifying one of Barber's four character types, the active-positive, which presents him in a favorable light; however, Barber also noted possible limitations in McGovern's performance if elected president.

8. Speculation on these matters in mid-July of 1973, when I had an opportunity to revise an earlier draft that had been written before the Watergate scandal began to unravel in March of 1973, seemed not only hazardous and premature, but also necessarily of limited value to those who would read this review some six or more months later. Accordingly, in revising the manuscript I decided to make no alterations in the substance of my earlier assessment of Barber's book which might benefit in some way from Watergate hindsight. However, I have permitted myself to *add* a few observations that have come to mind since then in reflecting on the emerging Watergate scandals.

9. With Watergate hindsight, I would emphasize this point even more. Some aspects of Nixon's behavior which appear to have contributed substantially to the crisis of his presidency occurred in situational contexts other than those that Barber singled out as being most germane.

10. Barber, "Classifying and Predicting Presidential Styles: Two 'Weak' Presidents," *Journal of Social Issues,* xxiv (July 1968), pp. 62, 78.

11. See, for example, the well-developed typologies of the various functions in the role of legislator, and the typologies of the ways in which each of these functions can be defined by the role-incumbent. J. Wahlke and others, *The Legislative System* (New York 1962).

While useful for a differentiated study of the variance in role orientations adopted by legislators, these typologies are not relevant for study of the role definitions of other political positions, nor do they provide a direct and useful way, as Barber's concept of style does, for assessing the interaction between role and personality in the incumbent's performance in the legislature.

12. Barber, "Adult Identity and Presidential Style: The Rhetorical Emphasis," *Daedalus,* XCVII (Summer 1968), pp. 938–68.

13. This point is emphasized particularly by Philip Geyelin, *LBJ and the World* (New York 1966); see also Nelson W. Polsby, *Congress and the Presidency* (Englewood Cliffs, N.J. 1971), pp. 33–41, 64–66.

14. Particularly useful approaches for conceptualizing the relationship between personality and role are to be found in Edwin J. Thomas, "Role Theory, Personality, and the Individual," in E. R. Borgatta and W. Lambert, eds., *Handbook of Personality Theory and Research* (New York 1968); R. C. Hodgson and others, *The Executive Role Constellation: An Analysis of Personality and Role Relations in Management* (Boston 1965).

15. Harold D. Lasswell, *Power and Personality* (New York 1948), pp. 101–4. The adverse impact small-group dynamics can have on political decision making is intensively explored by Irving L. Janis, *Victims of Groupthink* (Boston 1972).

16. The shift of emphasis from style to character can be seen by comparing the two articles Barber published in 1968 (both of which focus on style with hardly any mention of character) with his paper, "The President and His Friends," given at the annual meeting of the American Political Science Association in New York, September 1969, in which the importance of character begins to be stressed. A further shift in emphasis from style to character—and the conversion of his earlier typology of style into the present one of character—took place during the revision of this APSA paper for subsequent publication under a new title, "The Interplay of Presidential Character and Style: A Paradigm and Five Illustrations," in Fred I. Greenstein and Michael Lerner, eds., *A Source Book for the Study of Personality and Politics* (Chicago 1971), pp., 384–408.

See also Barber's "Some Consequences of Pluralization in Politics," in Harvey S. Perloff, ed., *The Future of the United States Government: Toward the Year 2000* (New York 1971).

17. One can sympathize with his desire to avoid becoming drawn into the quagmire of competing and unsatisfactory theories of character. Barber is not the first (nor will he be the last) political scientist to discover that the task of borrowing responsibly from the neighboring field of psychology cannot be discharged by attempting to find a single, neatly packaged, authoritative book or article written by a psychologist that tells you all you need to know about the problem.

For a review of developments in psychoanalytic conceptions of character, see chap. 2 of Ernst Prelinger and Carl N. Zimet, *An Ego-Psychological Approach to Character Assessment* (New York 1964).

18. "Why might we expect these two simple dimensions to outline the main character types? Because they stand for two central features of anyone's orientation toward life. In nearly every study of personality, some form of the active-passive contrast is critical; the general tendency to act or be acted upon is evident in such concepts as dominance-submission, extraversion-introversion, aggression-timidity, attack-defense, fight-flight, engagement-withdrawal, approach-avoidance" (p. 12).

19. The brief statement in Appendix A of *The Lawmakers* (New Haven and London 1965) was cautious, carefully qualified, and, it must be said, only a small step in this direction. In it, Barber suggested that one can find "some reflections, some common themes" similar to his own types in the accounts of those "who have observed humans acting in similar circumstances." He referred the reader to specific portions of some thirty studies where "relevant evidence or theory" could be found. However, limitations of space did not permit Barber to quote, summarize, or analyze these materials; thus the reader was left to pursue the matter for himself.

20. The second dimension ("positive-negative affect toward one's activity") constitutes a significant reformulation of what Barber called "commitment to

the office" (or "willingness to return") in *The Lawmakers,* ibid., pp. 18, 212. This reformulation and reconceptualization of the second dimension, as Fred Greenstein suggests [personal communication], was apparently necessary in order to accommodate to the fact that the vicissitudes of presidential recruitment are likely to screen out those who utterly reject the presidential role.

21. Post-Watergate hindsight makes more noticeable the importance of old-fashioned moral character and the difficulty of incorporating this concept into character typologies such as Barber's.

22. Before we can attribute a validating function of some kind to the case studies of the presidents, we have to consider whether the character-type constructs themselves have been formulated in part via induction and incorporation of findings from the case studies. Thus, if some of the postulated psychodynamics of a general character type are drawn from the historical case studies, an element of circularity may be involved. To the extent that the type constructs are extracted partly from the case studies, they cannot be assessed and validated by those case studies.

Admittedly, exploratory research and circularity are often hard to distinguish; the issue is of secondary importance for the development and statement of a theory as against its testing. Barber is not too clear in indicating how he arrived at the composite of characteristics he imputes to each type. That the case studies are part of the empirical material from which the theory is derived is suggested by some of the language Barber employs in summarizing and drawing together "the main character themes emerging from these three cases" (Wilson, Hoover, and Johnson). He notes that the "active" and "negative" variables that define this type were "relatively accessible to even the casual observer" of the biographical materials on these three presidents. Continuing, Barber then makes a statement which suggests that he enriched the skeletal active-negative category via the case studies of the three presidents: "What makes these simple dimensions interesting beyond mere description is their power in highlighting a whole range of personality qualities *which emerge from the case studies* and which explain why we find in the presidency men who strive so mightily and enjoy it so little" (p. 95; emphasis added).

23. Sometimes the validity of the four character types is boldly asserted in Barber's biographical profiles of the presidents. Thus, for example, Harding is said clearly to display "the *typical* passive-positive theme: the hunger for love, the impelling need to confirm one's lovableness" (p. 199; emphasis added). As for Coolidge and Eisenhower, "Both shared *with other passive-negative people in politics* a propensity for withdrawal" (p. 172; emphasis added). The clear implication of such language is that a much larger number of political leaders have been studied from the same characterological perspective and that the results have confirmed the clustering of characteristics under each of Barber's types. For this, however, no documentation is provided in *Presidential Character.* (On the other hand, perhaps such a "claim" is not intended and the statement should be regarded merely as a rhetorical embellishment of the descriptions of the presidents.) Nor can one find adequate

documentation in Barber's earlier book, *The Lawmakers*. That study contained few references to character *per se;* but some of the distinctive personality characteristics Barber inferred as being associated with his four legislative types ("Lawmakers," "Advertisers," "Spectators," and "Reluctants") do indeed bear a close resemblance to the characteristics he now imputes to his four character types. It should be noted, however, that the personality characteristics associated with his legislative types were impressionistically derived, being suggested by Barber's observations of Connecticut legislators. Indeed, with exemplary rigor and explicit caution, Barber noted that the hypotheses he advanced in *The Lawmakers* were "speculative generalizations, not verified results," and discussed in detail the methodological problems of his study (pp. 271, 16). Since the hypotheses advanced in *The Lawmakers* were evidently not subsequently assessed systematically against a new body of data, the earlier study offers useful impressionistic support at best; it does not contain rigorous empirical evidence on behalf of the validity of the four character types advanced in his latest work.

24. For a systematic discussion of the conditions under which personal variability among different actors may affect behavior in a given role, see Fred I. Greenstein, *Personality and Politics: Problems of Evidence, Inference, and Conceptualization* (Chicago 1969), 46–57. See also Greenstein's discussion of the circumstances under which ego-defensive needs are likely to manifest themselves in an actor's political behavior, ibid., pp. 57–61.

25. During the course of an individual's maturation and development, he develops a variety of constructive ego strategies in addition to his ego defenses. As Brewster Smith, Jerome Bruner, and Robert White noted many years ago, the early psychoanalytic account of ego defense mechanisms "failed to mention the tremendous importance of constructive strategies [employed by 'normal individuals'] as a means of avoiding the vicissitudes that make crippling defenses necessary . . . [They] often prevent things from occurring that might disrupt them or, more positively, they . . . plan events in such a way [so as to] operate effectively . . . " *Opinions and Personality* (New York 1956), p. 283; see also p. 22.

26. We should also take note of complicating factors: (1) the role and situational requirements that impinge on a political actor may contain conflicting or ambiguous elements that make it more difficult for him to exercise effective control and constructive regulation of his personality needs; (2) the politician's role may itself include aberrant requirements which activate personality motives and needs that are ordinarily kept under control. In other words, as Willard Gaylin, M.D., has emphasized, the nature of politics and what it takes to be successful in politics—as in business—may attract sociopathic and paranoid personality types: "The capacity to be ruthless, driving and immoral, if also combined with intelligence and imagination, can be a winning combination in politics as well as commerce. . . . Sociopathic and paranoid personality traits that are most dangerous in people of power are precisely those characteristics most suitable for the attainment of power in a competitive culture such as ours." "What's Normal?," *New York Times Magazine*, April 1, 1973.

27. There is ample evidence that cognitive dissonance mechanisms distorted Hoover's perception of reality vis-à-vis the scope and depth of the suffering of the unemployed. Arthur Schlesinger, Jr., notes striking examples of Hoover's tendency to downgrade and dismiss reports of suffering and malnutrition, and to favor more optimistic reports. He also notes that "the strain of maintaining his principles in the face of the accumulating evidence of human need doubtless led both to anxiety and to self-righteousness." A. M. Schlesinger, Jr., *The Crisis of the Old Order* (Boston 1957), pp. 241–243.

But cognitive dissonance occurs in many circumstances other than the type of characterological rigidification postulated by Barber. Hoover evidently experienced an acute conflict at the cognitive level between his humanitarian values and his political philosophy, which he resolved in favor of the latter. One cannot exclude, of course, that the conflict experienced at the cognitive level was *reinforced* by personality needs and anxieties. But the precise nature of this personality involvement is, as I have suggested, another matter.

As this discussion implies, students of personality need to develop better ways of distinguishing and differentiating between explanations of behavior in terms of *cognitive* variables and explanations in terms of *psychodynamic* patterns aroused by the situation. In recent years attention has frequently been called to the danger of confounding these two explanatory variables. In addition to the need for finding indicators that will enable the investigator to discriminate between the two, ways must be found to investigate the relationship between cognitive and psychodynamic variables.

28. Thus, Barber concludes the chapter "Three Tragic Tales" with a general observation that fits into the explanation of Wilson's tragedy but not into that of Hoover and Johnson. Speaking of the way in which the process of rigidification leaves the active-negative president locked in mortal combat with an opponent who personifies a threat felt at the personal level, Barber states that for the beleaguered president "surrender is suicide, an admission of guilt and weakness. Having invested all his moral capital in the cause, he will—he must—plunge on to the end" (p. 57). Since such a prediction would be falsified by the Hoover and Johnson policy reversals, questions are raised regarding the adequacy of Barber's characterological theory which implies that an active-negative president loses the possibility of controlling or cutting short the process of rigidification once it has started.

29. Rather, he tries to explain why the characterological propensities to rigidification were not evident earlier in Wilson's (as well as Hoover's and Johnson's) careers (p. 99).

30. Compare Barber's emphasis on Nixon's negative affect towards his activity with White House correspondent Hugh Sidey's observation: "Nixon wears the Presidency like a comfortable coat of armor. It has been dented here and there and it has a few tarnished spots, but it fits him and it feels good. He loves the job." *Life Magazine,* November 17, 1972, p. 4.

Bruce Mazlish, too, finds that Nixon "obviously enjoys his new role" as president, and that "in the office of President, Nixon believes that his role and his self have finally come together." *In Search of Nixon* (New York 1972), p. 76.

31. It may be noted in passing that Barber evidently assumed that the kind of political tragedy he predicted would be plainly visible in public events. This would seem to exclude from the scope of the effort of prediction such events as the secret illegal activities of the special investigation unit Nixon set up in the White House in 1971. At first glance, it does not appear that the personality factors that may have entered into Nixon's authorization of such activities are the same as the psychodynamic process of rigidification postulated in Barber's theory. On the other hand, retrospective analysis of these recently disclosed activities may offer Barber an opportunity for a "correction by evidence" that would attempt to show that these activities, although not initially predicted by his theory, are at least consistent with an amplified and revised version of it.

32. However, this coping strategy may in turn create a different set of risks for performance in the role. Long before the disclosures associated with the Watergate scandal, observers called attention to the dangers of isolation stemming from the President's preference for a staff system of tight buffers around him.

33. Mazlish's interpretation of the Haynsworth-Carswell affair emphasizes even more than Barber's that Nixon overreacted and became personally involved, experiencing his defeat as a humiliation (fn. 30, 127–31).

34. The backlash against the Cambodian invasion would seem to provide precisely the kind of challenge to Nixon's power, virtue, etc., that, according to Barber's theory, should have triggered the ruinous process of rigidification in Nixon. In fact, the opposite occurred (as Barber reports without recognizing its possible significance as a "test" that *dis*confirms his prediction); for when "the reaction [to the Cambodian venture] exploded across the country, *Nixon began to back-pedal.* On May 5 he pledged to Congressional committees meeting in the White House that the Cambodian venture would be over in three to seven weeks, with all Americans withdrawn, and that he would not order troops deeper into Cambodia than 21 miles without seeking Congressional approval . . ." (pp. 439–40; emphasis added).

35. In stating this reinterpretation of the materials Barber provides, I draw also on an unpublished study of Nixon's political personality and political style by Richard Born (Stanford 1970). Born concludes that both in his prepolitical period and during his political career Nixon consistently evinced a strong need for respect rather than for power. As criteria that a high value is placed on respect by the person, Born utilizes Harold D. Lasswell's three indicators of this need: (1) constant need for reassurance about "how am I doing?"; (2) sensitivity to the admiration of others; and (3) reactions of wounded pride and resentment to slights, real or imagined. See "Democratic Character," in *The Political Writings of Harold D. Lasswell* (Glencoe, Ill. 1951), p. 499. Whether Lasswell's indicators are adequate is less germane than the fact that some set of explicit indicators is necessary to avoid the dangers of a purely impressionistic judgment.

The difficult problem of identifying valid indicators of a power need and related problems connected with this concept and Lasswell's general hypothesis regarding the compensatory nature of power need are discussed in George,

"Power as a Compensatory Value for Political Leaders," *Journal of Social Issues,* XXIV (July 1968), pp. 29–49.

36. A useful and incisive account of the ambiguities that plagued much of the earlier research on the authoritarian type, with direct relevance to the problems encountered in the construction of Barber's character types, is provided by Fred I. Greenstein, *Personality and Politics: Problems of Evidence, Inference and Conceptualization* (Chicago 1969), chap. 4.

37. For discussion of these developments see, for example, Thomas E. Cronin, *The State of the Presidency* (New York 1974); Richard T. Johnson, *Managing the White House* (New York 1974).

38. Neither does Barber mention or refer to the possible significance, if any, of Nixon's consultations, while Vice President, with Arnold Hutschnecker, M.D., who in 1951 had written a book on psychosomatic medicine—leading to rumors later on that Nixon had seen a psychiatrist. In an article written in 1969, Dr. Hutschnecker states unequivocally that "during the entire period that I treated Mr. Nixon, I detected no sign of mental illness in him." He also states that, because of the rumors, he and Nixon came to "an understanding, years before the 1960 elections, that we should discontinue our doctor-patient relationship." Hutschnecker also refers to having had "an amicable personal relationship" with Nixon "over the years" during which time they "became friends and, as such, we discussed many subjects in an open and relaxed manner." A. A. Hutschnecker, M.D., "The Mental Health of Our Leaders," *Look Magazine,* July 15, 1969, pp. 51–54.

39. The possibility of change and maturation in personality is dealt with more explicitly and with some degree of plausibility in Mazlish's psychohistorical interpretation of Nixon. While finding that Nixon has not changed "in any fundamental sense" (fn. 30, 143), Mazlish sees evidence that Nixon achieved a release from old emotions and attained stronger and more effective ego controls. Ibid., pp. 105, 125, 144–45.

40. Similar observations about Nixon's "crisis" behavior are offered by Mazlish, ibid., pp. 26, 77, 87–88, 92, 127, 138; and by Arthur Woodstone's psychoanalytically inspired journalistic study, *Nixon's Head* (New York 1972).

41. Among the changes Mazlish sees in Nixon's development since the nadir in his political career is that "his control of impulse, his planning and deliberation were greater than ever" (fn. 30, 125).

42. For a fuller discussion see George, "Adaptation to Stress in Political Decisionmaking: The Individual, Small-Group, and Organizational Contexts," in G. V. Coelho, D. A. Hamburg, and J. Adams, eds., *Coping and Adaptation* (New York 1974). See also Ole R. Holsti and Alexander L. George, "The Effects of Stress on the Performance of Foreign Policy-makers" (forthcoming).

43. Greenstein (fn. 36), especially pp. 65–68, 95–96, 102–44. For a briefer account somewhat differently stated, see Greenstein, "Personality and Politics," prepared for *The Handbook of Political Science* (forthcoming). Harold Lasswell employs a different terminology ("nuclear," "co-relational," and "developmental") in discussing similar problems. See his "A Note on Types of Political Personality: Nuclear, Co-Relational, Developmental," in *Journal of Social Issues,*

xxiv (July 1968), pp. 81–92; a helpful introduction to Lasswell's article is provided by Greenstein and Lerner (fn. 16), pp. 231–32. Greenstein's terms (phenomenology, dynamics, genesis) are used here because their substantive referents are clearer and more relevant for our purposes than Lasswell's terminology.

44. Carl Gustav Hempel, *Aspects of Scientific Explanation* (New York 1965), p. 157. See also the article on "Typologies" by Edward A. Tiryakian, in *International Encyclopedia of the Social Sciences*, xvi, pp. 177–86.

45. In *The Lawmakers,* Barber himself warned against the beguiling nature of typologies such as his own: "At a certain stage in the development of a typology, one experiences a peculiar intellectual seduction. The world begins to arrange itself in fourfold tables. The lines separating the categories get blacker and thicker, the objects near the margins move quietly toward the centers of the cells or fade into invisibility . . . " (p. 261).

46. Hempel (fn. 44), pp. 158 and 151–54; see also Tiryakian (fn. 44), p. 183.

47. This and the following paragraphs draw on an earlier, more detailed discussion in George, "Some Uses of Dynamic Psychology in Political Biography," reprinted in Greenstein and Lerner (fn. 16), pp. 78–98.

48. If the active-passive dimension is treated as a continuum, the objection may be raised that this obscures the conditions under which a person is active and the conditions under which he is not active.

49. On this point see, for example, Edrita Fried, *Active Passive: The Crucial Psychological Dimension* (New York 1971).

50. A similar observation is made by Fred Greenstein, who comments that Barber's two dimensions "need amplification to take account of individuals who exhibit mood and behavior swings and for emotionally ambivalent individuals." "Political Psychology: A Pluralistic Universe," prepared for *The Handbook of Political Psychology,* Jeanne N. Knutson, ed. (forthcoming).

51. In addition, special problems seem to arise in applying the dimension of positive-negative affect to the compulsively oriented active-negative type. Positive-negative, it will be recalled, refers to whether a person generally enjoys what he is doing. Barber finds that the euphoric reactions an active-negative person like Nixon displays are rare and short-lived and, besides, tinged with "a masochistic element" (p. 350). This acknowledges, at least, that the emotions a compulsive person experiences while at work, and the nature of his emotional reward, cannot be described very well with reference to the simple positive-negative dimension. While a compulsive person "worries" a decision, applying himself conscientiously to it, he also gains important satisfactions thereby. In some compulsives there may be a need to deny open or full expression of the positive affect experienced, as a kind of superstitious way of warding off danger and bad luck. Reliance on surface behavior for scoring a compulsive person on the positive-negative dimension involves the risk of overlooking the element of secret or controlled pleasures and the more complex nature of affect derived from activity.

52. Interesting from this standpoint is James Payne's effort to modify Barber's approach in order to avoid characterological issues. Payne, together with

Oliver Woshinsky, has formulated a number of "incentive types" to character-ize political activists and political leaders. The authors emphasize that "incen-tive" describes only a fraction of any individual politician's personality. See James L. Payne and Oliver H. Woshinsky, "Incentives for Political Participa-tion," *World Politics,* xxiv (July 1972), pp. 518–46.

53. For a fuller account of this possibility, see Hempel (fn. 44), pp. 152–54, 158–59.

54. Erwin C. Hargrove, *Presidential Leadership: Personality and Political Style* (New York 1966).

55. For a review of several recent efforts of this kind, see Robert Coles, "Shrinking History—Part Two," *New York Review of Books,* xx (March 8, 1973). My own views and those of my wife, Juliette L. George, are elaborated in "Psycho-McCarthyism," *Psychology Today,* vii (June 1973), pp. 94–98.

56. Indeed, this direction has been taken with great caution by the Group for the Advancement of Psychiatry in its recent study, "The VIP with Psychi-atric Impairment," VIII. Report #83 (January 1973).

6

Presidential Management Styles and Models

Alexander L. George and Eric Stern

EVERY NEW PRESIDENT FACES the task of deciding how to structure and manage high-level foreign-policymaking in his administration. The task is a formidable one since responsibility for different aspects of national security and foreign policy is distributed over a number of departments and agencies. Relevant information, competence, and influence over policy is widely dispersed within the executive branch as well as outside of it. This imposes on the president and his assistants the task of mobilizing available information, expertise, and analytical resources for effective policymaking. In addition, the president and his closest associates have the responsibility for providing policy initiative and coherence throughout the executive branch.

To discharge these tasks effectively requires internal coordination within the government. Those parts of the executive branch that have some responsibility for and/or contribution to make to a particular policy problem must be encouraged to interact with each other in appropriate ways. Left to themselves, these various agencies, of course, would interact voluntarily and achieve some measure of "lateral coor-

Alexander George is the author of the first part of this chapter, taken from his *Presidential Decisionmaking in Foreign Policy* (Boulder: Westview Press, 1980). He is coauthor with Eric Stern of the sections on Presidents Carter and Reagan, and Stern wrote the sections on Presidents Bush and Clinton.

Stern wishes to thank Lina Svedin for research assistance and Paul 't Hart for useful comments on the previous draft of the section on President Clinton.

dination" in formulating policy. But it is essential for the president (and each department or agency head) to ensure lateral coordination by institution of various procedures and mechanisms, such as ad hoc or standing interdepartmental committees, policy conferences, liaison arrangements, a system of clearances for policy or position papers, and so on.

However important lateral coordination is, it cannot be counted upon to produce the caliber of policy analysis, the level of consensus, and the procedures for implementation required for an effective and coherent foreign policy.

Moreover, lateral coordination may be weakened and distorted by patterns of organizational behavior and the phenomenon of "bureaucratic politics" that create impediments to and malfunctions of the policymaking process. Accordingly, all presidents have found it necessary to impose mechanisms for control and coordination of policy analysis and implementation from above—either from the White House itself or from the National Security Council (NSC)—or have fixed responsibility for achieving control and coordination with the State Department; or have adopted a combination of these mechanisms.

The traditional practice for seeking improvement in the performance of the foreign-policymaking system was to undertake *structural reorganization* of the agencies and the mechanisms for achieving their coordination and cooperation. Periodically—indeed, at least once in each presidential administration—the foreign-policymaking system was reorganized.[1] But the results of reorganizations have been so disappointing that the "organizational tinkering" approach has fallen into general disrepute. Instead, greater attention is being given to the *design and management of the processes* of policymaking.

Coupled with this shift in focus from organizational structure to process is a new awareness among specialists in organization and public administration that their past efforts to identify a single standardized model of policymaking that would be optimal for all presidents was misguided. Instead, it is now recognized that each president is likely to define his role in foreign-policymaking somewhat differently and to approach it with a different decisionmaking and management style. Hence, too, he will have a different notion as to the kind of policymaking system that he wishes to create around him, feels comfortable with, and can utilize. In brief, the present emphasis is on designing organizational structures to fit the operating styles of their key individuals rather than attempting to persuade each new top executive to accept and adapt to a standardized organizational model that is considered to be theoretically the best.

As this implies, the first and foremost task that a new president faces is to learn to define his own role in the policymaking system; only then can he structure and manage the roles and relationships within the policymaking system of his secretary of state, the special assistant for national security affairs, the secretary of defense, and other cabinet members and agency heads with responsibilities for the formulation and implementation of foreign policy.

The president's basic choice is whether to give his secretary of state the primary role in the foreign-policymaking system or to centralize and manage that system from the White House itself. Still another model is that of a relatively decentralized system that is coordinated from the White House for the president by his special assistant for national security affairs.

A new president may receive advice on these matters from specialists in organization or in foreign policy, but in the last analysis his choices in these matters will be shaped by preferences of his own that stem from previous experience (if any) in executive roles and the extent to which he regards himself as knowledgeable and competent in foreign policy and national security matters. Finally, as all president-watchers have emphasized, the incumbent's personality will shape the formal structure of the policymaking system that he creates around himself and, even more, it will influence the ways in which he encourages and permits that formal structure to operate in practice. As a result, each president is likely to develop a policymaking system and a management style that contain distinctive and idiosyncratic elements.

Detailed comparison of past presidents from this standpoint suggests that a variety of personality characteristics are important, of which three can be briefly noted.[2] The first of these personality dimensions is *"cognitive style."* Cognitive psychologists have found it useful to view the human mind as a complex system for information processing. Every individual develops ways of storing, retrieving, evaluating, and using information. At the same time the individual develops a set of beliefs about the environment, about the attributes of other actors, and about various presumed causal relationships that help the person to explain and predict, as best he can (correctly or incorrectly), events of interest to him. Beliefs of this kind structure, order, and simplify the individual's world; they serve as models of "reality." Such mental constructs play an important role in the individual's perception of what is occurring in his environment, in the acquisition and interpretation of new information, and in the formulation and evaluation of responses to new situations.

At the same time, individuals differ in their approaches to processing and evaluating information, and this is generally what is meant by "cognitive style." There is as yet no standardized approach to characterizing the dimensions of cognitive style. For present purposes, the term is used to refer to the way in which an executive such as the president defines his informational needs for purposes of making decisions. "Cognitive style" also refers to his preferred ways of acquiring information from those around him and making use of that information, and to his preferences regarding advisers and ways of using them in making his decisions.

Defined in these terms, as we shall note, an individual's cognitive style plays an important role in his preference for one management model as against others. Cognitive styles do vary among presidents, and it simply will not work to try to impose on a new president a policymaking system or a management model that is uncongenial to his cognitive style.[3]

A second personality dimension that influences a president's choice of a policymaking system is *his sense of efficacy and competence* as it relates to management and decisionmaking tasks. In other words, the types of skills that he possesses and the types of tasks that he feels particularly adept at doing and those that he feels poorly equipped to do will influence the way in which he defines his executive role.

A third personality dimension that will influence the president's selection of a policymaking model is his general *orientation toward political conflict* and, related to this, toward interpersonal conflict over policy among his advisers. Individuals occupying the White House have varied on this personality dimension, too. Thus, we find that some chief executives have viewed politics as a necessary, useful, and perhaps even enjoyable game while other presidents have regarded it as a dirty business that must be discouraged or at least ignored. The personal attitude toward conflict that a president brings into office is likely to determine his orientation to the phenomena of "cabinet politics" and "bureaucratic politics" within his administration as well as to the larger, often interlinked game of politics surrounding the executive branch. Individuals with a pronounced distaste for "dirty politics" and for being exposed to face-to-face disagreements among advisers are likely to favor policymaking systems that attempt to curb these phenomena or at least shield them from direct exposure. They also are likely to prefer staff and advisory systems in which teamwork or formal analytical procedures are emphasized in lieu of partisan advocacy and debate.

Cognitive style, sense of efficacy, and orientation toward conflict (and of course, as noted earlier, the nature of any prior experience in executive roles and the level of personal competence and interest in foreign policy and national security affairs)—all these combine to determine how a new president will structure the policymaking system around him and how he will define his own role and that of others in it.

Three management models have been identified that characterize at least in general terms the approaches displayed by different presidents in recent times.[4] These are the "formalistic," "competitive," and "collegial" models. The formalistic model is characterized by an orderly policymaking structure, one that provides well-defined procedures, hierarchical lines of communication, and a structured staff system. While the formalistic model seeks to benefit from the diverse views and judgments of participants in policymaking, it also discourages open conflict and bargaining among them.

The competitive model, in contrast, places a premium on encouraging a more open and uninhibited expression of diverse opinions, analysis, and advice. To this end the competitive model not only tolerates but may actually encourage organizational ambiguity, overlapping jurisdictions, and multiple channels of communication to and from the president.

The collegial model, in turn, attempts to achieve the essential advantages of each of the other two while avoiding their pitfalls. To this end, the president attempts to create a team of staff members and advisers who will work together to identify, analyze, and solve policy problems in ways that will incorporate and synthesize as much as possible divergent points of view. The collegial model attempts to benefit from diversity and competition within the policymaking system, but it also attempts to avoid narrow parochialism by encouraging cabinet officers and advisers to identify at least partly with the presidential perspective. And by encouraging collegial participation in group problem-solving efforts, this approach attempts to avoid the worst excesses of infighting, bargaining, and compromise associated with the competitive model.

Truman, Eisenhower, and Nixon employed one or another variant of the formalistic approach. Franklin D. Roosevelt employed the competitive model, and John F. Kennedy the collegial one. As for Lyndon B. Johnson, he began by trying to emulate Franklin Roosevelt's style and gradually moved toward a formalistic approach but one that exhibited such idiosyncratic features that we have decided not to offer a description of it here. Carter, Reagan, Bush, and Clinton will be discussed in subsequent sections of this chapter.

Franklin D. Roosevelt

Let us begin with Franklin D. Roosevelt, whose unusual policymaking system is the prototype for the competitive management model. A dominant feature of FDR's personality was his strong sense of political efficacy. He felt entirely at home in the presidency, acting in the belief that there was close to a perfect fit between his competence and skills and some of the most demanding role requirements of the office. Then, too, FDR viewed politics and the games that go with it as a useful and enjoyable game and not, as others before him (for example, William Taft and Herbert Hoover) as an unsavory, distasteful business to be discouraged or avoided. FDR not only felt comfortable in the presence of conflict and disagreement around him; he also saw that, properly managed, it could serve his informational and political needs. Instead of trying, as his predecessor had, to take the politics out of the policymaking process, Roosevelt deliberately exacerbated the competitive and conflicting aspects of cabinet politics and bureaucratic politics. He sought to increase both structural and functional ambiguities within the executive branch in order better to preside over it. For Roosevelt, exposure to conflict among advisers and cabinet heads did not stir up anxiety or depression; nor did he perceive it as threatening in a personal or political sense. Not only did he live comfortably with the political conflict and, at times, near-chaos around him, but also he manipulated the structure of relationships among subordinates in order to control and profit from their competition. What is noteworthy is that Roosevelt did not attempt to create a for-

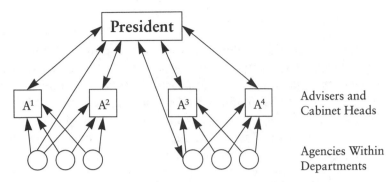

FIGURE 6.1   The Competitive Model (FDR)

mal, centralized model of the policymaking process (as advocated, for example, in later Hoover Commission proposals for reorganization of governmental agencies); rather, he deliberately created "fuzzy lines of responsibility, no clear chains of command, overlapping jurisdictions" in order to promote "'stimulating' inter-departmental conflict which could and did eventually land in his own lap."[5]

At the risk of simplification, it is possible to delineate some features of the distinctive communication network or patterns associated with FDR's competitive model (see Figure 6.1[6]).

Characteristic features of the competitive model (FDR): (1) the president deliberately encourages competition and conflict among advisers and cabinet heads by giving them overlapping assignments and ambiguous, conflicting jurisdictions in given policy areas; (2) there is relatively little communication or collaboration among advisers; (3) the president reaches down on occasion to communicate directly with subordinates of cabinet heads to get independent advice and information; (4) relevant information on important policy problems is forced up through the network to the president himself; competing advisers are forced to bring important policy problems to the president for resolution and decision; but (5) the president avoids risk of becoming overloaded or involved by operating this system selectively; on occasion (not depicted on the chart), he encourages or insists that subordinate officials settle things themselves and refuses to become identified with their policies or pet projects.

Harry S. Truman

Harry Truman adopted a different strategy for coping with the complex morass that governmental structure had become as a result of Roosevelt's style and administrative practices and the wartime expansion of agencies. Initially, Truman tried to tidy up the mess by clarifying and dividing up the jurisdictions. He also established the NSC in 1947 as a vehicle for providing orderly, balanced participation in foreign-policymaking deliberations. Truman tried to weaken the game of bureaucratic politics by strengthening each department head's control over his particular domain and by delegating presidential responsibility to him. New in the office, Truman took special pride in his ability to delegate responsibility and to back up those he trusted. He learned through experience, however, that to delegate too much or to delegate responsibility without providing clear guidance was to jeopardize the performance of his own responsibilities.

When faced with larger policy issues that required the participation of heads of several departments, Truman attempted to deal with them by playing the role of chairman of the board, hearing sundry expert opinions on each aspect of the problem, then making a synthesis of them and announcing the decision. Truman not only accepted the responsibility of making difficult decisions, but he also liked doing so, for it enabled him to satisfy himself—and, he hoped, others—that he had the personal qualities needed in the presidency. His sense of efficacy expressed itself in a willingness to make difficult decisions without experiencing undue stress. A modest man in many ways, Truman adjusted to the awesome responsibilities of the presidency suddenly thrust upon him by respecting the office and determining to become a good role player. By honoring the office and doing credit to it, he would do credit to himself. Included in this role conception was Truman's desire to put aside personal and political considerations as much as possible in the search for quality decisions that were in the national interest. He was willing to accept the political costs both to himself and to his party entailed in making controversial decisions, such as his policy of disengaging the United States from the Chinese Nationalists in 1949, his refusal to escalate the Korean War after the Chinese Communist intervention, his firing of General Douglas MacArthur, and his refusal to dismiss his loyal secretary of state, Dean Acheson, when he came under continuing attack. Truman's variant of

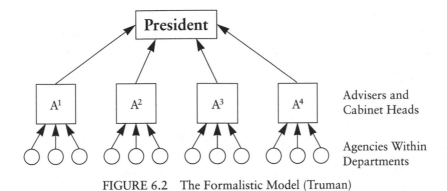

FIGURE 6.2   The Formalistic Model (Truman)

the formalistic model may be depicted, again in simplified terms, as in Figure 6.2.

Characteristic features of the formalistic model (Truman): (1) specialized information and advice flows to the president from each of his cabinet heads and advisers; (2) the president tends to define the role of each cabinet head as a functional expert on some aspect of national security or foreign policy; each official briefs the president authoritatively on that aspect of a policy problem for which he has jurisdiction; (3) each adviser receives information and advice from his subordinate units; (4) the president does not encourage his advisers to communicate with each other or to engage in joint efforts at policy analysis and problem solving; (5) the president sticks to channels and seldom reaches down to bypass a cabinet head to get independent information/advice from one of his subordinates; and (6) the president takes responsibility for intellectual synthesis of specialized inputs on a policy problem received from advisers.

Dwight D. Eisenhower

Dwight D. Eisenhower avoided personal involvement as much as possible in the bureaucratic politics aspects of policymaking within the executive branch and in less savory aspects of politics generally. At the same time, however, Eisenhower recognized that conflict and politics are inevitable and adapted to them by defining his own role as that of someone who could stand "above politics," moderate conflict, and promote unity. In doing so, Eisenhower expressed his special sense of efficacy that led him (and others) to believe that he could make a distinctive and unique contribution by seeming to remain "above politics" and by emphasizing the shared values and virtues that should guide governmental affairs. This did ñot prevent him, however, from engaging in political maneuvers of his own when he perceived that his interests required it.[7]

Eisenhower did not attempt (as Nixon would later) to depoliticize and rationalize the formal policymaking process completely. Rather, Eisenhower's variant of the formalistic model encompassed advocacy and disagreement at lower levels of the policymaking system, even though he wanted subordinates eventually to achieve agreement, if possible, on recommendations for his consideration. Moreover, formal meetings of the large NSC were often preceded by less formal "warm-up" sessions with a smaller group of advisers that provided opportunities for genuine policy debate. The conventional depiction of Eisenhower's NSC system as an unimaginative, bureaucratic body laden with the preparation and presentation of cautiously formulated positions, therefore, is not justified.[8]

What these observations about Eisenhower's policy system reveal is that a formalistic management model need not be highly bureaucratized. Examples of the formalistic management model, which always seem bureaucratized on the surface, need to be examined much more closely in order to determine how they actually function. As is well known, policymaking in complex organizations usually proceeds on *two* tracks: the formal, visible, official track and the informal, less visible track. Even the most formalistic of policymaking systems is accompanied by some kind of informal track that is utilized by the participants—including sometimes the president himself—in an attempt to "work with" or "work around" the formal procedures.

In particular, a president's use of surrogates as "chiefs of staff" in a formalistic management model needs close examination to determine to what extent he actually restricts his own involvement in policymaking and remains unaware or uninterested in the important preliminaries of information processing. Thus, in Eisenhower's case, recent archival research reveals that two of his "chiefs of staff"—Governor Sherman Adams and Secretary of State John Foster Dulles—were by no means as powerful as has been thought. "Adams was not the all powerful domestic policy gate-guard he is said to have been. He did

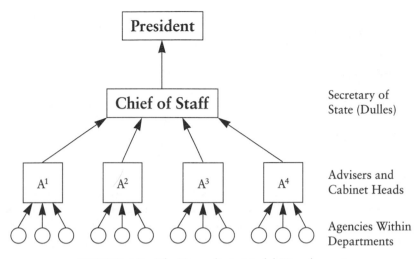

FIGURE 6.3   The Formalistic Model (Eisenhower)

not keep important information from Eisenhower's attention, nor did he make important decisions solo. . . . In the case of Dulles . . . not even the most obsequious Lyndon Johnson courtier could have been more assiduous about testing the waters. . . . Dulles was in touch with the president daily, and was consistently responsive to Eisenhower's directives."[9]

With these important caveats in mind, we can proceed to examine how the visible structure of his formalistic model differed from Truman's. This can be seen by comparing the chart for Truman's system with that for Eisenhower's presented in Figure 6.3.

Characteristic features of the formalistic model (Eisenhower): similar to Truman's variant of the formalistic model with two important exceptions: (1) a "chief of staff" position is created to be utilized, when the president wishes, as a buffer between himself and cabinet heads and to arrange for preparation of formal recommendations to the president (Sherman Adams performed this role for Eisenhower on domestic policy matters; in practice, Secretary of State John Foster Dulles came to assume a similar, though informal, role for Eisenhower in foreign policy, though not in defense matters); and (2) again, unlike Truman's version of the formalistic model, in this one the president attempts to protect himself from being overloaded by urging advisers/cabinet heads to analyze problems and resolve policy differences whenever possible at lower levels.

John F. Kennedy

John F. Kennedy felt much more at ease with the conflictual aspects of politics and policymaking than his predecessor; his sense of efficacy included confidence in his ability to manage and shape the interpersonal relations of those around him in a constructive fashion, and his cognitive style led him to participate much more actively and directly in the policymaking process than Eisenhower had or Nixon would later on. These personality characteristics contributed to forging a collegial style of policymaking based on teamwork and shared responsibility among talented advisers. Kennedy recognized the value of diversity and give-and-take among advisers, and he encouraged it. But Kennedy stopped well short of the extreme measures for stimulating competition that Roosevelt had employed. Rather than to risk introducing disorder and strife into the policymaking system, Kennedy used other strategies for keeping himself informed, properly advised, and "on top." He did not find personally congenial the highly formal procedures, the large meetings, and the relatively aloof presidential role characteristic of Eisenhower's system. Particularly after the Bay of Pigs fiasco, Kennedy employed a variety of devices for counteracting the narrowness of perspective of leading members of individual departments and agencies and for protecting himself from the risks of bureaucratic politics. Noteworthy is Kennedy's effort to restructure the roles and broaden the perspectives of top department and agency officials and to introduce a new set of norms to guide their participation in policymaking.

The kind of teamwork and group approach to problem solving that Kennedy strove to create—and achieved with notable success in the Cuban missile crisis at least—is often referred to as the "collegial" model to distinguish it both from the more competitive and the more formal systems of his predecessors. The sharp contrasts between Kennedy's collegial system and the competitive and formalistic models emerge by comparing Figure 6.4 with Figures 6.1, 6.2, and 6.3.

Characteristic features of the collegial model (JFK): (1) the president is at the center of a wheel with spokes connecting to individual advisers/cabinet heads; (2) advisers form a "collegial team" and en-

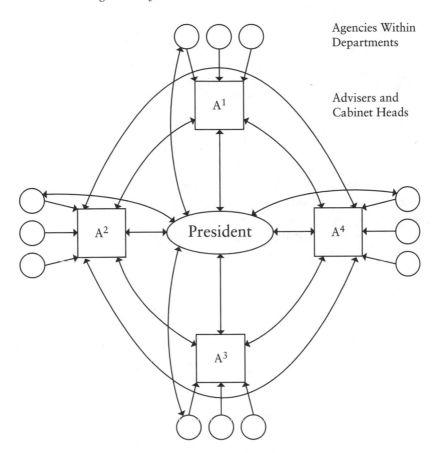

Agencies Within
Departments

Advisers and
Cabinet Heads

FIGURE 6.4   The Collegial Model (JFK)

gage in group problem-solving; (3) information flows into the collegial team from various points lower in the bureaucracy; (4) advisers
do not perform as individual filters to the president; rather, the group
of advisers functions as a "debate team" that considers information
and policy options from the multiple, conflicting perspectives of the
group members in an effort to obtain cross-fertilization and creative
problem solving; (5) advisers are encouraged to act as generalists,
concerned with all aspects of the policy problem, rather than as experts or functional specialists on only part of the policy problem; (6)
discussion procedures are kept informal enough to encourage frank
expression of views and judgments and to avoid impediments to in-

formation processing generated by status and power differences among members; and (7) the president occasionally gives overlapping assignments and occasionally reaches down to communicate directly with subordinates of cabinet heads in order to get more information and independent advice.

Richard M. Nixon

Richard Nixon strongly favored a formalistic model. As a number of observers have noted, several of Nixon's well-defined personality characteristics shaped his management style and approach to decisionmaking. During his earlier years, Nixon had developed a cognitive style that enabled him to cope with deeply rooted personal insecurities by adopting an extremely conscientious approach to decisionmaking. As described so well in his book *Six Crises,* the whole business of acquiring information, weighing alternatives, and deciding among them was, for Nixon, extremely stressful, requiring great self-control, hard work, and reliance upon himself. Dealing with difficult situations posed the necessity but also offered an opportunity for Nixon to prove himself over and over again. He experienced his greatest sense of self and of his efficacy when he had to confront and master difficult situations in which a great deal was at stake.[10]

Nixon's pronounced sense of aloneness and privacy, his thin-skinned sensitivity and vulnerability were not conducive to developing the kind of interpersonal relationships associated with a collegial model of management. Rather, as Richard T. Johnson notes, "Nixon, the private man with a preference for working alone, wanted machinery to staff out the options but provide plenty of time for reflection. . . . " Similarly, "with his penchant for order," Nixon inevitably "favored men who offered order," who acceded to his demand for loyalty and shared his sense of banding together to help him cope with a hostile environment.[11]

Nixon's preference for a highly formalistic system was reinforced by other personality characteristics. He was an extreme "conflict avoider"; somewhat paradoxically, although Nixon was quite at home with political conflict in the broader public arena, he had a pronounced distaste for being exposed to it face-to-face. Early in his administration, Nixon tried a version of multiple advocacy in which leading advisers would debate issues in his presence. But he quickly abandoned the experiment and turned to structuring his staff to avoid overt manifestations of disagreement and to avoid being personally drawn into the squabbles of his staff.[12] Hence Nixon's need for a few staff aides immediately around him who were to serve as buffers and enable him to distance himself from the wear and tear of policymaking.

It is interesting that Eisenhower's "chief of staff" concept was carried much further in Nixon's variant of the formalistic model. The foreign-policymaking system that Henry Kissinger, the special assistant for national security affairs, developed during the first year of Nixon's administration is generally regarded as by far the most centralized and highly structured model yet employed by any president.[13] Nixon was determined even more than Eisenhower had been to abolish bureaucratic and cabinet politics as completely as possible; but, more so than Eisenhower, Nixon also wanted to enhance and protect his personal control over high policy. To this end, a novel system of six special committees was set up operating out of the NSC, each of which was chaired by Kissinger. These included the Vietnam Special Studies Group, the Washington Special Actions Group (to deal with international crises), the Defense Programs Review Committee, the Verification Panel (to deal with strategic arms talks), the 40 Committee (to deal with covert actions), and the Senior Review Group (which dealt with all other types of policy issues).

Reporting to the Senior Review Group were six lower-level interdepartmental groups that were set up on a regional or functional basis (Middle East, Far East, Latin America, Africa, Europe, and Political-Military Affairs), each of which was headed by an assistant secretary of state. In addition, Kissinger could set up ad hoc working groups composed of specialists from various agencies and run by his own top staff aides.

Thus, not only did Kissinger's committee structure reach down into the departments and agencies, absorbing key personnel into various committees controlled by Kissinger or his staff aides, but also other committees that were created on an interdepartmental basis though chaired by assistant secretaries of state were given their assignments by Kissinger and reported to the Senior Review Group chaired by Kissinger. As a result, a novel, unconventional policymaking structure was created and superimposed upon the departments and largely superseded the traditional hierarchical policymaking system. Striking differences with Eisenhower's formalistic model can be noted (see Figure 6.5).

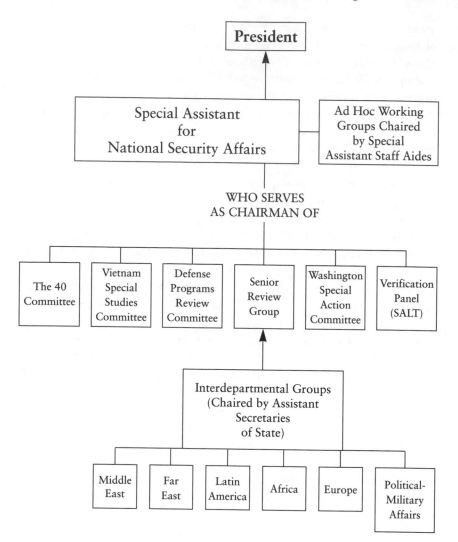

FIGURE 6.5   The Formalistic Model (Nixon)

Jimmy Carter

Comparing Jimmy Carter's publicly stated intentions with the evolution of his foreign policy management system during his four years in office yields somewhat ironic conclusions. Carter entered office with professed commitments to "cabinet government," intending to downgrade the role of national security adviser and to center foreign-policymaking in the State Department.[14] He left office with a significantly factionalized system that had evolved into one of the most White House–centered in modern history.[15]

Carter's management style embraced distinctive elements of both the collegial and the formalistic models. As one observer noted, Carter's national security policymaking system "is an amalgamation selectively drawn from the experiences of his predecessors."[16] Like Kennedy, Carter initially resisted a "chief of staff" system for organizing his work and contacts with others.[17] Carter's preference was a communications structure in the wheel configuration with himself at the hub, affording maximal opportunity for direct contact with officials and advisers. This was in part a post-Watergate reaction to Nixon's tightly hierarchical management system. Again like Kennedy (and Roosevelt), Carter wished to be actively involved in the policymaking process and at earlier stages, before the system had produced options or a single recommended policy for his consideration.[18]

At the same time, Carter differed from Kennedy in preferring a formally structured NSC system and retaining elements of the "formal options" system developed by Kissinger for Nixon.[19] Carter gradually restored the prestige of the NSC staff after the brief eclipse that occurred during the Gerald Ford administration when Kissinger was secretary of state, and he relied increasingly on its studies for help in making decisions.[20] Carter's preference for underpinning the collegial features of his management model with formalistic structure and procedures is not surprising given his naval training and experience as an engineer.[21]

In his somewhat technocratic approach to policymaking, experts and orderly study procedures played an essential role, and so the features of the collegial model that he valued had necessarily to be blended somehow with features of a formalistic model.[22] In this mixed system, policymaking was not meant to be as highly centralized as in the Nixon administration. Carter not only allowed relatively liberal access to the Oval Office but also maintained a more decentralized advisory system than Nixon had. This reflected not only his personality and management style but also the lessons that he and others drew from the experience of his predecessors. He was determined not to become isolated in the White House.

One of Carter's main concerns at the outset was to set up his foreign policy machinery in a way that would avoid the extreme centralization of power that Kissinger, as special assistant for national security affairs, had acquired during Nixon's first term and that led him to replace for all practical purposes the secretary of state. In Carter's administration, the special assistant (Zbigniew Brzezinski) was not meant to become as powerful or as public a figure as Kissinger had been. Instead Brzezinski was intended to be a behind-the-scenes source of intellectual insight, creativity, and a comprehensive strategic perspective.[23]

Carter's intention was for his secretary of state, Cyrus Vance, to be his chief diplomat and leading foreign policy spokesman and to be a key adviser.[24] In particular, Carter expected Vance to be a strong manager and team player who would not challenge the president's ambition to call the shots in the foreign policy realm. Despite some qualms, Carter apparently intended to rely on the State Department to play an important role in policy preparation.[25] In line with this concept and his general preference for organizational austerity, the number of committees in the NSC staff was reduced from what they had been in Nixon's administration, and Brzezinski did not chair all of the NSC committees as Kissinger had.[26] However, the committee he did chair, the Special Coordination Committee (SCC), over time became increasingly important at the expense of an alternative body, the Policy Review Committee (PRC), which was chaired at the cabinet secretary level.[27]

In his attempt to inhibit the special assistant from becoming the dominant actor in the system and a virtual "chief of staff,"[28] Carter planned to rely on collegiality among his principal national security advisers—the secretary of state, the secretary of defense, the special assistant, and the vice president—to achieve the necessary interaction and coordination.[29] Accordingly, the NSC organization under Carter was designed to be more modest than Nixon's in centrality, structure, staffing, and operations.

Although Carter's choice of organizational model was in part a response to the experiences of his predecessors, both his choice of this system and the functioning of the system in practice were also shaped to a considerable extent by his personality. Carter brought with him to the White House a cognitive style and sense of personal efficacy that gave him confidence in the possibility of mastering difficult problems and of finding comprehensive solutions for them.[30] This orientation was reflected, for example, in Carter's attraction to the idea of zero-based budgeting.[31] The realm of foreign policy was no exception.[32]

Ironically, this same sense of confidence may have inhibited Carter's ability to make best use of the advisory system he created. Several observers have noted that Carter exhibited an active leadership style in meetings that seemed designed to demonstrate his own mastery of the subject matter rather than to draw out the views of his colleagues.[33] This may also have encouraged anticipatory compliance on the part of cabinet members and aides. As Hamilton Jordan informed Carter in March 1980: *"A great premium is placed upon anticipating what you want instead of providing you with frank and hard analysis."*[34] Furthermore, it has been suggested that Carter had great difficulty in accepting criticism from others and admitting his own mistakes, which may have inhibited him from learning from experience.[35]

Carter's legendary appetite for written material initially aroused the approval of many observers.[36] However, this trait also had a downside that gradually became apparent.[37] Overloaded with detail that consumed time that might otherwise have been devoted to strategic reflection, Carter had a tendency to lose sight of the forest for the trees. According to C. Campbell, "He brought to his work a ponderous style that tended to ritualize consultation and caused him to devour factual information."[38] Attempts by aides to reduce Carter's reading burden met with resistance. Brzezinski writes, "Whenever I tried to relieve him of excessive detail, Carter would show real uneasiness, and I even felt some suspicion, that I was usurping his authority."[39]

Despite public perceptions of a warm and extroverted personality, some insiders suggest that Carter tended to be rather shy and conflict averse on an interpersonal level.[40] According to Bob Berglund (Carter's secretary of agriculture), Carter "didn't really like to mix it up in a meeting. He didn't like to debate or listen to arguments; he was very uncomfortable in that area."[41] Other observers note that Carter was particularly conflict averse regarding aides with whom he was personally unfamiliar and suggest that he was reluctant to sanction aides who did not perform well.[42]

This trait could help to explain why Carter, like Nixon, apparently preferred many policy conflicts to be spelled out on paper rather than in oral deliberations. However, other commentators concede that Carter was somewhat averse to intense personalized conflict but argue that he enjoyed the give-and-take of substantive debate among his advisers. In fact, according to A. Moens, Carter actually encouraged competitive behavior in his aides and cabinet members in order to widen his information base for policymaking.[43] Carter himself subsequently claimed: "The different strengths of Brzezinski and Vance matched the roles they played and also permitted the natural competition between the two organizations to stay alive. I appreciated those differences. In making the final decisions on foreign policy, I needed to weigh as many points of view as possible."[44]

How then did the system that Jimmy Carter created function in practice, and what attempts were made to adjust the system during the course of his term? Although Carter did succeed to some extent in avoiding a highly centralized, "closed" system of foreign-policymaking, it must also be said that he was much less successful in avoiding the potential difficulties of the mixed formalistic-collegial model that he created. A number of weaknesses quickly became evident in the Carter system that seriously affected its performance. The collegial model requires close contact and continuing interaction between the president, his secretary of state, and the special adviser. A considerable degree of contact and sustained interaction among these officials were sustained during much of the Carter administration, through a wide range of official and unofficial forums for consultation.[45]

However, their respective roles remained highly fluid and were not well defined.[46] For example, no clear arrangement for policy specialization and division of labor was maintained among these three principals. In contrast, the secretary of defense's role appears to have been more clearly defined; his participation in policymaking was noticeably less prone to responsibility conflicts with others.[47] In the absence of role definition and specialization, all three—the president, his secretary of state, and the special adviser—could and often did take an active posture in any important policy problem. A shared interest in major policy problems is to be expected in a collegial system, but some understandings must also be developed to regulate initiative, consultation, the articulation of disagreements, formulation of collective judgments, and relations with the mass media. Carter evidently counted on the fact that the three men knew and respected one another prior to his election to the presidency to make his collegial approach work. And, to be sure, for a time it seemed that the three men got along well. Yet more than a façade of cordiality is needed for effective policymaking in a collegial system.

Collegiality entails certain risks, and its preservation may exact a price. The evidence indicates that the preservation of cordiality in the early period of the Carter administration was accompanied by a perhaps partly unconscious tendency to subordinate disagreements over policy among the three men that should have been articulated, confronted, and dealt with in a timely fashion.[48] Carter may have contributed to this tendency to seek concurrence by reacting negatively to diversity in his briefing materials during the first six weeks of his administration.[49]

Another source of difficulties was Carter himself. He had a habit of suddenly taking the initiative or intervening in an important foreign policy matter, as in the case of his human rights initiative and the neutron bomb controversy,[50] leaving Vance and Brzezinski with the embarrassing and difficult task of making the best of it or of trying to modify the policy. Carter's colleagues and aides were greatly frustrated by their inability to curb this tendency to take over important matters, which also tended to deny them an adequate opportunity to advise Carter beforehand. According to Brzezinski's account, "At times, Carter's impatience produced circumstances in which he would make decisions ahead of the NSC coordinating process, prompting me to complain to him."[51]

Carter's style tended to leave the decisionmaking process open and the degree of policy maturity unclear. Closure became difficult to achieve as advocates were not provided with clear signals as to when to break off their advocacy on particular issues. According to Brzezinski, Carter was at times "like a sculptor who did not know when to throw away his chisel."[52]

Another weakness of Carter's system quickly developed and proved difficult to cope with. Foreign policy became badly fragmented in the first year of Carter's administration. The hybrid system "put a heavy burden on the president's time and attention and called for unusual interpersonal skills, which Carter was unable to provide, in mediating differences and maintaining teamwork."[53] The situation was characterized by: (1) overactivism—the floating of many specific policy initiatives within a relatively short period of time; (2) a tendency to initiate attractive, desirable policies without sufficient attention to their feasibility; (3) poor conceptualization of overall foreign policy and, related to this, a failure to recognize that individual policies conflicted with each other; (4) a poor sense of strategy and tactics; (5) a badly designed and managed policymaking system.[54]

These flaws cannot be attributed merely or even primarily to Carter's inexperience in foreign policy.[55] After all, his administration included various high-level officials with considerable expertise and experience in foreign-policymaking. Part of the explanation has to do with important aspects of his personality, which may well seem attractive in and of themselves. Carter is a man of high moral principles, as exemplified by his sincere commitment to human rights.[56] He wanted to imbue U.S. foreign policy with renewed moral purpose; he was an activist in this respect and took genuine pleasure in his administration's ability to launch so many worthwhile policy initiatives so quickly—and he could see no harm in pushing ahead simultaneously with so many good initiatives.

What was needed to safeguard against an overloading of the foreign policy agenda and the fragmentation of foreign policy was a strong policy planning and coordinating mechanism, one that would alert Carter to this problem and assist him in dealing with difficult trade-offs among conflicting policy initiatives by establishing priorities and generally better integrating the various strands of foreign policy. Such a policy planning and coordinating mechanism, however, was lacking. The need to develop it somehow fell between the two pillars of Carter's mixed collegial-formalistic model. Neither the formalistic nor the collegial components of Carter's system provided the necessary planning/coordinating mechanisms and procedures.

An increasingly significant problem during the latter two-thirds of the administration was that Vance and Brzezinski did develop important disagreements over policy, particularly on matters having to do with assessment of Soviet intentions and strategy and tactics for dealing with the Soviet Union. The effort to preserve collegiality in the first eighteen months of the administration led both men to paper over their disagreements and to avoid the difficult but necessary task of coming to grips with these fundamental policy questions. But these matters could not be avoided indefinitely, and after jockeying and competing with each other to influence Carter's position, first one way and then the other, the controversy between Vance and Brzezinski spilled out into the open. Brzezinski began speaking out aggressively to undermine the positions taken by the secretary of state. Among other things, Brzezinski wanted the administration to exploit the Sino-Soviet conflict, to "play the China card," in order to exert pressure on the Soviets. Vance opposed this effectively for some time. But Brzezinski continued his efforts and was successful in obtaining the president's approval for his trip to China. The special assistant's outspoken disagreements with the secretary of state became so damaging that Vance finally went to the president in the summer of 1978 and prevailed upon him to restrain Brzezinski from airing his disagreements publicly. This situation resulted in Brzezinski's adopting a somewhat lower public profile for a time.[57]

Yet a combination of institutional arrangements, personal chemistry, and the developing political context conspired to keep Brzezinski's star on the rise. The configuration of world events, especially the Soviet invasion of Afghanistan and the fall of the shah of Iran, tended to strengthen the hawkish Brzezinski's hand at the more dovish Vance's expense. Similarly, these situations kept the administration in a semi-permanent crisis mode during its final two years, which pushed formal interagency coordination toward the NSC's SCC, chaired by none other than Brzezinski. Buttressed by his positive personal relationship with Carter, Brzezinski became increasingly assertive, manipulating the process in order to pursue his policy agenda.[58]

The conflict between Vance and Brzezinski ultimately came to a head as a result of the April 1980 decision to attempt a military rescue of the American hostages being held in Iran. The preliminary deliberations were held in Vance's absence, leading to a provisional decision by Carter to go ahead with the mission. Upon his return, Vance was granted an opportunity to present his case at a formal NSC meeting. In spite of Vance's pleas, Carter decided to go ahead with the ill-fated mission, a decision that prompted Vance to resign in protest.[59] Carter promptly appointed Senator Edmund Muskie as his replacement, primarily on the basis of his usefulness as a foreign policy spokesman. Muskie was unable to challenge seriously Brzezinski's position in the waning months of the administration.[60]

There were other weaknesses in the management of Carter's foreign policy system. Under Brzezinski as special assistant, and given the character of his staff, the NSC did not function effectively in coordinating the various strands of foreign policy and helping Carter with his difficult task of managing the various contradictions and trade-offs between different foreign policy objectives. Neither Brzezinski himself nor his deputy, David Aaron (who apparently was selected in part for his ties to Vice President Walter Mondale), earned reputations for being good administrators or for defining their roles as high-level staff rather than as activists in making policy.[61] In fact, both were much more interested in influencing policy than in managing the policymaking process in a neutral, efficient manner. Moreover, many of the people Brzezinski brought onto the NSC staff to work with him were also eager to influence policy as best they could from the vantage point of the White House.

As a result, the fragmentation of foreign policy at the conceptual level,[62] to which many critics have called attention, was reinforced by the administration's failure to develop an effective central coordinating mechanism for the organization and management of the policy-making process.[63] In an attempt to cope with these problems in midstream, Carter turned to the creation of special task forces for each major policy issue in order to centralize authority in the White House and to improve coordination of agency and departmental officials on behalf of presidential policy. Following the successful use of ad hoc task forces to direct efforts to secure ratification of the Panama Canal treaty and to deal with other major issues, in late 1978 Carter established an executive committee headed by Vice President Mondale to be responsible for dealing with the president's agenda and priorities. The committee endorsed a plan for forming task forces for all major presidential issues for 1979. Task forces were established on a dozen issues of high priority, including domestic as well as foreign policy issues.

Ronald Reagan

Delving into foreign policy management during the Ronald Reagan administration reveals a turbulent image of a system in search of a stable personnel mix and organizational equilibrium that would take more than six years and a major foreign policy scandal to achieve. During those six years the system was relatively decentralized, undermanaged, and characterized by chronic and exhausting extremes of personal, ideological, and bureaucratic conflict. These conditions generated an unusually high degree of senior staff turnover. In the course of an eight-year term Reagan appointed two secretaries of state, two secretaries of defense, and *six* national security advisers—a record indicative of serious difficulties in establishing and maintaining a sound foreign-policymaking system.

Mindful of and wishing to distance himself from the precedent of the turbulent latter years of the Carter administration, Reagan wished to significantly modify the structure of the policymaking system. Even before taking office he indicated that he would reduce the scope and functions of the office of the adviser for national security affairs (NSA) in order to avoid a repetition of the damaging competitive relationship that had developed between Brzezinski and Vance in the Carter administration. Instead, he embraced the ideal of a State Department–centered foreign-policymaking system, trusting that coordination could be achieved through collegiality among his cabinet secretaries and through the good offices of a significantly downgraded national security adviser.[64] Thus Reagan proposed a synthesis of the formalistic and collegial models.[65]

It is fair to say that this model did affect Reagan's appointments and initial allocations of responsibility. Reagan selected Richard Allen as national security adviser, a minor figure who had served briefly on the Kissinger NSC staff. Reagan sharply reduced Allen's access and policymaking prerogatives, directing him to focus on the task of policy coordination and to refrain from taking part in public diplomacy, policy advocacy, and operational matters. Allen was directed to report to the president via Edwin Meese III. Meese, a Reagan crony who, though lacking experience in foreign policy, had had a brief career spanning both domestic and foreign policy, was one of a "troika" of White House officials who would collectively (and by most accounts effectively) enact the chief of staff role during Reagan's first term.[66]

For secretary of state, Reagan chose General Alexander Haig, another and more prominent veteran of the Nixon administration, where he had served as Kissinger's deputy and briefly as White House chief of staff.[67] Haig was promised the prime role in the foreign-policymaking process and the privilege of being chief foreign policy spokesman for the administration.[68] The secretary of defense post went to Caspar Weinberger, a longtime Washington hand and political ally of the president, known for his conservatism and his hawkish views. Reagan tapped William Casey—who had served in the Office of Strategic Services during World War II—for the CIA directorship, taking the relatively unusual step of granting Casey cabinet rank, a tacit indication that Reagan had an important role in mind for the agency.[69]

Let us now turn our attention to the man who made these initial choices and set the stage for what would be an eight-year administration. Reagan's relatively unusual cognitive style is deserving of comment as it affected both his choice of management model and, subsequently, the functioning of that system. As depicted by several of his most authoritative biographers and former associates, Reagan comes across as both intelligent and intellectually lazy.[70] He was often impatient with detailed presentation of policy material. He preferred oral briefings, briefing films, and "mini-memos" to reading lengthy reports. These preferences and characteristics contrast vividly with Carter's insatiable appetite for reading and tendency to immerse himself in the details of policy problems. Despite much publicity regarding memory lapses, Reagan apparently could demonstrate a remarkable ability to absorb orally presented material.[71]

Often described as "incurious," Reagan tended to be strikingly passive in information acquisition.[72] He generally asked few questions in deliberations. This passivity extended to consideration of policy options. Reagan generally accepted the options laid out by his advisers as given. Unlike Eisenhower, he rarely attempted to reshape options himself or question the way in which problems were framed.[73] Reagan was typically decisive when presented with clear choices, especially when they could be based on the bedrock of his convictions. Yet it seems that value conflicts raised by such choices tended to be suppressed and ignored rather than rigorously explored and resolved.[74]

One insightful biographer suggests that Reagan's mode of thought was more narrative than analytical, his cognitive processes driven by experience, stories, and analogy rather than deductive logic.[75] Furthermore, he allegedly tended to be rather unselective and uncritical regarding the sources of the information on which he relied, making him vulnerable "to arguments short on facts and long on theatrical gimmicks." That account reports that Reagan exhibited a credulity bordering at times on gullibility.[76]

Assessing Reagan's own sense of personal efficacy and competence is not an easy task. He appeared generally to enjoy the presidency, mastering the public aspects of the role to an extent unmatched by his recent peers. He drew great satisfaction from the positive response of his audiences. He was confident and active in his relationship with Congress, recalling Lyndon Johnson in his skill at face-to-face persuasion. Reagan has often been described as comfortable with decision.[77] In congressional testimony in 1987, George P. Shultz described Reagan as follows: "He is comfortable with himself. He is decisive, he steps up to things, and when he decides, he stays with it. And sometimes you wish he wouldn't, but anyway he does. He is very decisive and he's very strong."[78] Reagan possessed a set of core convictions that often enabled him to be decisive, even without having mastered the nuts and bolts of an issue.[79]

Yet, where those convictions were unable to provide guidance, Reagan could find himself confused and tentative. An astute observer suggests that: "The paradox of the Reagan presidency was that it depended entirely on Reagan for its ideological inspiration while he depended upon others for all aspects of governance except his core ideas and his powerful performances. In the many arenas of the office where ideology did not apply or the performances had no bearing, Reagan was at a loss."[80] Some commentators have focused on Reagan's limited experience in foreign affairs and apparent lack of motivation to take active steps to educate himself once in office.[81] It is possible that his sense of personal efficacy was somewhat diminished in this area, particularly early in his tenure when he focused much of his attention on his domestic agenda.

As a manager, Reagan was confident about his ability to pick people, set broad objectives, and delegate authority.[82] However, when this broad strategy ran into trouble he was quite reluctant about resorting to more hands-on types of management. In fact, he was so tentative that his management style could be characterized fairly as benign neglect, leaving colleagues frustrated at his reluctance to take steps to deal with personnel and organizational problems.[83]

Some of this tentativeness was probably the result of Reagan's attitude toward interpersonal conflict. According to a number of commentators, Reagan had a low tolerance for conflict among his cabinet and staff members and hated confrontations.[84] He would go to great lengths to avoid conflict and try to develop a consensus, thus giving dissenters considerable leverage. When confronted with serious differences of opinion among his advisers, he often tried to split the difference in order to avoid offending anyone. This often produced delay in policy formulation and a susceptibility to unhappy and unstable compromise policies.[85] Reagan hated to fire people and preferred to let staff handle such unpleasant situations. In keeping with his distaste for confrontation, Reagan rarely made decisions on contested matters in meetings. He preferred to listen to the opposing views and make the decisions subsequently in private. In this he resembled Nixon. Perhaps in part because of his aversion to confrontation and his general tentativeness on issues where his ideological impulses were conflicted or inapplicable, Reagan was allegedly vulnerable to being persuaded by the last adviser to have spoken with him alone before he made major decision.[86]

Reagan's personal relationship to his advisers and staff is also worthy of note. On the one hand, Reagan possessed a surface-level warmth, chronic good humor, and a personal charisma that tended to inspire loyalty in his aides (and support from the general public). He could exhibit a genuine, though often fleeting empathy that was triggered, for example, in spontaneous personal encounters with others in dire straits. However, many observers suggest that these qualities masked a fundamental detachment from those around him.

While his style made him heavily dependent on his staff, Reagan apparently was not fully conscious of this dependence and tended to take his people for granted. In contrast to George Bush, who was highly solicitous of his colleagues and staff, Reagan came across as relatively self-absorbed, "unthoughtful," and oblivious to the personal needs and predicaments of those around him. This quality appears to have had a corrosive quality on loyalty to the president and on staff morale in general, contributing to the high turnover rate among senior staffers and officials.[87]

Given this institutional design and this cast of characters, how did the system function in practice?[88] Despite Reagan's call for collegiality, serious conflict emerged in the system almost immediately as a result of personal and political rivalries. Secretary of State Haig's undisguised presidential ambitions (he had tested the waters in the early stages of the 1980 contest for the Republican nomination) could hardly have encouraged a benign view among the Meese-Deaver-Baker troika on the wisdom of allowing the secretary to place himself squarely astride the foreign-policymaking system in a way that might have overshadowed the White House. In the months that followed the inauguration, indications of conflict between Haig and Allen and their staffs began to appear in the media.[89]

That conflict should develop among Reagan's foreign policy team was not surprising or unexpected. Reagan had entered the White House without a well-developed set of position papers on security matters and foreign policy, which candidates for the presidency usually prepare during their campaigns. Indeed, his campaign advisers had decided not to attempt to articulate specific positions in order not to expose the latent disagreements among his supporters. While all his major foreign policy and security advisers shared the general view that a "tougher" posture toward the Soviet Union should be adopted and that U.S. military capabilities should be "strengthened," this so-called consensus was a shallow one, papering over major disagreements concerning the specific strategies and policies that should be adopted. Inevitably, therefore, intense competition set in among different factions within Reagan's administration to shape and control specific policies, a struggle that was to prove time consuming and costly.[90] This conflict rapidly reached levels of intensity that undermined rather than invigorated the policymaking process.

The administration soon became vulnerable to criticism that it was slow in formulating policy on key defense and diplomatic issues and lacked a coherent, consistent foreign policy. Though Haig was initially anointed by Reagan as his leading foreign policy adviser—his "vicar of foreign policy," as Haig referred to himself—the secretary of state found it difficult to take firm hold of the fragmented foreign policy apparatus. Operating from the State Department, Haig lacked the advantages that a position in the White House would have provided, and he could not count on its firm, consistent support. Haig's own more moderate foreign policy views and some of his early appointments to positions of influence in the department marked him in the eyes of those whose views were to the right of his in the Reagan entourage, in Congress, and among attentive opinion leaders. Secretary of Defense Weinberger and several of his associates in the Department of Defense were prominent members of this camp.

Even if Allen had been neutral in the policy competition that increasingly developed between Weinberger and Haig, he was ill equipped to play a role in the top-level foreign policy management system. Allen's office had been so downgraded in importance that he did not have direct access to the president as had his predecessors in previous administrations. With the passage of time it became increasingly evident that the task of coordinating the policymaking process at the White House level could not be managed effectively through the existing organizational arrangements. Visible evidence of feuding among leading foreign policy advisers damaged Reagan's standing at home and abroad.

Reagan himself contributed to the disappointing performance of his foreign-policymaking system during his first year in office. Not only did he attempt to delegate much of the foreign-policymaking burden to Haig and his other associates (reminiscent of the heavy delegation of responsibility to subordinates that he had displayed as governor of California), but also he was relatively uninterested in foreign policy and gave higher priority during the first year and a half of his presidency to his economic policies. As we have already noted, Reagan counted on collegiality among his top-level advisers to smooth the working of his administration. But though collegiality was preserved and indeed played an important role in the workings of the inner White House circle composed of Meese, Deaver, and Baker, it did not spread outward to lubricate the interactions of the principal advisers in the foreign-policymaking system—Haig, Weinberger, and Allen.

What emerged, therefore, was not a well-designed, smoothly working system that, while centered in a strong secretary of state, was complemented by additional high-level coordination and linkage to the president himself through the national security adviser. Rather, it was a fragmented, competitive, inadequately managed system in which distrust was ever present and which gave rise repeatedly to damaging intra-administration conflicts over policy.[91] Franklin Roosevelt's competitive system was designed to bring important issues up to the presidential level and to improve the quality of information and advice available to a president who was interested and actively involved in making the important decisions. In contrast, the competitive-conflictual features of Reagan's foreign policy machinery were the consequences of a poorly structured and inadequately managed system, one that did not engage the president's attention except sporadically, when international developments or intra-administration conflicts required his personal attention.

To his credit and that of his leading advisers, Reagan recognized well before the end of his first year in office that his foreign-policymaking system was not working and that it required reorganization and change of personnel. Early in 1982 Allen was replaced by William Clark, a close friend of Reagan and a former California Supreme Court justice whose foreign policy background consisted exclusively of a brief period as undersecretary of state under Haig.[92] In addition, Reagan now strengthened the position of the national security adviser; Clark would henceforth deal directly with the president on a daily basis and no longer report to Meese. A determined effort was made to enable Clark to discharge more effectively the traditional role of custodian-manager of the system.

During the first half of 1982 relations between Haig and Clark developed with a minimum of friction. Behind the scenes, however, lay still unresolved questions between the White House and the State Department as to the direction and control of foreign policy, a situation that was exacerbated by the clash of styles and personalities. With Secretary of State Haig's resignation in June 1982, it became evident that the new policy machinery created by the strengthening of the role of the adviser for national security affairs had not stabilized itself sufficiently to cope with new stresses that developed in connection with the president's trip to Europe and the Israeli invasion of Lebanon, both of which occurred in June.

Thus, less than eighteen months after his inauguration, President Reagan was forced to replace both his national security adviser and his secretary of state, an unprecedented admission of failure to develop an effective foreign-policymaking system.

Insofar as personality clashes and differences of style had contributed to Haig's departure, there was every reason to expect that these impediments would disappear with the choice of George Shultz as his replacement. What was also clear by mid-1982 was that Reagan had significantly modified his initial preference for a State Department–centered foreign-policymaking system. Thus Shultz would not have the luxury of starting out as the anointed primus inter pares among Reagan's foreign policy advisers. Instead, he would have to seek a modus vivendi with the other advisers and the confidence of the president.

By October 1983 Clark, weary of the travails of the job of national security adviser, seized an opportunity to move into a cabinet post as secretary of the interior and was replaced by his deputy, Robert McFarlane.[93] Like Allen, McFarlane had previously served as an aide to Kissinger, whom he reportedly saw as a worthy role model.[94] However, it should be said that during the two years that McFarlane served as national security adviser, he gradually consolidated his position and performed the difficult task of mediating major policy conflicts between State and Defense with increasing effectiveness. McFarlane also made important progress in gaining the president's trust and his ear, and he moved in a slow but purposeful way to enhance his own power and prestige.[95]

However, McFarlane found himself increasingly frustrated during the first year of Reagan's second term by the changes in White House operations introduced by Donald T. Regan, who replaced James Baker as chief of staff after the election. Just when he was needed most to follow up on the opportunities created by the Reagan-Gorbachev summit meeting at Reykjavik in November 1985, McFarlane could put up with the frustrations of his position no longer, and he resigned. He was replaced by his deputy, Vice Admiral John Poindexter, a person who clearly lacked the broad experience, political sophistication, and reputation needed to cope with the difficult tasks that had faced all his predecessors in the position of national security adviser to President Reagan.

Before proceeding to note Poindexter's fate, let us make some additional observations regarding the weakness and vulnerability of Reagan's management style. The formalistic chief of staff model that Reagan adopted to structure the White House policymaking system differed in important respects from that of Eisenhower. While Eisenhower gave considerable prominence to the formal NSC system and to the role of his secretary of state in foreign policy, in practice he exercised quiet but firm leadership to ensure that the formal machinery and his cabinet officers were responsive to his own policy views and judgments on major issues. In striking contrast, Reagan distanced himself to a surprising and dangerous degree from both the substance and the process of foreign-policymaking. Unlike Reagan, Eisenhower defined the role of his national security adviser in such a way as to complement his own leadership role and style, and this enabled the special assistant to serve as an effective "custodian-manager" of the system. The result was that Eisenhower's White House achieved reasonably effective interagency coordination of policy with State, Defense, and other agencies. In contrast, in his first six years in office Reagan failed to develop a model of how the national security adviser, the secretary of state, and the secretary of defense should work together to complement and compensate for, rather than to exacerbate the risks inherent in, his own modest involvement in foreign-policymaking. Moreover, Reagan's penchant for delegating responsibility to trusted advisers, a practice that had served him reasonably well in his first term, created substantial new problems when he replaced James Baker, a skillful and sophisticated political operator, with Donald Regan as chief of staff.[96]

Nonetheless, in his first five years in office, despite the forced resignation of one secretary of state and a succession of four national security advisers, Reagan's extraordinary personal popularity and his presidency remained unscathed, and he retained the possibility of finishing his second term with a defensible record in foreign policy. All this was placed in jeopardy with the revelation in the winter of 1986–1987 that the White House had been utilizing elements of the NSC staff to sell arms covertly to Iran in order to facilitate the release of American hostages in Lebanon, and that some of the proceeds of these sales were being diverted to the *contras* in Central America. National Security Adviser Admiral Poindexter and his subordinate Lieutenant Colonel Oliver North, who together had orchestrated the covert activities, were quickly relieved of their duties. As details of the Iran-Contra affair emerged, attention quickly focused on the glaring weakness of Reagan's management style and the gross inadequacies of his foreign-policymaking system. These criticisms were sharply stated and documented in the report of the Tower Commission, which the president had appointed and charged with bringing out all the facts of the Iran-Contra scandal and with making recommendations for improving the NSC system.[97]

Even before the Tower Commission issued its report, the president appointed Frank Carlucci, a person of stature and high-level government experience (most recently as deputy secretary of defense during 1981 and 1982), to replace Admiral Poindexter in late 1986.[98] The new national security adviser moved quickly to reorganize the staff and to replace many of its personnel. Ably assisting in this reform process was the newly appointed deputy national security adviser, Lieutenant General Colin Powell.[99]

Another casualty was Reagan's White House chief of staff, Donald Regan, who had assumed that position after the president's reelection. Regan's style and performance had been the object of considerable criticism even before the Iran-Contra scandal. Though not centrally implicated, Regan was damaged by the affair, and the president reluctantly removed him shortly after the Tower Commission issued its report. CIA director William Casey might well have had to resign also were it not for his removal from the scene by a severe and ultimately fatal illness before all the facts regarding his involvement emerged.

Regan's replacement, former Senator Howard Baker, was widely regarded as an excellent choice for the position. Together with Frank Carlucci, Baker contributed to restoring confidence in the operations of the White House staff. The president himself emerged from a period of semi-seclusion and struggled to reassert his leadership. At the president's order, and with Carlucci's assent, the NSC staff was directed to end its direct involvement in covert operations.[100]

Yet this is not to say that Carlucci intended to accept a drastically diminished role for the national security adviser and his staff. Carlucci envisioned combining a prioritized custodian-manager role with the provision of policy advice:

> My first responsibility is to be an honest broker. . . . Now, what right do I have to offer personal advice to the president? The president has every right to say to his staff: "What do *you* think I ought to do?" . . . There is nothing in the constitution or in any statute which says that the national security adviser or the staff cannot give the president independent advice if the president asks for it.[101]

Carlucci's NSC staff also retained an operative role with regard to so-called "special missions," which would come to include even a Carlucci visit to the Nicaraguan *contras*.[102] Similarly, the NSC staff continued to operate back channels to communicate with the Soviets.

Some significant friction between Carlucci and Shultz would emerge by mid-1987 over such matters. Shultz also objected to what he perceived as Carlucci's bid to use the recommendations of the Tower Commission to strengthen the national security adviser's policy coordination role via a radical restructuring of the decisionmaking process in a document entitled NSDD 276. It was ultimately approved over Shultz's objections.[103] Furthermore, the long-standing conflict between Shultz and Weinberger over arms control and the U.S.-Soviet relationship continued to hamper policymaking in that area.

By the autumn of 1987 an arms control agreement on intermediate nuclear forces (INF) appeared to be in sight. Growing cooperation between Shultz and Carlucci and the president's growing confidence in Gorbachev and desire for an agreement left Weinberger out in the cold. Citing the ill health of his wife, Weinberger announced his resignation in October. Weinberger's departure triggered a major reshuffling of the national security team. Carlucci was given the defense portfolio and Colin Powell (who had developed a solid working relationship with Shultz) was promoted to national security adviser.

These moves ushered in a period of collegiality that would last through the end of the administration. Weinberger's departure put an end to the ideological and personal polarization that had weakened the administration's foreign-policymaking for almost seven years.

Furthermore, Colin Powell defined his national security adviser's role as serving "all of the NSC principals, not just the president."[104] Powell thus placed a heavy emphasis on maintaining collegiality: "By early 1988, national security assistant Powell was hosting intimate, 7:00 A.M. sessions every weekday morning in his White House office in which he and the secretaries of state and defense would briefly go over all the immediate national security issues of the upcoming day."[105] Though the new willingness to compromise was a refreshing change from the turmoil (to borrow Shultz's phrase) of the earlier phases of the administration, it may have had a downside as well. According to one assessment, the collegial system tended to produce policies that reflected the common denominator of the relevant agencies.[106]

The new collegiality also resulted, however, in a consensus in favor of exploring cooperation with the Soviet Union on arms control and regional issues, which contributed to a number of high-profile outcomes widely regarded as positive. These included the INF agreement signed at the December 1987 Washington summit and ratified in time for the Moscow summit in May 1988; substantial movement toward a strategic arms limitation treaty (START); and progress on regional conflicts such as in Afghanistan (where a Soviet commitment to withdraw was achieved) and Namibia. Thus Reagan proved able or fortunate enough to put the crisis of public and personal confidence caused by the Iran-Contra affair behind him and end his administration on a note of harmony among his staff and achievement abroad.

Reflection on foreign-policymaking during the Reagan presidency reveals a number of surprises, ironies, and apparent paradoxes. A president uncomfortable with conflict and hoping for collegiality had to endure more than six years of bitter personal and policy conflict before achieving a collegial atmosphere in his foreign-policymaking system. A strong leader capable of captivating a nation with his vision was revealed as a weak manager who had great difficulty in placing his own house in order and maintaining discipline among his staff and an orderly foreign-policymaking process. An apparently inveterate anticommunist accused of "black and white thinking" and prone to referring to the Soviet Union as an "evil empire" presided over what was probably the most fundamental and positive transformation of U.S.-Soviet relations during the postwar period.[107] Commonly seen as a prototypical conservative, Reagan proved capable of truly radical thinking when it came to nuclear weapons, as evidenced by his apparently sincere desire to abolish nuclear arms and replace deterrence with strategic defense.[108]

George Bush

To a greater extent than any of his predecessors since John F. Kennedy, George Bush succeeded in developing a foreign policy *team* in the literal sense of the term. This feat was accomplished and maintained through careful recruitment and active management on the part of the president. Bush's personal style and foreign policy management approach contrasted sharply with Reagan's in many respects, despite his "friendly take-over" of the reins of power as Reagan's anointed successor.

Bush chose to assemble a team and develop an organizational framework that would suit his own mode of operation and demonstrate that his was not simply a third Reagan administration, minus Reagan himself. Despite the fact that Reagan left a generally highly regarded set of foreign policy advisers in place at the time of the transition, resignations were requested without exception.[109] In moves more reminiscent of a transition from opposition, Secretary of State George Shultz, Defense Secretary Frank Carlucci, and National Security Adviser Colin Powell were set aside in favor of a new team with close ties to the president.

Intent on developing a more collegial atmosphere than the confrontational climate of the previous administration, Bush set out to create what might be called a kinder, gentler, foreign policy process. He began by tapping longtime friends and colleagues who would be comfortable working with him and with each other in implementing his key foreign policy initiatives and national security policies. Bush's long public service and emphasis on cultivating personal relationships provided him with a valuable asset: a network of talented, experienced, and loyal individuals. Bush was able to draw on this network in selecting members of his cabinet and staff, as well as for ad hoc consultation on particular policy matters.

Before discussing the key members of this team and the functioning of Bush's foreign policy system, let us pause to consider Bush's personality and style. Bush took office with a marked sense of personal efficacy in the realm of foreign policy.[110] As one keen observer noted: "In dramatic contrast to the detached, chairmanlike Reagan, Bush was knowledgeable and very interested in foreign policy and both willing and able to be at the center of discussions on that topic."[111] Bush clearly wished to keep his hands on the policymaking process, preferring early and sustained involvement rather than being presented with options to check off.[112] As a result, he has been described as "more decisive than Jimmy Carter and more in charge than Ronald Reagan."[113]

A good part of Bush's sense of efficacy probably stemmed from his long years of on-the-job training; few presidents have had such impressive foreign policy credentials when taking office. Bush's experience as ambassador to the United Nations during the Nixon administration, as envoy to China and director of the CIA during the Ford administration, and as Reagan's vice president are worthy of mention in this regard.[114] Some commentators have suggested that Bush's sense of efficacy may have at times resulted in overconfidence and excessive reliance on his own knowledge and instincts. For example, it has been alleged that Bush relied heavily on his own knowledge of the Middle East (and consultation with foreign leaders), engaging in only cursory consultation with academic or departmental experts during the Gulf War.[115] However, this alleged tendency does not show up clearly in the realm of U.S.-Soviet relations, where Bush did in fact consult regularly with Soviet experts inside and outside of government.[116]

The conventional wisdom on Bush's cognitive style emphasizes his pragmatic approach to decisionmaking. One astute observer describes him as "a problem solver rather than a visionary, a doer rather than a dreamer."[117] Bush's consensus building stands in sharp contrast to Reagan's more ideologically driven approach. Bush, we are told, was more comfortable with plain facts than with grand theories. Lacking a clear compass or strategic vision ("that vision thing"), his political course tended to be buffeted by the winds of expediency.[118] Bush is often described as cautious rather than bold, as conciliatory rather than confrontational.

Yet this image seems incomplete. Bush's behavior in office suggests that hot cognitions may well have displaced cool calculation on occasion. A limited set of strongly held principles, or perhaps, strong historically driven analogies, may have taken over and driven his thinking. This appears to be the case in the Persian Gulf crisis, where Saddam Hussein's aggression apparently triggered strong associations with the Munich analogy and Bush's own combat experience as a naval aviator in World War II.[119] Alternatively, it has been suggested that lasting and intensive criticism (such as the legacy of the "wimp factor" from the election campaign and of a Panama policy perceived as ineffectual and indecisive) served as a catalyst for aggressive behavior.[120]

Once he was convinced and engaged on an issue, Bush could display a considerable degree of stubbornness.[121] This trait comes across clearly in the case of the Tower nomination. Bush refused to withdraw his nomination of John Tower for secretary of defense, despite mounting evidence that a potentially costly early defeat in Congress was imminent. Tower was ultimately rejected by the Senate on the grounds that his history of heavy drinking would pose a risk to national security in such a sensitive post.[122]

Similarly, the conventional image of Bush (held especially prior to the Gulf War) as "more *reactive* than *proactive,* more *adrift* than *imaginative*"[123] neglects part of the Bush legacy. While the "new world order" rhetoric remained underspecified and perhaps overambitious through the end of his tenure, Bush did set an important precedent in his collaboration with the newly undeadlocked United Nations Security Council during the Gulf War. The humanitarian military intervention in Somalia in the twilight days of his administration, also conducted under UN auspices, should be seen as another milestone in the history of international cooperative action.[124] Still, the inability of the administration, regional institutions, and the international security community to engage constructively in managing the dissolution of Yugoslavia was a setback to the vision of a new world order.

A number of commentators have suggested that Bush had a tendency to allow personal relationships (of both positive and negative affect) to color his thinking on policy issues.[125] Bush's personal antipathy to Manuel Noriega and Saddam Hussein and his tendency to view their defiance as insults to himself and his office almost certainly contributed to the decisions to intervene in Panama and to escalate the Persian Gulf crisis.[126] Similarly, Bush's reluctance to diversify the U.S. relationship with the Soviet Union/Russia by distancing himself somewhat from Gorbachev (with whom he had a warm relationship) and establishing better ties to Boris Yeltsin (whose "earthy" style offended Bush's sensibilities) lends itself to being understood in these terms.[127]

Like Roosevelt and Reagan, Bush favored acquiring information through conversation. His telephone was constantly in use as he employed his broad network of foreign and domestic contacts to gather information on the policy issues before him. Not a reader by nature, he generally preferred oral briefings and policy memos to long reports. Still, from time to time he would study intensively when facing a major challenge. For example, Bush reportedly geared up for the Malta summit with an intensive program of readings, seminars, and informal consultations. Brent Scowcroft provided some twenty memos, and "tutorials were held in the Oval Office and at Camp David by government specialists, outside experts, and former officials."[128]

The balance of available evidence suggests that Bush's personality is characterized by a moderate to high tolerance of interpersonal conflict. In contrast to the reclusive Nixon or the somewhat passive and harmony-seeking Reagan, Bush reportedly enjoyed the give-and-take of heated debate over policy issues.[129] In his own words, his approach was to "get good strong experienced people, encourage them to express their views openly, encourage them not to hold back."[130]

However, it is important to distinguish between the different stages of the decision process when assessing Bush's tolerance of dissent and free communication. Bush was most tolerant of dissent in the earlier brainstorming stages of a decision, where he often used his advisers as sounding boards. However, as presidential commitment to a line of action increased and choices were made, tolerance for dissent tended to give way to the expectation that his advisers would behave as team players taking direction from their captain.[131] Once a presidential decision had been made, Bush expected his advisers to be good soldiers: "I want them to be frank; I want them to fight hard for their position. And then, when I make the call, I'd like to have the feeling that they'd be able to support the president."[132]

This expectation raises an important issue: What happens if the president commits prematurely to a course of action, *before* key advisers have had an opportunity for frank debate on the character of the problem and the merits of alternative options? Clearly, this would place advisers in a difficult situation, one in which norms of candor and a robust, deliberative process would be in danger of being undermined by presidential expectations of solidarity and support. This issue will be taken up in more detail later.

Bush has been accused of valuing loyalty over expertise in his key personnel choices.[133] In fact, when it came to his foreign policy national security team, Bush was largely spared such trade-offs. For the most part, Bush was able to fill his key positions with individuals who were both "professionals *and* buddies" (emphasis added).[134] For national security adviser, Bush chose a friend who actually had prior experience in that role: Brent Scowcroft. Scowcroft, a retired Air Force general, had served with distinction as national security adviser during the Ford administration and on several presidential commissions, including the Tower Commission.[135] Experienced White House and congressional hand Richard Cheney was named secretary of defense following the Tower nomination defeat. Cheney had served as Ford's chief of staff and as the senior Republican on the House Select Committee that investigated the Iran-Contra affair. Longtime friend and political confidant James Baker III was appointed secretary of state. Baker had served as undersecretary of commerce in the Ford administration and as chief of staff and secretary of the treasury in the Reagan administration. Baker's experience profile suggested strength in international economic policy; although "[c]onspicuously absent from Baker's resume was any direct experience in U.S.-Soviet relations or other traditional major foreign policy issues."[136] However, Bush's own strength in these areas (as well as Scowcroft's) compensated for this potential weakness. Other members of Bush's inner circle included Vice President Dan Quayle, Chief of Staff John H. Sununu, Deputy National Security Adviser Robert Gates (later CIA director), and ultimately Colin Powell, chairman of the Joint Chiefs of Staff.

Working with this cast of characters, how did Bush choose to structure his foreign policy process and how did the system function in practice? The Bush system appears to be the best example of a predominantly collegial system since the Kennedy administration.[137] Like Kennedy, who had made himself accessible to staff and cabinet (see Figure 6.4), Bush placed himself at the center of an information network in the wheel configuration. Interestingly, the lines of communication in this network were strong not only along the spokes between the president and his individual advisers but also along the circumference (among the advisers themselves). It is this feature that leads us to emphasize the team quality of Bush's management system.

As Richard T. Johnson has noted, maintaining a collegial policy group demands a great deal of a leader. Bush appears to have been well equipped temperamentally to meet this challenge. In marked contrast to his predecessor, Bush was consistently solicitous of the egos and feelings of his subordinates. In particular, he tried to demonstrate his continued faith in them following setbacks in their areas of responsibility or when they came out on the losing side of disagreements over policy.[138] Despite the otherwise relatively centralized White House operation under Chief of Staff Sununu,[139] these officials retained direct and easy access to the president. Access to the president lubricated the policy process, while Bush's hands-on style helped to keep potential conflicts from festering. These arrangements and dispositions help to explain how Bush was able to keep his national security team intact throughout his entire term, a dramatic achievement in comparison with the high turnover that plagued the Reagan administration.

It has been suggested that the relatively homogeneous and cohesive Bush advisory group may have been prone to premature concurrence seeking, a tendency exacerbated by Bush's penchant for ad hoc informal consultation.[140]

James Pfiffner suggests that Bush did not make use of any systematic strategy, such as multiple advocacy, formal options, or structured group deliberations, in order to guard against premature concurrence seeking: "Aside from occasional consultations with outside and governmental Middle East specialists, Bush dealt primarily with members of his war council. And even then, at crucial decision points he neglected to consult Cheney, Baker or Powell at different times (for example, the decisions to make the liberation of Kuwait U.S. policy, the decision to double U.S. forces, and the decision to offer the Baker trip to Iraq)."[141]

This raises a more general issue. Were Bush's advisers sufficiently diverse in their views and candid in the expression of those views to expose the president to a broad range of opinion on major policy issues? In the case of the Gulf War, the record suggests that Bush's advisers were in fact divided. Powell and Baker apparently favored giving sanctions (the strangulation option) more time to work before taking military action. Although several commentators maintain that Powell had insufficient opportunity to make the case for sanctions in formal settings, it seems certain that Baker (privileged by his close friendship with the president) would have had the opportunity and the "idiosyncrasy credit" to make his views known privately to the president.

In the realm of U.S.-Soviet/Russian relations, President Bush was regularly presented with a diversity of views on the prospects for reform and of particular leaders (Gorbachev and Yeltsin) and on appropriate U.S. arms control postures. At times these differences were aired publicly, such as when Cheney predicted in April 1989 that Gorbachev would ultimately fail, just when the administration was increasing its commitment to a working relationship with Gorbachev.[142] More often, the conflict was largely behind the scenes. Close examination reveals a series of relatively civil, though substantively serious, disagreements between key advisers over issues such as the Conventional Forces in Europe (CFE) treaty, START, and whether U.S. policy should focus exclusively on Gorbachev or diversify and forge links with Yeltsin. Interestingly, the alliances tended to shift across issues, a fact that helped to maintain lines of communication and inhibit the development of antagonistic factions.[143]

Especially striking was the constructive relationship between Secretary of State Baker and National Security Adviser Scowcroft. In contrast to the bitter rivalry that has been all too common in relationships between secretaries of state and national security advisers, the two men appear to have worked together in a relatively smooth fashion despite differences at times over policy issues. A number of factors help to explain this cooperation. Both officials enjoyed close relationships with and virtually unlimited access to the president, which provided balance and stability.[144] Scowcroft's relatively low-key style reduced the potential for friction, as did Baker's commitment to being "the White House's man at State, rather than State's man at the White House."[145] Finally, deliberate efforts were made to create secondary channels of communication through senior aides. For example, Baker reportedly selected Lawrence Eagleburger as a deputy in part for his close relationship with Scowcroft.[146]

Although closer consideration of Scowcroft's performance in his second tour of duty as national security adviser is not possible here, his general role in Bush's foreign policy management system should be described. A number of commentators have suggested that Scowcroft's role in the Bush administration differed markedly in several respects from his role in the Ford administration. He apparently took on a time-consuming role as personal counselor to the president, no doubt at Bush's instance, and this may at times have eroded his ability to act as custodian-manager of the policy process. Because he engaged in considerable public as well as private policy advocacy, it may have been more difficult for him to perform credibly as an honest broker mediating among the other advisers.[147]

The emphasis on collegiality up to this point of the analysis does not imply that Bush's policymaking system did not at times exhibit features of the other models. A revamped system of formal policy coordination was created by Scowcroft shortly after his appointment, in line with the Tower Commission's findings. The system consisted of three levels: the NSC ("Principals Committee") chaired by Scowcroft in the president's absence, the Deputies Committee chaired by Scowcroft's deputy national security adviser, and twelve midlevel policy coordination committees.[148] However, the tendency among senior officials to set aside formal policy development tracks in favor of a more collegial, less structured, and less formal mode of operation undermined the effectiveness of these arrangements. General disappointment with the early (and much publicized) formal review of U.S.-Soviet policy (NSR-3) may also have contributed to the turning away from these formal structures.[149]

Bush preferred to rely on multiple channels for policy information and development. These included informal small advisory groups, formal bodies such as the NSC system just described, and wide-ranging consultations in person and on the telephone with members of his network, including foreign leaders. In this, as well as in an alleged penchant for compartmentalizing information on sensitive issues and springing surprises on aides, his style and system recall some aspects of FDR's style, but they did not develop the conflictful features of Roosevelt's competitive model.[150]

Bill Clinton

In our discussion of the Bill Clinton management style and organizational model as it appears at the start of his second term, we must emphasize that our analysis is tentative, as the information base regarding these matters is still both limited in scope and contradictory. What information is available is likely to be tainted by political motivations and affected by the inclination of the mass media to focus on less flattering aspects of the foreign-policymaking process and the behavior of the principal players.

As we shall see, Clinton created an organizational model that seemed to be an uneasy blend of collegiality and formalism explicitly designed, at least initially, to limit the extent of presidential engagement in foreign-policymaking—and allow him to focus on his domestic agenda. Over the course of a turbulent first term, he would change these priorities and in so doing significantly alter the mode of operation of his advisory system and improve its performance.

Like many of the presidents we have discussed here, Clinton drew selectively on the experiences of his predecessors in constructing his foreign-policymaking system. Following the example of his early political role model, John F. Kennedy, Clinton wished to create a system that would encourage open communication and broad participation among his advisers. At the same time, Clinton desired a system that would systematize policy analysis and ensure that those units of the government with a stake in a particular issue would have a chance to air their concerns and bring their expertise to bear. The latter priority was in part a reaction to charges that a handful of top Bush administration officials tended at times to make important policy decisions while bypassing departmental and agency expertise.

Another central lesson was drawn from the latter part of the Carter administration, specifically regarding the negative consequences of excessive rivalry between the secretary of state and the national security adviser. The Carter experience, though more than a decade in the past, was quite vivid and salient for Clinton and his advisers for two very good reasons. First, the Carter administration was the last Democratic tenure of the White House and as such a natural source of vicarious experience for a new Democratic president. Second, and perhaps more important, one of the coheads of the transition team was Warren Christopher, who had bitter firsthand experience of the increasingly open and destructive infighting between Zbigniew Brzezinski and Cyrus Vance while serving as Vance's deputy.[151]

Clinton held Christopher in particularly high esteem as a fellow lawyer and an elder statesman of experience, integrity, and political judgment. Furthermore, though of humble origins like Clinton himself, Christopher offered a link to the foreign policy establishment, a potentially valuable asset to an "outsider" president. While serving as Vance's deputy, Christopher played a major role in overseeing the prolonged negotiations with Iran over the hostage crisis and earned a reputation for unflappable calm, caution, and patience.[152] Because he was mindful of the importance of a good working relationship between the secretary of state and the national security adviser, Clinton selected Anthony Lake for the other major foreign policy position. Lake, who had figured prominently in the Clinton campaign, offered a relatively unusual combination of academic credentials (postgraduate work at Cambridge and most recently a professorship at Mount Holyoke College) and governmental experience. Lake's academic qualifications, it was hoped, would provide conceptual sophistication and strategic vision to the foreign policy mix.[153] Unlike Kissinger (for whom Lake had worked during the Vietnam era) and Brzezinski, Lake was reputed to have a relatively low-key personality and to be a good team player. This expectation was reinforced by the fact that he enjoyed a cordial relationship with Christopher dating back to Lake's service as director of policy planning in the Carter administration State Department.[154] A self-avowed neo-Wilsonian who had devoted a substantial portion of his academic career to the study of Africa, Lake reportedly intended to shift a traditionally Eurocentric foreign policy toward a greater emphasis on North-South relations and the promotion of democracy. Since he had coauthored a well-known book criticizing the U.S. foreign-policymaking process,[155] his views on the role of the NSA were on the record. Lake seemed slated for a largely behind-the-scenes role as a custodian-manager of the policy process.

Clinton tapped Les Aspin as secretary of defense. Aspin, a veteran congressman and former chairman of the House Armed Services Committee, had a deserved reputation as a defense intellectual promising to combine an open and creative approach to defense policymaking, with deep knowledge of weapons systems, arms control, and legislative politics. One keen observer described Aspin as an "idea machine of staggering proportions," suggesting that Aspin would be an activist defense secretary in the Robert McNamara mode.[156] Clinton felt that Aspin's qualifications made him well prepared to take on the daunting task of rethinking U.S. defense policy in the post–Cold War world.

Another potentially key player on the Clinton foreign-policymaking team was Vice President Al Gore. Though vice presidents have traditionally been delegated funeral duty and have not uncommonly been excluded from the inner circle on foreign policy matters, Gore enjoyed a privileged position. Gore, known as a "policy wonk," had during his Senate career and preparations for his own bids for the presidency, developed several policy specialties that seemed likely to prove relevant to the Clinton administration. Like Aspin, Gore had mastered the arcane minutiae of arms control, an area in which Clinton's own experience was limited. Gore's main focus in recent years had been the global environment, an area emphasized in the campaign and one likely to be a higher priority for the Clinton administration than for the Bush team. Not to be underestimated either was the importance of the personal rapport and friendship that reportedly developed between Clinton and Gore in part during their celebrated bus tours together during the grueling presidential campaign.[157]

Clinton's choice of organizational model reflects a number of competing priorities deriving from his view of the experience of his predecessors, his personality and preferences, and the contemporary political context.[158] At the same time, Clinton reportedly planned to delegate a considerable amount of the day-to-day management of foreign policy to his advisers. This, he hoped, would enable him to focus on the most important issues—initially defined as including Russia, the Middle East, and the global economy—and reserve much of his energy and efforts for his ambitious domestic policy agenda.[159]

Thus in contrast to Kennedy, who set up a collegial system in order to be more closely and personally involved in the policymaking process, Clinton apparently intended to set up a collegial system geared toward a relatively low level of presidential engagement.[160] According to one early report: "Clinton has essentially delegated foreign-policy formulation to Secretary of State Warren Christopher, Defense Secretary Les Aspin, the national security adviser, W. Anthony Lake, and Mr. Lake's deputy, Samuel R. Berger. On domestic policy issues, Mr. Clinton is personally absorbed in the give and take. But on foreign policy, he has basically asked these aides to work out solutions and submit them to him to be approved or rejected."[161]

Clinton planned to depend on these officials to bring important matters to his attention, to brief him on their progress, and to strictly ration his own participation in foreign-policymaking, in keeping with his campaign promises.[162] In turn, his role would be to set the broad guidelines for major policies and to make the final decisions.[163]

This planned mode of operation led Clinton to concentrate a considerable degree of responsibility in the hands of the national security adviser, a choice often associated with a formalistic model. Lake apparently was intended to be a virtual chief of staff for foreign policy (although not by any means an all-powerful one) and a surrogate manager of the policy process.[164] He was assigned a central role as a liaison between the president and the foreign policy team, including control over much of the paper flow to Clinton on foreign policy matters. In a mid-1993 interview Lake described a difficult balancing act between gatekeeping and burdening the president: "I really wanted to avoid becoming the guard-all shield between the President and the rest of the foreign policy community, but at the time make sure he wasn't being buried in all kinds of different memos and meetings. That's not what the President wants in any case."[165]

Lake was one of a handful of officials included in the daily morning CIA briefing to the president.[166] Immediately afterward he met privately with Clinton for consultations on pressing foreign policy issues. Clinton himself often did not attend top-level interagency meetings on foreign policy even on issues such as Somalia, Bosnia, and Haiti. Instead the president relied on Lake and others to keep him informed of developments. Lake was given the responsibility for chairing the bi-weekly interagency "principals meetings" on high-priority issues. Lake's deputy, longtime Clinton friend and fellow lawyer Samuel Berger, chaired the parallel "deputies committee," which met four or more times per week to develop options to be presented to the principals, reinforcing the strategic positioning of the White House national security contingent.[167] All in all, it seems fair to say that Lake's position was at the hub of the information network.[168]

It is important to say, however, that Lake seemed unlikely to exploit this privileged position and close access to the president in order to marginalize the State Department. A former foreign service officer himself, Lake had long advocated increasing the influence of career diplomats in the policymaking process.[169] His long-standing concern with maintaining the integrity of the policy process also made him appear unlikely to try to take unfair advantage of his strategic position.[170] In addition, Lake's good personal relationship with Christopher made the prospects for a good working relationship between the secretary of state and the NSA better than is often the case.

Clinton placed particular emphasis on trying to preempt a perennial source of friction between the State Department and the White House by making it clear that Secretary of State Christopher was intended to be the chief spokesman for the administration on foreign policy issues. Thus Lake's powerful "inside" position was to be balanced in part by Christopher's undisputed "outside" prerogatives. This is not to say that Christopher was not meant to be a key inside player as well. In fact, Christopher reportedly was one of Clinton's most trusted advis-

ers, weighing in not only on foreign policy but also on domestic issues.[171] Lake's access to Clinton was thus also balanced by daily communication between the president and Christopher.

Proceeding from the premise that regular communication among the
three leading foreign policy officials promised to promote cooperative
relations, a regular Wednesday lunch meeting was instituted. This was
meant to provide an opportunity for these principals to exchange ideas
informally over sandwiches and keep each other informed on major
developments. Early reports asserted that the watchwords for the policymaking system were to be secrecy, efficiency, and consensus.[172]

Let us now turn to the personal qualities and preferences of the
leading man in this cast of players. We will begin by discussing Clinton's cognitive style. Most observers seem to agree that Clinton possesses an agile and sophisticated mind.[173] Like Jimmy Carter before
him (and like his vice president, Al Gore), Clinton likes to delve
deeply into the details of policies that interest him. In other words, he
too is a policy wonk.[174] These skills were already on public display
during the transition, when Clinton received rave reviews for the
much-publicized Arkansas economic "summit and teach-in," where
he demonstrated an impressive command of theoretical and applied
economics and the ability to direct an orchestra of nationally
renowned academic specialists and leading industrialists.

A lawyer by training, Clinton reportedly enjoys the give-and-take of
policy deliberations and debate. He is often described as a good listener and an open-minded participant in policy discussions. He is able
to see and argue both sides of complex and difficult issues. Allegedly,
he is uncomfortable with a quick consensus among his advisers and
prone to take the devil's advocate role himself if no one else does.
Without the energy and critical examination typical of an argumenta-
tive discussion, he is unsure that the issue has been sufficiently
probed. He apparently feels most comfortable in making a decision
and promoting a policy after he has gone through this process and "internalized" the issue.[175] This may be a time-consuming and exhausting
ordeal for Clinton and his aides. Critics have suggested that as a result
of this style, Clinton's decision meetings tend to resemble academic
seminars or "bull sessions."[176]

Observers differ to some extent in their assessment of the degree to
which Clinton is able to integrate the complexities that emerge from
his own study (he is reputedly a voracious reader)[177] and from his ses-

sions with experts from within and outside the administration. Some argue that Clinton has an unusual capacity to forge a robust and sophisticated position out of the sometimes chaotic process of deliberation and consultation and suggest that he is "the Great Synthesizer."[178] Others contend that he has difficulty in making up his mind and bringing the deliberative process to closure.[179] Similarly, there is disagreement over the extent to which Clinton is able to master his enthusiasm and boldness and prioritize in order to focus on a limited number of central issues.[180]

Clinton seems to have a relatively mixed reaction to conflict. As already noted, he thrives on intellectual conflict—encouraging and deriving satisfaction from policy debate. At the same time, he seems moderately uncomfortable with personal conflict and confrontation.[181] It has often been suggested that he has a strong need to be liked and that he does not like to say no.[182] For example, he reportedly hates to fire subordinates and tends to rally to the support of those responsible for major fiascoes.[183] With his apparently unusually empathetic personality, Clinton has a tendency to take the views and concerns of his discussion partners to heart.[184] In fact, he tends to incorporate the best arguments of his critics into his repertoire and concede their merit in discussions with his advisers.[185] Clinton's political opponents have lampooned this tendency, labeling him the "Me-Too President." These behaviors and traits have led some observers to conclude that Clinton is a political chameleon, empathizing intensely (but ephemerally) with each of his audiences and discussion partners in turn.[186]

When it comes to political persuasion and the exercise of power, Clinton seems more at home with the carrot than the stick.[187] This is not to say that Clinton is possessed of a particularly placid disposition. In fact, when under stress, Clinton is given to short-lived, highly intense fits of rage that may be triggered by even the most minor provocation. These episodes are a common enough feature of the Clintonian landscape to have been dubbed "earthquakes" or "morning vents" by aides. These seem to be primarily a mechanism for venting frustration.[188] Once the storm has passed, the episodes apparently leave few lasting traces. Clinton himself professes an inability to hold a grudge, a potential liability in politics: "I don't hate anyone. I forget the people I'm supposed to hate."[189]

Clinton clearly possesses a strong sense of personal political efficacy in general. He is drawn to taking bold positions, to addressing issues that others have not dared to tackle. In the domestic arena this orientation led him to take on controversial problems such as deficit reduction, health care reform, and welfare reform. It may have also contributed to his vocal criticism during the campaign of what he characterized as overly timid Bush administration policies with regard to trouble spots such as Haiti and Bosnia or human rights violations in China. This boldness of campaign rhetoric carries with it the risk of creating expectations that may not always be easy to fulfill once the successful candidate is in power, as the Clinton team would discover during the frustrating first eighteen months of the administration.[190]

Yet Clinton's confidence level in the realm of foreign policy was not quite as high as in other policy areas. At the outset, at least, Clinton did not see himself as having mastered the details of foreign-policy-making. Given that Clinton's background and experience as governor of Arkansas and within the Democratic Party organization were clearly tilted in favor of domestic issues,[191] that his campaign stressed Bush's neglect of domestic problems in favor of foreign policy, and that he had declared his intention to focus on the economy "like a laser beam," it is difficult to avoid the impression that Clinton at times saw his responsibility for foreign policy as a burden of office rather than an area of passionate interest and a primary focus of endeavor.

A number of observers have suggested that Clinton has a strong sense of political mission dating back to his youth. In a letter explaining his decisions regarding the Vietnam draft, he discusses his desire to maintain his viability within the system and his expectation of a political career.[192] This sense of mission helps to explain his attraction to bold political projects. It may also help to explain the pragmatism that many see as a hallmark of the Clinton administration. His basic sense of morality and purpose may help him to rationalize political expediency in the short run. The imperatives of his political ideals (defined at a high level of abstraction) give way to the imperatives of deal making. Thus Clinton is able to practice the maxim that "politics is the art of the possible" secure in the assurance that his was the best possible policy (or else he would not have chosen it).[193] In other words, Clinton seems able to compromise his policies without compromising his self-image.

Other personality traits worthy of mention are Clinton's unusual levels of energy, endurance, and ability to tolerate stress. He has been known to describe himself as "almost compulsively overactive."[194] Clinton expects a lot of himself and his aides, at times driving himself to the point of exhaustion.[195]

Furthermore, he demonstrated in the campaigns and throughout much of a stormy first term an impressive ability to maintain his composure in the face of biting and sustained criticism and allegations of financial and sexual misconduct. As a result, he does appear to have earned another of his nicknames, "the Comeback Kid." Similarly, at least one relatively credible inside account suggests that Clinton rises to the occasion in crisis situations, where he displays calm, determination, and decisiveness even in the face of hard choices and heavy stress.[196]

Finally, according to several commentators, Clinton characteristically demonstrates a laissez-faire approach to managing his advisers and staff.[197] Clinton's inclination is to focus his attention on gathering bright, talented, and pleasant[198] people around him and on engaging challenging policy problems head-on. He tends to pay less attention to how the work is organized and to whether the policymaking system is functioning properly. In fact, he apparently thrives on an atmosphere of "creative chaos."[199] This suggests that Clinton may be dependent on the effectiveness of surrogate "chiefs of staff" to keep an eye on these questions for him. To the extent that they fail him in this regard, serious problems are to be expected.

Now let us turn to a brief examination of how the Clinton foreign-policymaking system has functioned in practice. The early performance of Clinton and his advisers was heavily criticized by the mass media and the academic and public affairs communities.[200] Clinton himself was painted as insufficiently attentive, chronically indecisive, imprudent in his speech, and either unwilling or unable to shoulder the mantle of leadership in foreign policy. His advisers were vilified as bland, incompetent, impractically idealistic, or morally bankrupt. The system as a whole was derided as ponderous and inefficient, a "government by committee" turning out a foreign policy characterized by hypocrisy, fits and starts, proliferating initiatives, and inadequate follow-through, and an inability to exercise leadership at home or abroad. Derogatory comparisons with the Carter administration were common.

The administration itself conceded that the handling of some issues did not always live up to the standards of consensus, efficiency, and secrecy the team set for itself and that serious coordination difficulties had emerged at times. Spokespersons admitted that policymaking on particular issues such as Bosnia and Somalia may have got off to a poor start. However, they claimed that the administration quietly succeeded in managing the most important issues and relationships, such as foreign trade policy (including the General Agreement on Tariffs and Trade [GATT] and the North America Free Trade Agreement [NAFTA], and relations with the major European and Asian trading partners), nuclear nonproliferation policy, and promoting democratization and stability in Russia and other parts of the former Soviet Union. They asserted that perceptions of inadequacy derived more from failures of communication and public relations than from fundamental weaknesses of personnel, management, organization, or "vision." In response to allegations of a lack of strategic vision, friendly observers pointed to the concept of "democratic enlargement" (launched by Lake in 1993) as a conceptual and strategic foundation of the administration's foreign policy and providing an integrative perspective for dealing with geo-economic as well as more traditional types of security issues.[201]

Several adjustments to the system intended to redress these perceived difficulties were made early on. As it became clear that Christopher was achieving mixed success in speaking for the administration on foreign policy issues, some of this responsibility was delegated to others, such as David Gergen, who was brought aboard in May 1993. Gergen, a well known journalist who had served in several Republican administrations, had a reputation as a seasoned Washington hand skilled in dealing with the White House press corps.[202] Gergen was first instructed to work closely with Lake in order to communicate more effectively the administration's message to the media.[203] Lake himself began to take and maintain a more public profile later that year, granting interviews, making speeches, and publishing articles explaining the administration's policy and policymaking process.[204]

Apparently Lake and Gergen developed personal conflicts[205] that led to Gergen's reassignment to support Christopher instead as part of a late 1994 reshuffle of the White House staff. This shake-up also included the replacement of Chief of Staff Thomas McLarty, who was widely regarded as ineffective, by former Office of Management and Budget director Leon Panetta.[206] Gergen's influence gradually waned and he eventually left the administration. The energetic and experienced Panetta, however, brought a new level of organizational discipline and legislative insight to the White House staff, especially on the domestic side.[207] Some accounts suggest that Panetta also tightened up aspects of the White House operation relevant to foreign-policymaking, including improved management of the president's schedule, facilitation of direct communications with foreign leaders, and oversight of the paper flow.

An important question raised by the way in which Clinton chose to organize the foreign-policymaking process is whether a significantly collegial foreign policy system can function effectively with a president who wishes to maintain a relatively high degree of detachment from the policy process. Collegial systems generally have been seen as a way of immersing the president in the policymaking process as well as a means of bringing the collective experience of the advisers to bear on policy issues, rather than compartmentalizing responsibility. Yet, as we have noted, collegial systems require a great deal of management and "maintenance" in order to keep the lines of communication clear and to prevent substantive conflict from spilling over into personal conflict or into the public domain. Rules of the game must be established in order to delineate appropriate dissent from obstructionism and political gamesmanship. Finally, collegial systems may lead to the opposite problem—an unwillingness to confront differences of opinion squarely—and, as a result, a tendency to compromise by adopting policies that represent the least common denominator and to postpone difficult decisions that threaten the comfortable atmosphere.

A number of indications suggest that a sincere desire among the principals to avoid the severe conflict and bureaucratic warfare of the late Carter administration may have resulted in a tendency to fall into the trap of the early Carter administration—the repression of disagreement.[208] A large number of early press reports alleged excessive tendencies toward consensus. Lake himself asserted in an October 1993 interview that such a problem might have existed: "I think when people work well together, you can take the edge off the options." He vowed to be more alert to the risks of "groupthink," alluding explicitly to Irving Janis's well known concept.[209]

One early fiasco, apparently the result of a combination of disorganization, honeymoon optimism, and a tendency toward consensus seeking, was the souring of Operation Restore Hope in Somalia. Specifically, the decision in question had to do with whether U.S.

forces should make retaliatory strikes and participate in the efforts to arrest Somalian strongman Mohammed Farah Aidid following a June 5, 1993, attack that resulted in the deaths of two dozen Pakistani UN peacekeepers. After this incident the Clinton administration abandoned the strict constraints on the duration and scope of the U.S. intervention imposed by the Bush administration. This fateful decision to change the rules of engagement for U.S. forces in Somalia was taken on the basis of only the most cursory and, it would turn out, overly optimistic deliberations. Sadly, in developments all too reminiscent of the Reagan administration's misadventure in Lebanon, the new policy led to the U.S. forces' being perceived as having taken sides in the Somali conflict rather than as impartial peacekeepers and providers of humanitarian aid. After an ambush in which eighteen elite U.S. soldiers were killed and the body of a dead American soldier publicly desecrated before the eyes (and television cameras) of the international press corps, a policy review was undertaken. "According to at least one account, this tragedy had a profound impact on Lake, leading him to offer Clinton his resignation and disposing the national security assistant against sending U.S. peacekeepers to Rwanda in 1994."[210] The Somalia policy review led to the withdrawal of the U.S. contingent in Somalia a half year later.[211]

The tendency toward consensus seeking that contributed to the Somalia fiasco clearly did not extend to all policy questions. A rash of uncoordinated statements by senior officials and Clinton himself indicated that significant conflicts over policy were occurring over trouble spots such as Bosnia and policy dilemmas such as China policy. In the Bosnia case, an activist faction reportedly including National Security Adviser Lake, Vice President Gore, Defense Secretary Aspin and UN Ambassador Madeleine Albright was in favor of vigorous measures such as the use of force (particularly air power) and terminating the arms embargo that placed the Bosnian government at a disadvantage.[212] Others, most notably Warren Christopher and Bush administration holdover Joint Chiefs of Staff chairman Colin Powell, argued forcefully against a more aggressive U.S. policy, the former emphasizing the need for continued negotiation and consensual multilateralism, and the latter the risks entailed in heightened military engagement.[213] How was this early conflict handled? A compromise of sorts was worked out and accepted by Clinton. The administration continued advocating an activist posture (at this point entailing the possible use of air strikes and selective lifting of the weapons embargo) but refrained from proceeding unilaterally pending the emergence of a broader consensus among North Atlantic Treaty Organization (NATO) members and with other key actors such as Russia. The approach to coalition building was tentative rather than forceful, and the resistance of the Europeans in conjunction with the strong disapproval of the Russians resulted in a relatively modest policy not altogether unlike that of the Bush administration. This policy would remain in place—with relatively minor adjustments—until a number of contextual developments and staff changes enabled the adoption of a more activist policy.

One such staff change was the replacement of Powell by Polish-born General John M. Shalikashvili in October 1993. Shalikashvili did not share Powell's highly restrictive conception of the role of military force in the pursuit of foreign policy and humanitarian aims. Another such change was the solicited resignation in December 1993 of the controversial secretary of defense, Aspin, whose "academic" and disorganized style had not gone over well at the Pentagon. Aspin was replaced by his deputy, William Perry, who, it would turn out, was disposed toward a more muscular U.S. internationalism.[214] These staff changes, particularly Powell's departure, contributed to a noticeable shift in the balance of factional power in favor of interventionism on Bosnia and other similar issues.

Another contentious issue during much of the first term was China policy. For one thing, the Clinton program emphasized the elevation of economic issues to the level of national security. As a result, promoting trade with China—a developing market of enormous potential—was an important priority. Second, issues of weapons proliferation (particularly the spread of technologies of mass destruction such as chemical weapons, nuclear weapons, and ballistic missiles) were slated for high-priority treatment. China stood out on this issue as a major arms exporter in its own right and one of the only states in the world with significant influence over North Korea—an unpredictable "rogue state" on the threshold of acquiring nuclear weapons. Finally, the Clinton rhetoric emphasized the imperative of taking the moral high ground and elevating the status of human rights issues in foreign-policymaking. Clinton had criticized Bush for "coddling" China in the wake of the violent 1989 crackdown against the Tiananmen Square demonstrators. These difficult value trade-offs resulted in a turbulent policymaking process.

The issue was first brought to a head by the need to decide whether or not to renew China's most favored nation (MFN) status in June 1993. As the deadline approached, a policy compromise was worked out. The MFN status was renewed for another year. At the same time, a "strong" message was sent to the Chinese leadership that the status would not be renewed in 1994 unless significant progress was made on human rights issues. This effectively put off the decision for a year, but did not resolve the value conflict. As the next deadline approached, most observers agreed that the Chinese had not modified their policies in order to address the U.S. concerns. As a result, a difficult choice had to be made. In the end, the status was again renewed, leading many observers to surmise that the administration had compromised principle for pragmatism.

These early policy choices suggest that Clinton's own inclinations toward policy compromise and procrastination may have been reinforced by the collegial aspects of the policymaking system. In both of these cases an inability to face up to difficult choices seems to have resulted in situations in which the administration ended up squandering credibility by going public with ambitious rhetoric that it did not have the will and backing (on the part of key domestic and foreign constituencies) to sustain.

These problems seemed to be evident in the handling of the protracted crises over the North Korean nuclear program and the Haitian junta's coup against President Jean-Bertrand Aristide. In both cases, the administration went public with relatively bold rhetoric and was seen—at least for a time—as having been forced to retreat. Interestingly enough, former president Jimmy Carter appears as a central figure in both of these cases. In the former case, Clinton and his advisers initially and publicly declared that nuclear weapons in North Korea could not be tolerated under any circumstances and seemed to imply that the United States would be prepared to take drastic action if the North Koreans allowed their participation in the nonproliferation treaty "safeguards system" to lapse. Faced with apparent North Korean intransigence, the U.S. rhetoric and the apparent risk of military confrontation continued to escalate. The North Korean government defied U.S. pressure with impunity while the administration remained largely passive, which raised questions about its credibility. The impasse was broken to a considerable extent by a mediation effort by Carter. Carter's mission paved the way for a controversial agreement signed in October of 1994 under which the North Koreans agreed to freeze their nuclear program and *eventually* (the accord envisioned a five-year transition period) place their nuclear sites under International Atomic Energy Agency (IAEA) safeguards. The agreement also included a commitment to phasing out North Korean reactors capable of producing weapons-grade nuclear materials. In exchange the United States and its allies (most notably South Korea, which was intended to foot most of the bill) offered economic and technical inducements, including assistance in building safer light-water reactors less suited for military purposes. The accord diffused a potentially dangerous situation, but how well its complex reciprocal arrangements would be implemented remained to be seen. Relations with North Korea would remain turbulent throughout the first term, marred by a series of military incidents and scares.[215]

The administration's early policy on Haiti for the first eighteen months seemed to be cut from the same cloth of retrenchment and policy patience. A first highly visible retreat took place regarding an aspect of the Haiti problem with potentially explosive domestic implications. During the campaign, Clinton criticized Bush for indifference to the plight of the Haitian refugees. Already during the transition, Clinton and his advisers shifted their tone and began to use language obviously intended to deter Haitian refugees from trying to reach the United States.[216] The new administration rapidly settled into a mode characterized by aggressive rhetoric in support of the exiled President Aristide, patient negotiation with the junta, and an intensification of the economic sanctions in place against Haiti—a posture that would be maintained for more than a year.

However, the patience of President Clinton and his advisers came to an end in the second half of 1994 and the Haiti crisis was brought to a head. During the summer of 1994 a familiar pattern emerged. The State Department representatives (led by Warren Christopher and Deputy Secretary of State Strobe Talbott) pushed for a firm ultimatum to the Haitian junta and an invasion should they fail to yield. Defense Secretary William Perry opposed those options, arguing that the economic sanctions should be allowed more time to work and that more positive inducements should be offered. Despite lukewarm public and congressional support for a U.S. intervention, the administration chose to escalate its combination of threats and inducements designed to convince the junta to step aside during the late summer and early autumn. By mid-September, all preparations for an invasion were in place and it appeared that Clinton would follow in the footsteps of Reagan in Grenada and Bush in Panama and use force to change the government of a small neighboring country. In a last-ditch attempt to gather public support, Clinton made an impassioned speech castigating the junta for their heinous crimes against human rights. In the eleventh hour, however, at Lake's initiative (and reportedly over State Department opposition) Jimmy Carter was drafted once again as a crisis intermediary in what appeared to be a rapidly escalating situation. This time, Carter was accompanied by former chairman of the Joint Chiefs General Powell, and Senator Sam Nunn. The crisis envoys succeeded in brokering an agreement that enabled the U.S. troops to land unopposed. By mid-October U.S. forces were firmly in control of the island, the junta leaders had departed, and Aristide was in charge once again. In this case, the administration's patient approach apparently paid off—although, as in the case of Bosnia, at the cost of the human suffering that took place in the meantime and diminished accountability for those responsible for human rights abuses. The policy also entailed U.S. acceptance of a considerable degree of responsibility for Haiti's future, a responsibility that some feared might lead to "another Somalia"—a nightmare scenario that fortunately has not materialized.

As the administration approached the midterm congressional elections, the political context and presidential preferences began to change. The Clinton team's domestic agenda—including health care and welfare reform—became increasingly blocked as a more conservative mood emerged in the country. At the same time, the revamped and restaffed foreign policy operation had a number of successes in addition to the Haiti and North Korea agreements, including the Israel-Jordan peace agreement, the apparently successful deterrence of Saddam Hussein (who had once again massed troops near the Kuwaiti border), and improvements in U.S.-Russian relations marked by such actions as Russian troop withdrawals from the Baltic states.

These achievements reportedly stemmed at least in part from a new more hands-on and proactive presidential attitude with regard to foreign affairs. According to several accounts, Clinton had been devoting more of his time and effort to foreign affairs during much of 1994. Several explanations have been offered for this shift. One focuses on some of the early fiascoes, such as Somalia, which convinced the president that he had to be more personally involved in foreign-policymaking. Another focuses on the increasingly gridlocked domestic situation, suggesting that foreign policy problems may have seemed more tractable and satisfying to work with than their domestic counterparts. The Republican congressional victories in the 1994 midterm elections (and subsequently in the 1996 elections) suggested that the difficult domestic legislative situation was likely to persist.

Other accounts suggest that a key factor in the administration's successes was National Security Adviser Lake's adoption of a more assertive role during this period, which allegedly helped to steady the tiller guiding Clinton foreign policy. Lake, despite some chronic minor health problems and the deterioration of his marriage (both thought to have been exacerbated by the stressful demands of his position) shifted the balance of his role from policy broker toward policy advocate during this period. As a result Lake became, as one journalist would later describe him, "Clinton's chief gatekeeper, confidant, loyalist, and propagandist on foreign policy."[217] This more active role would persist throughout the rest of Clinton's first term and would have important implications for administration policy with regard to NATO expansion as well as several of the policy success stories already mentioned. According to J. De Parle, Lake led a faction within the administration in favor of expanding NATO in order to extend protection to several former Warsaw Pact nations—a policy opposed vehemently by other officials daunted by persistent and vocal Russian opposition.[218]

A number of analyses point to Vice President Gore as another source of decisiveness and stability within the foreign-policymaking system to a far greater extent than has generally been the case for occupants of his position. Along with Lake and longtime Clinton friend Deputy Secretary of State Strobe Talbott, Gore came to play an important role in shaping U.S.-Russian relations in general (meeting regularly with Boris Yeltsin's prime minister, Viktor S. Chernomyrden) and on arms control issues in particular. According to several accounts, Gore also played an important role as monitor and troubleshooter for the policymaking system at large—acting to break logjams and to help keep the president on track. However, in so doing, Gore generally acted in the mode of high-leverage advocate as opposed to honest broker.[219]

Did these changes in the mode of operation of the foreign policy system affect the handling of troublesome issues such as China policy and Bosnia? The available evidence suggests that it did. Clinton and his team eventually made progress in resolving the difficult tensions between security, trade, and human rights considerations in the relationship with China by committing to a policy of "engagement." This entailed maintaining China's MFN status and curbing inclinations to allow human rights questions to sour the U.S.-China relationship. This is not to say that the bilateral relationship was problem-free. Serious tensions between China and Taiwan over indications that the latter was moving toward formal independence erupted in the early months of 1996 and threatened to entangle the United States in a potentially dangerous conflict. The Clinton administration ultimately made use of a stick and carrot strategy, moving U.S. naval vessels to the vicinity when a crisis punctuated by provocative Chinese military exercises in the Taiwan Strait developed. At the same time, the United States sent strong signals that the "one China" policy in place since the Nixon administration would not be changed. The crisis de-escalated after relatively cordial consultations between Lake and his Chinese counterparts, which took place in Virginia in early March. It is noteworthy that Lake, in this case, engaged in the kind of direct statesmanship for which he had previously criticized his predecessors Kissinger and Brzezinski.[220]

This "new look" extended to management of the Bosnia situation as well. Internally, the Perry-Shalikashvili team succeeded in modifying the Weinberger-Powell line, thus facilitating the use of limited force in "unconventional" missions in support of diplomacy. Following a series of highly publicized atrocities against civilians in Bosnia, including the fall of the UN safe haven at Srebrenica, it became possible for a more determined Clinton national security team led by Lake to secure European support for (and Russia's reluctant acceptance of) a more coercive policy toward the Bosnian Serbs. This tougher policy came to include a campaign of air strikes in September 1995. Strongarm diplomacy spearheaded by, among others, Assistant Secretary of State Richard Holbrooke resulted in the Dayton Agreement of November 21, 1995, and U.S. participation not only in air support, but also in ground operations in Bosnia under NATO auspices.

To sum up this necessarily brief and preliminary assessment, we find that the Clinton foreign-policymaking system suffered through a difficult and uneven early phase characterized by chronic presidential inattention, inadequate coordination, tendencies toward consensus seeking on some issues and toward poorly managed policy conflict on others, which persisted through most of the first two years of the administration. The period immediately preceding and following the midterm election marked the emergence of new phase of presidential attentiveness, significantly more effective, organized, and proactive management of the policy process, and the development of mechanisms (including the more active policy advocacy role of the national security adviser) for coping with policy conflict within the advisory system and creating a more stable basis for policy formulation and implementation.

Clinton's reelection in November 1996, ironically enough on a record that emphasized foreign policy achievement and continuity, led to a radical restructuring of the foreign-policymaking system. Secretary of State Christopher, who reportedly had been considering leaving government since at least December 1994, left the team. Clinton appointed Madeleine Albright to replace him. Albright had already established herself as an important player in her role as ambassador to the United Nations. Like Lake, the new secretary of state had an academic as well as a policy background, having been a college professor prior to her government service. Like Shalikashvili, she was foreign born—a refugee from Czechoslovakia for whom the Munich and Yalta agreements were major formative experiences. Albright, the first woman secretary of state in U.S. history, was reportedly chosen for her ability to communicate and "sell" U.S. policy (which was not, as some observers argued, Christopher's strong suit) as well as for an unusual combination of toughness and inclination toward team play. These qualities, it was hoped, would enable her to take direction from the increasingly confident President Clinton and maintain collegiality with the other principals. This is not to say that Albright lacks convictions; she is known as a fervent believer in the U.S. mission in the world as a champion of the oppressed (as indicated by her strong support for U.S. intervention in Bosnia and Rwanda) and of human rights.[221]

In a gesture toward a bipartisan foreign policy reminiscent of Kennedy's appointment of the liberal Republican Robert S. McNamara, Clinton (reportedly at the urging of Vice President Gore) tapped maverick Republican Senator William S. Cohen to replace William Perry as secretary of defense. Cohen, a mainstream Republican on most issues and a chronic critic of the first Clinton administration's defense policies, had demonstrated his independence by occasionally breaking ranks with his party to criticize what he viewed as gross misconduct in cases such as Watergate and the Iran-Contra scandal. Unlike McNamara, who was a former Fortune 500 executive, Cohen has had very limited management experience, raising concern regarding his ability to master the Pentagon bureaucracy.[222] Another question, more poignant in light of the failure of the Gergen experiment in bipartisanship, is whether the others would be able to accept the prickly Cohen as a full member of the team.

In another dramatic postelection move, National Security Adviser Lake, a pivotal player during most of the first-term team, was nominated to the CIA directorship, slated to replace John Deutch. Press accounts suggested that Lake had been worn down by the demands of the NSA position and lacked the stamina to continue. Lake's poor personal relationship with Madeleine Albright (whom Lake had reportedly treated brusquely when she was ambassador to the United Nations) and deteriorating relations with his own deputy (and close Clinton friend), Sandy Berger, may also have contributed to Clinton's decision to move Lake out of the White House.[223] Some observers questioned whether the new post, viewed by most observers as a demotion, would capitalize on Lake's strategic talents and academic bent, traits that may have been more suited to his previous position. Similarly, his ability to take charge of the large and macho CIA bureaucracy and see the CIA through the travails of the post–Cold War era was called into question. However, others pointed to Lake's relationship with the president and record of support for covert operations as assets that might serve him in good stead in the new position. Although he was initially seen as a safe bet in the confirmation process, Lake met unexpectedly fierce resistance, leading him to withdraw his name from consideration and retire, for the time being at least, from public life.

Lake was replaced by his former deputy, Samuel L. Berger, a longtime Clinton confidant known for his diplomatic skills, which often came into use in lubricating the relationships among the principals during the first term. The manner in which Berger defines and exercises his role is likely to be an important determinant of the new team's performance and the degree of and nature of policy conflict to be expected within the system. Similarly, the replacement of Chief of Staff Panetta by his former deputy, Erskine Bowles, raises some questions as to whether friction will emerge over the extent of the White House chief of staff's prerogatives in the realm of foreign policy.

Experience suggests that it may take some time for the new team and its leader to find its equilibrium despite the fact that most of the players—the main exception being Defense Secretary Cohen—were drawn from within the first Clinton administration. Coordination difficulties and role conflicts are to be expected as the members of the new team adjust to their new roles and new modes of interaction. The heavy emphasis on collegiality in Clinton's second-term appointments presents the risk that some of the early problems with conformity and consensus seeking may reemerge as a result of the shake-up. Ironically, Clinton's own more hands-on role may make this more likely. On the other hand, the fact that many of the players know the president and each other well should serve to mitigate this risk. It thus remains to be seen whether the advisory system equilibrium, so painstakingly achieved during the first term, can be rapidly developed and maintained by the new Clinton team.[224]

Conclusion

Each of the three management models—competitive, formalistic, and collegial—tends to have certain advantages and to incur certain risks. These are discussed in some detail by Richard T. Johnson with respect to each of the six presidents he studied (see Table 6.1).[225]

In addition, Johnson makes a number of useful suggestions for reducing the shortcomings and risks of each of these three management models:

> For example, a President who adopts the formalistic approach might choose [as Eisenhower did on occasion] to establish more fluid machinery or reach further down the information channels when facing a decision of particular importance to his Administration. [Similarly] a Chief Executive who adopts the competitive style might commission [as FDR did on occasion] formal study groups to ensure careful staff work on complex policy questions. . . . A President who chooses the collegial approach might utilize [as Kennedy did on occasion] a more formalistic structure for routine matters in order to concentrate his energies on the more sensitive policy areas.[226]

In concluding this discussion of the different management styles generally favored by different presidents, we should remind ourselves once again that our depiction of the communication structures associated with each of them necessarily oversimplifies the more complex

TABLE 6.1   Three Management Models

Benefits	Costs
Formalistic Approach	
Orderly decision process enforces more thorough analysis.	The hierarchy which screens information may also distort it. Tendency of the screening process to wash out or distort political pressures and public sentiments.
Conserves the decisionmaker's time and attention for the big decision.	
Emphasizes the optimal.	Tendency to respond slowly or inappropriately in crisis.
Competitive Approach	
Places the decisionmaker in the mainstream of the information network.	Places large demands on decisionmaker's time and attention.
Tends to generate solutions that are politically feasible and bureaucratically doable.	Exposes decisionmaker to partial or biased information. Decision process may overly sacrifice optimality for doability.
Generates creative ideas, partially as a result of the "stimulus" of competition, but also because this unstructured kind of information network is more open to ideas from the outside.	Tendency to aggravate staff competition with the risk that aides may pursue their own interests at the expense of the decisionmaker.
	Wear and tear on aides fosters attrition and high turnover.
Collegial Approach	
Seeks to achieve both optimality and doability.	Places substantial demands on the decisionmaker's time and attention.
Involves the decisionmaker in the information network but somewhat eases the demands upon him by stressing teamwork over competition.	Requires unusual interpersonal skill in dealing with subordinates, mediating differences, and maintaining teamwork among colleagues.
	Risk that "teamwork" will degenerate into a closed system of mutual support.

SOURCE: Richard T. Johnson, *Managing the White House* (New York: Harper and Row, 1974). Reproduced with minor changes and additions in *The Stanford Business School Alumni Bulletin,* Fall 1973.

reality and working of each system.[227] To some extent, elements of two or even all three models may be present in different mixes, with different emphases, in the policymaking system of each president. As has been evident in the foregoing accounts, the typology offered by Richard Johnson has been useful only as a starting point for characterizing each president's management style. In addition, it has been necessary to provide a detailed analysis of the ways in which each president has organized, managed, and used an information and advisory system.

Over the years, as the foreign policy activities in which the U.S. government is engaged have multiplied, the organizational arrangements for dealing with them within the executive branch have proliferated. To some extent, the sheer magnitude and complexity of the foreign policy enterprise forces every modern president to rely at least to some extent on formalistic procedures. It would be difficult in the modern era for even so gifted a politician and leader as Franklin Roosevelt to rely heavily on a competitive model. Of particular importance, therefore, are studies of variants of formalistic models that, in addition, attempt to make use of elements of the competitive and/or collegial models as well.

Finally, although each of these three management models has certain advantages and disadvantages, the effort to improve their performance by introducing modification of one kind or another encounters serious limits. The search for improvement in policymaking systems must go beyond general management models of this kind to more discriminating ways of improving information processing. Three procedures for widening the range of information, options, and judgment available to a president have often been recommended. They are the "devil's advocate," the "formal options system," and "multiple advocacy."[228]

Notes

1. For a history and critical analysis of these efforts at reorganization, see I. M. Destler, *Presidents, Bureaucrats, and Foreign Policy* (Princeton: Princeton University Press, 1972), chapter 2. Nonetheless, as Destler and other students of the problem recognize, organization design and structural parameters do affect foreign policy performance. For a sophisticated discussion, see Graham Allison and Peter Szanton, *Remaking Foreign Policy: The Organizational Connection* (New York: Basic Books, 1976); see particularly chapter 1, "The Argument:

Organization Matters." For a more general discussion applying not merely to foreign policy but the presidency as whole, see Stephen Hess, *Organizing the Presidency* (Washington, D.C.: Brookings Institution, 1976).

2. The following paragraphs draw on A. L. George, "Adaptation to Stress in Political Decision-making," in George V. Coelho, David A. Hamburg, and John E. Adams, eds., *Coping and Adaptation* (New York: Basic Books, 1974).

3. This general point is emphasized repeatedly also by Graham Allison in his study for the Commission on the Organization of the Government for the Conduct of Foreign Policy. For example: "The critical variable affecting which mechanisms [of centralized management] are used is the president: his personal preferences and style. . . . It follows, therefore, that efforts to legislate structure for high-level centralized management cannot succeed." Graham T. Allison, ed., *Adequacy of Current Organization: Defense and Arms Control*, vol. 4, Appendices, Commission on the Organization of the Government for the Conduct of Foreign Policy, June 1975 (Washington, D.C.: U.S. Government Printing Office, 1976), p. 35; see also pp. 10, 58.

4. These three management styles are described and evaluated in Richard T. Johnson, *Managing the White House* (New York: Harper & Row, 1974). See particularly chapters 1 and 8. A useful discussion of the evolution of the modern presidency and of the styles of different presidents is provided by Stephen Hess, *Organizing the Presidency* (Washington, D.C.: The Brookings Institution, 1976).

5. Richard Fenno, *The President's Cabinet* (New York: Vintage Books, Knopf, 1959), pp. 44–46. See also Arthur Schlesinger, Jr., *The Age of Roosevelt*, vol. 2, *The Coming of the New Deal* (Boston: Houghton Mifflin, 1959), chapters 32–34, and Richard E. Neustadt, *Presidential Power* (New York: Wiley, 1960), chapter 7.

6. The following figures (with the exception of the one describing Nixon's variant of the formalistic model) are taken directly, with minor adaptations, from John Q. Johnson, "Communication Structures Among Presidential Advisers" (seminar paper, Stanford University, September 1975). The seminal work on communication networks is that of Alex Bavelas, "Communication Patterns in Task-Oriented Groups," *Journal of Acoustic Society of America* 22 (1950):725–730. A summary of early work of this kind appears in Murray Glanzer and Robert Glaser, "Techniques for the Study of Group Structure and Behavior," *Psychological Bulletin* 58 (1961):2–27.

7. Recently available archival materials at the Eisenhower Library evidently necessitate a substantial revision of the conventional image of Eisenhower as an apolitical military man, one who was generally uninformed about and not very attentive to his executive responsibilities, one who was prone to overdelegate his responsibilities, and one who was naive about the art of governing. What emerges, rather, is a different executive style that Fred Greenstein refers to as Eisenhower's "invisible hand" mode of leadership in which he sought actively to secure his goals by indirection (Fred I. Greenstein, "Presidential Activism Eisenhower Style: A Reassessment Based on Archival Evidence" [paper delivered to the 1979 meeting of the Midwest Political Science Association, January 1979]).

8. Ibid., p. 9. See also Douglas Kinnard, *President Eisenhower and Strategy Management: A Study in Defense Politics* (Lexington: University of Kentucky Press, 1977), and Murray Kempton, "The Underestimation of Dwight D. Eisenhower," *Esquire* (September 1967).

9. Greenstein, "Presidential Activism Eisenhower Style," p. 10.

10. See, for example, James David Barber, *The Presidential Character* (Englewood Cliffs, N.J.: Prentice-Hall, 1972), and Johnson, *Managing the White House*, pp. 199–229.

11. Johnson, *Managing the White House*, pp. 210–211.

12. Ibid.

13. For a particularly detailed account of the structure, evolution, and performance of Nixon's NSC, *see* Chester Crocker, "The Nixon-Kissinger National Security Council System, 1969–1972: A Study in Foreign Policy Management," vol. 6, Appendices, Commission on the Organization of the Government for the Conduct of Foreign Policy, June 1975 (Washington, D.C.: Government Printing Office, 1976), pp. 79–99.

14. I. Destler, L. Gelb, and A. Lake, *Our Own Worst Enemy* (New York: Simon & Schuster, 1984), p. 217.

15. Carter's national security adviser, Zbigniew Brzezinski, in his memoirs (*Power and Principle* [London: Weidenfeld & Nicholson, 1983, p. 74]), goes so far as to assert that "Carter's was perhaps formally the most centralized [decisionmaking system] of all in the post-war era."

16. Don Bonafede, "Brzezinski—Stepping Out of His Backstage Role," *National Journal*, October 15, 1977, p. 1598. See also Elizabeth Drew, "A Reporter at Large: Brzezinski," *New Yorker*, May 1978, and Marilyn Berger, "Vance and Brzezinski: Peaceful Coexistence or Guerrilla War," *New York Times Magazine*, February 13, 1977.

17. As criticism mounted, Carter ultimately retreated on this point and formally assigned Hamilton Jordan to the chief of staff role in 1978. Jordan occupied that post until the campaign for the 1980 election got under way, when Jack Watson took over the position. See J. Burke, *The Institutional Presidency* (Baltimore: Johns Hopkins University Press, 1992), p. 136, and James Pfiffner, "The President's Chief of Staff: Lessons Learned," *Presidential Studies Quarterly* (Winter 1993), p. 78. A. Moens (*Foreign Policy Under Carter*, Boulder: Westview Press, 1990, pp. 34–35) argues with some justification that despite the formal title, Jordan was never allocated responsibility for the core functions associated with the chief of staff role, namely, controlling the paper flow to the president, access, and the presidential schedule.

18. See Burke, *The Institutional Presidency*, p. 120.

19. For example, Burke (*The Institutional Presidency*, p. 123) describes Carter's use of decision memoranda in which the president was offered boxes to check in order to indicate his policy preferences.

20. Bonafede, "Brzezinski."

21. Several commentators suggest that the training Carter received in the Navy through his participation in Admiral Hyman George Rickover's famous nuclear submarine program may provide clues to the development of his problem-solving style. See, e.g., C. Campbell, *Managing the Presidency* (Pitts-

burgh: University of Pittsburgh Press, 1986), p. 166. For a more detailed treatment of Carter's naval career, see B. Glad, *Jimmy Carter: In Search of the Great White House* (New York: Norton, 1980), pp. 58–68.

22. Glad (*Jimmy Carter*, p. 483), characterizes Carter's problem-solving style as "mechanical," referring to his systematic approach, his proclivity for lists, and his reductionist-analytic approach.

23. Burton Ira Kaufman, *The Presidency of James E. Carter* (Lawrence: University Press of Kansas, 1993), p. 37.

24. Former secretary of state Cyrus Vance, in his memoirs (*Hard Choices* [New York: Simon & Schuster, 1983], p. 34), describes his understanding with Carter regarding the division of labor within the system: "first, that it be made clear that I would be the president's spokesman on foreign policy; second, that I had no objection to Brzezinski's offering Carter independent policy advice . . . but that I must be able to present to him my own unfiltered views before he made any foreign policy decision."

25. Brzezinski (*Power and Principle*, p. 63) argues that Carter sought personal control and balance among his chief foreign policy officials: "I knew full well that Carter would not wish me to be another Kissinger. At the same time, I also felt confident that he would not let Vance become another Dulles. He wanted to be the decision maker and, even more important, to be perceived as one." Kaufman (*The Presidency of James E. Carter*, p. 38), basing his argument on Carter's memoirs, suggests that Carter was suspicious of what he perceived as an overly elitist, bureaucratized, and tradition-bound State Department and intended to use the "intellectual ferment" of the NSC staff as a counterweight.

26. According to Presidential Directive/NSC-2, two major NSC committees were established: the Policy Review Committee (PRC) chaired by the relevant cabinet secretary, and the Special Coordination Committee (SCC) chaired by National Security Adviser Brzezinski. The former was intended to cover issues with interagency implications in foreign policy, defense policy, intelligence, and economic issues. The latter was given a mandate for oversight of matters such as covert operations, arms control, and crisis management. For the declassified text of NSC-2, see the documentation of the Senate Foreign Relations Committee hearing, *The National Security Adviser: Role and Accountability* (April 17, 1980, Washington D.C.: Government Printing Office), p. 49.

27. For a description of the NSC under Carter, see Bonafede, "Brzezinski," and Lawrence J. Korb, "The Structure and Process of the National Security Council System in the First Year of the Carter Administration" (paper delivered at the annual meeting of the International Studies Association, Washington, D.C., 22–25 February 1978). See also the Senate Foreign Relations Committee materials cited earlier.

28. Brzezinski did control much of the paper flow to the president on national security matters, a traditional prerogative of a chief of staff. Destler, Gelb, and Lake (*Our Own Worst Enemy*, pp. 218, 221) contend that this arrangement provided Brzezinski with a major structural advantage in policy conflicts. See also Brzezinski, *Power and Principle*, pp. 61–63.

29. Vice President Walter Mondale reportedly received the same daily intelligence briefings as the other three principals (Carter, Vance, and Brzezinski)

and came to play an important role in assessing the domestic political consequences of alternative foreign policy postures. Carter was apparently reluctant to think in such terms; Mondale filled the gap. See also Brzezinski, *Power and Principle*, p. 34, and Kaufman, *The Presidency of James E. Carter*, p. 66, for treatments of Mondale's role.

30. For a remarkably incisive set of observations regarding aspects of Carter's personality and outlook that adversely affected the organization of his advisory system and his performance generally, see the series of articles published by his former speechwriter, James Fallows, "The Passionless Presidency," *Atlantic Monthly* (May and June 1979); Jimmy Carter's Theory of Governing," *The Wilson Quarterly* 1 (Winter 1977). For an in-depth, thoroughly researched critical appraisal of Carter's personality and career, see Glad, *Jimmy Carter*.

31. Kaufman, *The Presidency of James E. Carter*, p. 10.

32. Destler, Gelb, and Lake (*Our Own Worst Enemy*, p. 215) state that Carter's high levels of interest and activism in foreign affairs were one of the great surprises of the early part of his presidency.

33. See, e.g., Fallows, "The Passionless Presidency," p. 35, and Burke, *The Institutional Presidency*, pp. 119–120. See also Moens, *Foreign Policy Under Carter*, p. 48.

34. Cited in Kaufman, *The Presidency of James E. Carter*, p. 34.

35. Glad, *Jimmy Carter*, pp. 501, 504.

36. Barber, *The Presidential Character*, pp. 430–433.

37. According to Moens (*Foreign Policy Under Carter*, p. 35), Carter consumed an average of three to four hundred pages of written material per day, a prodigious achievement given the other demands of a modern presidential schedule.

38. Campbell, *Managing the Presidency*, p. 60.

39. Brzezinski, *Power and Principle*, p. 71.

40. Glad (*Jimmy Carter*, pp. 497–498) notes that "Carter's warmth towards others can be turned on and off like a spigot—sometimes without apparent reason" and emphasizes his fundamental detachment from other people.

41. Cited in Burke, *The Institutional Presidency*, p. 120.

42. See Burke, *The Institutional Presidency*, pp. 137–139. Brzezinski's account undermines the proposition that Carter was reluctant to sanction his aides and colleagues. Brzezinski (*Power and Principle*, p. 18) reports that "[Carter] never thanked me for anything, nor did he ever rebuke me sharply (which he did occasionally to every one of his senior officials, including Vance and Brown)." It is interesting to note that this description of Carter's style echoes Carter's description of his early role model, Admiral Rickover (cited in Barber, *The Presidential Character*, p. 408).

43. Moens, *Foreign Policy Under Carter*, pp. 36–37.

44. Cited in Moens, *Foreign Policy Under Carter*, p. 37.

45. The so-called VBB (Vance, Brzezinski, and Brown) Thursday afternoon lunches and the Friday morning breakfast meetings (which included Carter) were particularly important informal forums for consultation and coordination.

46. This appears to be an example of "a recurring problem of the Carter presidency: weak or conflicting delegation of authority" (Kaufman, *The Presidency of James E. Carter*, p. 25).

47. According to Brzezinski (*Power and Principle*, p. 45), more serious conflicts between Brown and Vance developed during the latter part of the administration, conflicts that were not ameliorated by Vance's resignation and subsequent replacement by Muskie. Vance does not emphasize such conflicts in his own memoirs. For an overview of Brown's role in the foreign policy process, see Moens, *Foreign Policy Under Carter*, pp. 43–44.

48. One of the main theses of Moens's *Foreign Policy Under Carter* (pp. 40, 170) is that multiple advocacy foundered during the early days of the Carter administration due to insufficient diversity of views and proposed options on many key foreign policy issues. In a recent study, for example, B. Jentleson ("Discrepant Response to Falling Dictators: Presidential Belief Systems and the Mediating Effects of the Senior Advisory Process," *Political Psychology* 11 (1990), p. 367) found that despite differences over nuances Vance and Brzezinski were basically united in their support for the shah of Iran through late 1978.

49. In a February 1977 memo to Brzezinski, Carter complained of the diversity and fragmentation of foreign policy briefings: "Get together and from now on give me *one coordinated* briefing book, collected from the myriad sources" (emphasis in original, cited in Kaufman, *The Presidency of James E. Carter*, p. 39).

50. Kaufman, *The Presidency of James E. Carter*, pp. 95–96.

51. Brzezinski, *Power and Principle*, p. 71.

52. Ibid., p. 522. According to Destler, Gelb, and Lake (*Our Own Worst Enemy*, p. 219), "Carter's determination to make detailed decisions himself without reference to any overarching strategy—*and his willingness to remake and remake them*—meant that no single subordinate would have his constant backing" (emphasis added).

53. Burke, *The Institutional Presidency*, p. 119.

54. See, for example, Stanley Hoffman, "The Hell of Good Intentions," *Foreign Policy* 29 (Winter 1977-1978), Thomas L. Hughes, "Carter and the Management of Contradictions," *Foreign Policy* 31 (Summer 1978), and Kaufman, *The Presidency of James E. Carter*, pp. 28, 94, 97.

55. Some scholars are inclined to accord more importance to the inexperience factor. Campbell (*Managing the Presidency*, p. 59) asserts that "deep bureaucratic dissatisfaction with the administration developed as it became clear that Carter and his most trusted aides were hobbled by inexperience. This defect—lack of familiarity with the Washington scene—presented the administration with very painful learning experiences in virtually all its significant initiatives."

56. Carter was fond of quoting Reinhold Niebuhr: "The sad duty of politics is to establish justice in a sinful world" (cited in Glad, *Jimmy Carter*, p. 478).

57. See Destler, Gelb, and Lake, *Our Own Worst Enemy*, p. 221.

58. Burke (*The Institutional Presidency*, p. 127) cites examples of Brzezinski's manipulation of such forums to include or exclude participants from other de-

partments virtually at will. See also Kaufman, *The Presidency of James E. Carter,* p. 128.

59. See Vance, *Hard Choices,* pp. 409–412, for his account of these events. For analyses of the decisionmaking process that led to the raid, see the early twin case studies by S. Smith: "Groupthink and the Hostage Rescue Mission," *British Journal of Political Science* 15 (1985), and "Policy Preferences and Bureaucratic Position: The Case of the American Hostage Rescue Mission," *International Affairs* 61 (1985). See also B. Glad, "Personality, Political, and Group Process Variables in Foreign Policy Decision Making: Jimmy Carter's Handling of the Iranian Hostage Crisis," *International Political Science Review* 10 (1989).

60. Destler, Gelb, and Lake (*Our Own Worst Enemy,* p. 224) report that during this period Carter made remarks such as "Zbig, we won't let the State Department push us around." Muskie was prone to finding himself out of the loop even on major initiatives such as PD-59, a massive procurement program designed to enhance U.S. counterforce potential vis-à-vis the USSR, announced in July 1980 (Kaufman, *The Presidency of James E. Carter,* pp. 186, 192).

61. David Aaron had served as Senator Mondale's foreign policy adviser before coming to the NSC (Brzezinski, *Power and Principle,* p. 58).

62. For a review of the debate concerning the degree of conceptual coherence in foreign policy exhibited by the Carter administration, see Jerel A. Rosati, "Continuity and Change in the Foreign Policy Beliefs of Political Leaders: Addressing the Controversy over the Carter Administration," *Political Psychology* 9 (1988), pp. 471–495. Rosati argues that "the Carter Administration initially had an optimistic worldview which was shared by the principal policymakers, but a dramatic reversal of its collective image took place over time, reflecting the continuity and change in the images of the individual policymakers" (p. 471).

63. Not surprisingly, Brzezinski himself is adamant in his rejection of these criticisms. See his *Power and Principle,* pp. 56, 526.

64. See J. Prados, *Keeper of the Keys: A History of the National Security Council from Truman to Bush* (New York: William Morrow & Co., 1991), pp. 447–459, for an account of Reagan's approach to foreign policymaking, institutional changes, and profiles of key players. See also H. Smith, *The Power Game: How Washington Works* (New York: Ballantine, 1988), pp. 558–561.

65. Burke, in *The Institutional Presidency,* labeled his chapter on Reagan "The Travails of Collegial Formalism." See also Bruce Buchanan, "Constrained Diversity: The Organizational Demands of the Presidency," in J. Pfiffner, ed., *The Managerial Presidency* (Pacific Grove, CA: Brooks/Cole, 1991), pp. 85–103.

66. The other two were White House Chief of Staff James Baker and presidential aide Michael Deaver. For an analysis of the workings of the troika, see J. Pfiffner, "The President's Chief of Staff: Lessons Learned," *Presidential Studies Quarterly* 23:1 (1993), pp. 86–87.

67. According to Lou Cannon (*President Reagan: The Role of a Lifetime* [New York: Simon & Schuster, 1991], p. 73), recommendations from Richard Nixon heavily influenced Reagan's appointments and approach to foreign policy management during the transition and early period of his administration.

68. Prados, *Keeper of the Keys*, p. 450.

69. Ibid., p. 453.

70. See, e.g., Martin Anderson's *Revolution* (New York: Harcourt Brace Jovanovich, 1988) and Lou Cannon's *President Reagan*, p. 55.

71. Surprisingly, Anderson (*Revolution*, p. 51) suggests that Reagan literally possessed a photographic memory, a useful talent for public speaking. It is thought-provoking that Reagan recently disclosed that he had been diagnosed as suffering from Alzheimer's disease. One is led to wonder whether some of his absent-mindedness in the latter part of his administration was the result of early effects of this condition.

72. B. Rockman, "The Style and Organization of the Reagan Presidency," in C. O. Jones, ed., *The Reagan Legacy: Promise and Performance* (Chatham, N.J.: Chatham House, 1988), p. 8.

73. Fred I. Greenstein, "Ronald Reagan: Another Hidden-Hand Ike?" *PS Political Science and Politics* (March 1990), p. 12.

74. Cannon, *President Reagan*, pp. 35, 761.

75. Ibid., p. 139.

76. Ibid., pp. 128, 152, 180. See also Smith, *The Power Game*, p. 584.

77. As Anderson puts it (*Revolution*, p. 286), Reagan "doesn't fret and doesn't change his mind."

78. George Shultz, *Turmoil and Triumph* (New York: Scribners, 1993), p. 920.

79. Richard Neustadt, *Presidential Power and the Modern Presidents: The Politics of Leadership from Roosevelt to Reagan* (New York: Free Press, 1990), pp. 276–279, and Cannon, *President Reagan*, p. 281.

80. Cannon, *President Reagan*, pp. 9, 373.

81. K. Mulcahey and C. Crabbe, "Presidential Management of National Security Policy Making, 1947–1987," in J. Pfiffner, ed., *The Managerial Presidency*, p. 262. Mulcahey and Crabbe (p. 262) assert, perhaps unfairly, that Reagan was "the least prepared of any recent chief executive in the realm of foreign affairs."

82. Ronald Reagan, *An American Life* (New York: Simon & Schuster, 1990), p. 161.

83. For example, George Shultz confesses in his memoirs, *Turmoil and Triumph*, his frustration with Reagan's "unwillingness to come to grips with the debilitating acrimony among his national security advisers."

84. See, e.g., Smith, *The Power Game*, p. 572. Cannon (*President Reagan*, pp. 176, 210) suggests that Reagan's distaste for conflict among his family of staff may derive from his childhood experiences as the child of an alcoholic.

85. Cannon, *President Reagan*, p. 308.

86. Several accounts suggest that advisers regularly engaged in Machiavellian maneuvers in order to capture eleventh-hour consultations with the president, in order to get the last word in on a contested issue. See, e.g., Smith, *The Power Game*, p. 576, and Prados, *Keepers of the Keys*, p. 481.

87. The rash of "kiss and tell" memoirs that appeared during the administration is indicative of this phenomenon.

88. The following account of the Reagan system in practice draws heavily

on a previously published article by A. L. George entitled "The President and the Management of Foreign Policy: Styles and Models," in C. W. Kegley and E. R. Wittkopf, eds., *Domestic Sources of American Foreign Policy: Insights and Evidence* (New York: St. Martin's Press, 1988), especially pp. 121–125.

89. Allen's gradual adoption of a more prominent public role probably contributed to bringing this conflict out in the open. See B. Patterson Jr., *The Ring of Power: The White House Staff and Its Expanding Role in Government* (New York: Basic Books, 1988), p. 125.

90. See Smith, *The Power Game*, pp. 559, 567–586, for an illustrative account of the factional tug-of-war over the Reagan administration's policy regarding the SALT II agreements.

91. For a discussion of the negative consequences of such "undermanaged" systems, see S. Kernell, "The Evolution of the White House Staff," in J. Pfiffner, ed., *The Managerial Presidency*, p. 51.

92. Prados, *Keeper of the Keys*, p. 462.

93. Reagan's tendency to promote deputies when the NSA position became vacant was pronounced, he did it three times.

94. McFarlane's attempt to emulate Kissinger's success in establishing a relationship with the People's Republic of China by covertly seeking a rapprochement with Iran would have dire consequences for the administration. See, e.g., Smith, *The Power Game*, p. 589.

95. See the major article in the *New York Times Magazine* by Leslie H. Gelb, "Taking Charge: The Rising Power of National Security Adviser Robert McFarlane," *New York Times*, May 26, 1985, and Prados, *Keeper of the Keys*, pp. 481–496.

96. For a more extensive and systematic comparison of the Reagan and Eisenhower foreign policy management styles, see Fred I. Greenstein, "Ronald Reagan: Another Hidden-Hand Ike?"

97. For an authoritative account of the Iran-Contra Affair, see T. Draper, *A Very Thin Line: The Iran-Contra Affairs* (New York: Hill & Wang, 1991). Iran-Contra is also extensively treated in Lou Cannon's *President Reagan*. See also United States, President's Special Review Board, *The Tower Commission Report* (New York: Bantam Books, 1987), and Lawrence E. Walsh, *Final Report of the Independent Counsel for Iran/Contra Matters* (Washington, D.C.: U.S. Court of Appeals for the District of Columbia Circuit, Division for the Purpose of Appointing Independent Counsel, 1993).

98. See Prados, *Keeper of the Keys*, pp. 538–540, for an account of Carlucci's career and a summary of the changes he brought to the NSC staff.

99. Powell, who had known Carlucci since a brief fellowship at the Office of Management and Budget during the 1970s, had previously been serving as Weinberger's military aide at the Defense Department (Prados, *Keeper of the Keys*, p. 543).

100. Prados, *Keeper of the Keys*, p. 540.

101. Quoted in Patterson, *The Ring of Power*, p. 104, emphasis in original.

102. Prados, *Keeper of the Keys*, p. 540.

103. For Shultz's account of these matters, see *Turmoil and Triumph*, pp. 902–903, 906–908, 924.

104. Prados, *Keeper of the Keys*, p. 544.

105. Patterson, *The Ring of Power*, p. 95. See also Shultz, *Turmoil and Triumph*, pp. 1080–1081.

106. Prados (*Keeper of the Keys*, pp. 544–545) argues, for example, that the administration's involvement in what came to be known as the "tanker war" in the Gulf, which resulted in the twin tragedies of the Iraqi attack on the USS *Stark* that left thirty-five U.S. crewmen dead and the USS *Vincennes*'s accidental downing of an Iranian passenger aircraft that killed 290 passengers, was the result of poorly specified objectives and rules of engagement.

107. For a rather pessimistic early assessment of Reagan's personality, cognitive style, and capacity for subtlety and change, see Glad, "Black and White Thinking." For accounts written from the vantage point of the early 1990s emphasizing Reagan's personal dynamism and relatively greater degree of cognitive openness, see Shultz, *Turmoil and Triumph*, pp. 1135–1136, and Cannon, *President Reagan*, passim. See also B. Glad and J. Garrison, "Ronald Reagan and the INF Treaty: Whatever Happened to the 'Evil Empire'?" (paper presented at the Annual Scientific Meeting of the International Society of Political Psychology, Cambridge, Mass., July 1993).

108. This capacity for strategic radicalism, which shocked the nuclear weapons establishment on a number of occasions, was most clearly revealed in the Strategic Defense Initiative ("Star Wars") and at the Reykjavik summit. See Cannon, *President Reagan*, for useful accounts of these developments.

109. James P. Pfiffner, "Establishing the Bush Presidency," *Public Administration Review* (January-February 1990), p. 65.

110. It is an interesting question whether that sense of confidence extended to other policy realms to the same extent. Perhaps Bush's early reliance on the Cabinet Council and working-group system set up by Special Assistant for Domestic and Economic Affairs Roger Porter and subsequent reliance on White House Chief of Staff Sununu reflected a somewhat lesser sense of efficacy than that exhibited in foreign policy issues. See Burke, *The Institutional Presidency*, pp. 162–163.

111. D. Oberdorfer, *The Turn* (New York: Poseidon Press, 1991), p. 332.

112. Burke, *The Institutional Presidency*, p. 162.

113. L. Berman and B. Jentleson, "Bush and the Post–Cold War World," in C. Campbell and B. Rockman, eds., *The Bush Presidency: First Appraisals* (Chatham, N.J.: Chatham House, 1991), p. 99.

114. For a detailed, if rather friendly, account of Bush's service in these posts, see F. Green's *George Bush: An Intimate Portrait* (New York: Hippocrene Books, 1989), chapters 9, 12, and 14. Kerry Mullins and Aaron Wildavsky ("The Procedural Presidency of George Bush," *Political Science Quarterly* 107:1 [Spring 1992]) make the rather bold claim that Bush's emphasis on consensus and his contextually driven worldview inhibited him from learning in a cumulative fashion from his prior government experience.

115. See J. T. Preston and M. D. Young, "An Approach to Understanding Decision Making: The Bush Administration, The Gulf Crisis, Management Style,

and Worldview," p. 25 (paper presented at the annual meeting of the International Studies Association, Atlanta, April 1–4, 1992). See also A. R. Hybel, *Power Over Rationality: The Bush Administration and the Gulf Crisis* (Albany: State University of New York Press, 1993), p. 8.

116. See M. Beschloss and S. Talbot, *At the Highest Levels* (Boston: Little, Brown, 1993) for accounts of these consultations.

117. Pfiffner, "Establishing the Bush Presidency," p. 66; Beschloss and Talbot (*At the Highest Levels*, p. 4) make similar observations.

118. B. Rockman, "The Leadership Style of George Bush," in Campbell and Rockman, eds., *The Bush Presidency: First Appraisals*, pp. 29, 31. See also Mullins and Wildavsky, "The Procedural Presidency," p. 63.

119. Many scholars emphasize the importance of the "Munich analogy" in the minds of Bush and his key advisers. See, e.g., Preston and Young, "An Approach to Understanding Decision Making," p. 22, and Hybel, *Power over Rationality*, p. 8–9. For accounts of Bush's war record, see F. Green, *George Bush*, chapter 3, and J. Hyam, *Flight of the Avenger: George Bush at War* (New York: Berkley Books, 1992).

120. Mullins and Wildavsky ("The Procedural Presidency," p. 35) suggest that "sustained criticism alluding to personal weakness seems to spur Bush to more aggressive behavior."

121. F. Green, *George Bush*, p. 77.

122. Pfiffner, "Establishing the Bush Presidency," p. 69.

123. Berman and Jentleson, "Bush and the Post–Cold War World," p. 94.

124. For an assessment of the Gulf War's impact on the United Nations and the prospects for collective security, see D. Puchala, "The President, the Gulf War, and the United Nations," in Marcia Lynn Whicker, James P. Pfiffner, and Raymond A. Moore, eds., *The Presidency and the Persian Gulf War* (Westport, Conn.: Praeger, 1993). See also A. George, "The Gulf War's Possible Impact on the International System," in S. Renshon, ed., *The Political Psychology of the Gulf War* (Pittsburgh: University of Pittsburgh Press, 1993).

125. B. Woodward (*The Commanders*, New York: Pocket Star Books, p. 59) notes Bush's reputation for grudges and vindictive political actions, suggesting that even Secretary of Defense Richard Cheney was afraid of crossing Bush. See also Beschloss and Talbot, *At the Highest Levels*, pp. 127, 166, and Mullins and Wildavsky, "The Procedural Presidency," p. 36.

126. B. Glad ("Figuring out Saddam Hussein," in Whicker, Pfiffner, and Moore, eds., *The Presidency and the Persian Gulf War*) suggests that Bush's propensity to demonize Saddam Hussein may have had negative effects on the prospects for managing the Gulf crisis toward outcomes short of war. Another clue to Bush's willingness to use force in pursuit of U.S. foreign policy objectives may be found in his choice of presidential role model. Apparently Bush looked to Theodore Roosevelt as his inspirational "hero." According to Berman and Jentleson ("Bush and the Post–Cold War World," pp. 98–99), Bush placed a portrait of Roosevelt in the Cabinet room and no fewer than two sculptures of the former Rough Rider in the oval office.

127. Mullins and Wildavsky ("The Procedural Presidency," pp. 36–37) make a parallel argument emphasizing Bush's alternative modes of dealing with in-

siders and outsiders. Bush, they suggest, negotiates with insiders and deals harshly with outsiders. Accordingly, Bush tended to be indulgent toward the Chinese leadership (defined as insiders as a result of relationships forged during Bush's service in China) after the Tiananmen Square crackdown. In contrast, he was initially suspicious of Gorbachev (first an outsider). As a personal relationship developed between the two, Gorbachev was placed in the insider category. Though they do not make this point, the long suspicion of Yeltsin as an outsider fits nicely with this perspective.

128. Briefers included Henry Rowen, Arnold Horelick, Stephen Meyer, Alan Greenspan, Robert Zoellick, Richard Nixon, James Schlesinger, Jeane Kirkpatrick, and Zbigniew Brzezinski. Beschloss and Talbot, *At the Highest Levels,* pp. 43, 139–141.

129. See, for example, Burke, *The Institutional Presidency,* p. 162, and Pfiffner, "Establishing the Bush Presidency," p. 67.

130. Quoted in Pfiffner, "Establishing the Bush Presidency," p. 67. See also Green, *George Bush,* p. 254.

131. Emphasizing this facet of Bush's personality, Preston and Young ("An Approach to Understanding Decision Making," p. 38) find him to be a group leader with a low tolerance for conflict, on the basis of their analysis of decisionmaking during the Gulf War.

132. Ibid.

133. Preston and Young, "An Approach to Understanding Decision Making," p. 38.

134. According to Berman and Jentleson ("Bush and the Post–Cold War World," pp. 99–101), "Bush's principal foreign policy appointees have two characteristics in common: (1) They are all professionals, with substantial previous foreign policy or other relevant government experience, and (2) they are all long-time friends or associates of George Bush." For short biographies of the Bush cabinet and White House staff, see *President Bush: The Challenge Ahead* (Washington, D.C.: Congressional Quarterly Inc., 1989).

135. In fact, according to I. Destler ("A Job That Doesn't Work," *Foreign Policy* 38 [Spring 1980], p. 86), Scowcroft's first performance, including his working relationship with Ford and Secretary of State Kissinger, was so strong as to serve as the role model for the position.

136. *President Bush: The Challenge Ahead,* p. 71.

137. It is interesting to note that a broader assessment of the Bush policy system (including economic and domestic policy realms in addition to foreign policy) would probably lead to attribution of a collegial-formalistic synthesis along the lines of the Carter model. For example, the Cabinet Councils and issue-specific task forces were reportedly major features of Bush policymaking in these issue areas.

138. According to Burke (*The Institutional Presidency,* p. 175), "Bush's attempts at showing continued personal trust in aides who have suffered setbacks or who are perceived to be in disfavor has [sic] reinforced a sense of collegiality and reduced the temptation to engage in bureaucratic politics and court intrigue." Burke points to Bush gestures such as inviting Baker to Camp

David during the latter stages of the Gulf War, in order to counter press reports of an NSC advantage vis-à-vis the State Department.

139. For an analysis of Sununu's domineering style as Bush's chief of staff, see James P. Pfiffner, "The President's Chief of Staff," *Presidential Studies Quarterly* 23:1 (1993), pp. 90–98. Sununu was ultimately replaced by the less autocratic Sam Skinner, who had been serving as secretary of transportation.

140. C. Campbell ("The White House and the Cabinet Under the 'Let's Deal' Presidency," in Campbell and Rockman, eds., *The Bush Presidency: First Appraisals*, pp. 208–210) argues that Bush's foreign policy process was insufficiently collective and suggests that consultation on key decisions was often incomplete. Examples he cites include the missed opportunity of the coup attempt against Manuel Noriega, the invasion of Panama, and post–Tiananmen Square China policy. Furthermore, he submits that an inadequately structured interagency coordination process resulted in a missed opportunity to deter Saddam Hussein from invading Kuwait in the first place. He alleges that Baker's focus on U.S.-Soviet relations and Scowcroft's preoccupation with his role as personal adviser to the president contributed to delaying a hardening of U.S. policy toward Iraq, which might have headed off the invasion of Kuwait.

141. J. Pfiffner, "Presidential Policy-Making and the Gulf War," in Whicker, Pfiffner, and Moore, eds., *The Presidency and the Persian Gulf War*, pp. 7–8. He asserts that Bush's key advisers included Scowcroft, Cheney, Baker, and Powell, as well as Gates, Sununu, and Quayle.

142. According to Beschloss and Talbot (*At the Highest Levels*, pp. 54–55), the damage control effort was managed by close coordination between Secretary of State Baker and National Security Adviser Scowcroft. In fact, they quote Baker's immediate reaction in a phone call to Scowcroft: "Dump on Dick with all possible alacrity."

143. Ibid., passim. See also Oberdorfer, *The Turn*.

144. In fact, Bush maintained an overall balance in his reliance on these two leading foreign policy advisers. While he relied heavily on Scowcroft's counsel with regard to the Gulf War, the realm of U.S.-Soviet (and post-Soviet) relations reveals a more evenly balanced picture. When Baker and Scowcroft disagreed, Bush did not consistently side with either of them.

145. K. Mulcahey, quoted in Burke, *The Institutional Presidency*, p. 170. Baker's alleged White House orientation was not cost free. This posture was apparently maintained by heavy reliance on a small circle of appointees at State which created friction with the career service.

146. Burke, *The Institutional Presidency*, p. 168–171, and Beschloss and Talbot, *At the Highest Levels*, p. 27.

147. For these critiques, see Campbell, "The White House and the Cabinet," p. 207–208, and Burke, *The Institutional Presidency*, pp. 169–170.

148. See Burke, *The Institutional Presidency*, p. 170.

149. Beschloss and Talbot, *At the Highest Levels*, pp. 43–45.

150. Woodward, *The Commanders*, p. 25; Campbell, "The White House and Cabinet," p. 208, and Burke, *The Institutional Presidency*, p. 168.

151. See B. Woodward, *The Agenda* (New York: Simon & Schuster, 1994), p. 59.

152. Woodward, *The Agenda,* p. 59.

153. Lake served for a brief period in the early 1970s as one of Kissinger's assistants on the NSC staff. Lake ultimately resigned in protest against the bombing of Cambodia.

154. Lake also seemed likely to get along with Defense Secretary Les Aspin, whom he had known since his days as a junior foreign service officer in Vietnam. In fact, Lake also had close ties to Undersecretary of State Peter Tarnoff and Undersecretary of State Frank Wisner dating from that period. See L. H. Gelb, "'Chris' and Aspin and Lake," *New York Times,* January 13, 1993.

155. Destler, Gelb, and Lake, *Our Own Worst Enemy.*

156. Gelb, "'Chris' and Aspin and Lake."

157. For an overview of the organizational changes with an emphasis on the implications for the State Department, see D. Newsome, "The Clinton Administration and the Foreign Service," *Foreign Service Journal* (April 1993), pp. 24–27.

158. See, e.g., T. Friedman, "Clinton Keeping Foreign Policy on a Back Burner," *New York Times,* February 8, 1993, p. A9.

159. M. Elliott et al., "Damned Yankees," *Newsweek,* October 25, 1993, p. 24.

160. A. Moens ("Clinton's Foreign Policy Decision-Making Process," preliminary draft of a paper, May 1995, p. 8) suggests that relatively little effort was devoted to reflection on the design of Clinton's foreign policy advisory system. In our view, this is somewhat misleading. It may be true that Clinton generally tends to be somewhat insensitive to matters of organization, as noted by F. Greenstein ("Political Style and Political Leadership: The Case of Bill Clinton," in S. Renshon, ed., *The Clinton Presidency: Campaigning, Governing, and the Psychology of Leadership* [Boulder: Westview Press, 1995], p. 141). However, the evidence suggests that Clinton's system was the product of several relatively deliberate design choices, as we have outlined.

161. Friedman, "Clinton Keeping Foreign Policy on a Back Burner," p. A9.

162. E. Drew, *On the Edge: The Clinton Presidency* (New York: Simon & Schuster, 1994), p. 28. See also D. Brinkley, "Democratic Enlargement: The Clinton Doctrine," *Foreign Policy,* 106 (Spring 1997), pp. 120, 124.

163. It is noteworthy that Hillary Rodham Clinton, by all accounts one of Clinton's closest advisers on domestic policy, apparently is uninterested in foreign policy and is reportedly not a key player (Elliott et al., "Damned Yankees," p. 24).

164. Available accounts of the Clinton administration foreign-policymaking process do not emphasize the role of White House Chief of Staff Thomas McLarty, who apparently devoted most of his energies to the domestic realm.

165. G. Ifill, "Security Official Guides U.S. Aims at Conference," *New York Times,* July 5, 1993, p. 5.

166. Other regular participants in the CIA briefing included Vice President Gore and Deputy National Security Adviser Samuel Berger. Chief of Staff Thomas McLarty attended sporadically.

167. L. Gelb, "Where's Bill?" *New York Times,* March 11, 1993; Friedman, "Clinton Keeping Foreign Policy on a Back Burner," p. A9.

168. According to the view of one White House official quoted anonymously in the *New York Times* (July 5, 1993, p. 5), "there's no question who's driving foreign policy in terms of the decisionmaking process. That would be Mr. Lake." See also J. De Parle, "The Man Inside Clinton's Foreign Policy," *New York Times Magazine*, August 20, 1995, pp. 32–39, 46, 55, 57.

169. S. A. Holmes, "Choice for National Security Adviser Has a Long Awaited Chance to Lead," *New York Times*, January 3, 1993, p. 10.

170. An NSC staff member interviewed by Eric Stern in 1993 suggested that the concern with an orderly process exhibited by Lake and the other foreign policy officials bordered on the obsessive.

171. *New York Times*, June 1, 1993, p. 3.

172. *New York Times*, July 5, 1993, p. 5.

173. P. Suedfeld's "President Clinton's Policy Dilemmas: A Cognitive Analysis," *Political Psychology* 15:2 (1994), an impressionistic analysis of the media commentary on Clinton's cognitive style, finds a consensus that he exhibits a high degree of cognitive complexity (differentiation). Ironically, Suedfeld's own systematic content analysis of Clinton's statements resulted in findings of rather low levels of complexity. Furthermore, the findings did not reflect the usual pattern of increased complexity as a political leader moves from the campaign to the governing context. See also P. Suedfeld and M. Wallace, "President Clinton as a Cognitive Manager," in Renshon, ed., *The Clinton Presidency*, pp. 215–233.

174. A major asset in such policy work (and in politics) is Clinton's good memory for facts, figures, and people. For example, Jim Moore (*Clinton: Young Man in a Hurry* [Fort Worth, Texas: The Summit Group, 1992], p. 43) makes the seemingly extravagant claim that Clinton remembers virtually everyone who has ever assisted him in a political campaign by name and personality. While this may be something of an exaggeration, this skill undoubtedly helped Clinton greatly in his political career.

175. M. Duffy, "The State of Bill Clinton," *Time*, February 7, 1994, pp. 28–29.

176. Stanley Hoffman, quoted in the *New York Times*, June 1, 1993, p. 3. In fact, Clinton has experience from the academic realm; he taught law at the University of Arkansas for several years in the early 1970s (Moore, *Clinton*, pp. 39–41). The latter phrase is Colin Powell's (*An American Journey*, New York: Random House, 1995, p. 576).

177. T. Friedman and E. Sciolino, "Clinton and Foreign Issues: Spasms of Attention," *New York Times* (international edition), March 22, 1993.

178. This characterization was suggested by a presidential aide quoted in S. Blumenthal, "The Education of a President," *New Yorker*, January 24, 1994, p. 37.

179. This seems to be the basic thrust of Woodward's account in *The Agenda*, for example.

180. The presidential scholar Fred Greenstein ("The Two Leadership Styles of William Jefferson Clinton," *Political Psychology* 15:2 [1994], pp. 351–352) resolves these competing images by suggesting that Clinton alternates between two modes of leadership: "a no holds barred style of striving for numerous policy outcomes with little attention to establishing priorities or accommodating to political realities, and a more measured, pragmatic style of focusing on

a limited number of goals and attending closely to the politics of selling his program." Greenstein suggests that clear external feedback of the impending failure of the former mode seems to trigger a retrenchment to the latter.

181. M. Hermann ("Presidential Leadership Style, Advisory Systems, and Policy Making," *Political Psychology* 15:2 [1994], pp. 369–370) suggests that Clinton appears to be extremely sensitive to the political context and uncomfortable with confrontation.

182. S. Renshon ("A Preliminary Assessment of the Clinton Presidency: Character, Leadership, and Performance," *Political Psychology* 15:2 [1994], p. 381) lists a number of commentators emphasizing this aspect, which he argues is exaggerated.

183. Woodward, *The Agenda,* pp. 78, 175.

184. It is possible that this empathy may have developed in part as a result of Clinton's experience as a child living with an alcoholic parent (see, e.g., Moore, *Clinton,* p. 24). Such children learn to be unusually sensitive to the moods of the drinker and others in their attempts to avoid triggering unpleasant episodes. See, e.g., S. Brown, *Safe Passage: Recovery for Adult Children of Alcoholics* (New York: J. Wiley and Sons, 1992), p. 27.

185. Woodward, *The Agenda,* p. 277.

186. For a persuasive and psychologically sensitive account emphasizing this point, see M. Kelley, "The President's Past," *New York Times Magazine,* July 21, 1994. See also Woodward, *The Agenda,* pp. 185–186.

187. Woodward, *The Agenda,* p. 297.

188. Ibid., e.g., pp. 55, 161, 255, 278, 280. See also S. Renshon, "A Preliminary Assessment," p. 381.

189. Quoted in Woodward, *The Agenda,* p. 324.

190. Moens, "Clinton's Foreign Policy," p. 3.

191. Clinton did exhibit a high level of interest in foreign affairs as a young man. His undergraduate major at Georgetown University was "international government studies" and he worked part time as a staffer on Senator William Fulbright's Senate Foreign Relations Committee while in college (Moore, *Clinton,* pp. 27, 30).

192. Kelley, "The President's Past," p. 26.

193. Ibid., pp. 24–26; Hermann, "Presidential Leadership Style," p. 373.

194. Quoted in Moore, *Clinton,* p. 35.

195. Woodward, *The Agenda,* p. 34.

196. Colin Powell's *An American Journey* provides several approving examples of Clinton's composure in crisis situations.

197. Greenstein (*The Two Leadership Styles,* p. 356) goes so far as to suggest that "insensitivity to organization" is one of Clinton's most fundamental leadership shortcomings. See also Greenstein, "Political Style," pp. 141–142, and Woodward, *The Agenda,* e.g., pp. 38, 210, 324, 328.

198. According to Renshon ("A Preliminary Assessment," p. 389), "Clinton relies heavily on 'chemistry' (which can be translated as 'They get along with me and I with them') as a major basis for selecting many advisers."

199. Duffy, "The State of Bill Clinton," p. 26.

200. See, e.g., L. Berman and E. Goldman, "Clinton's Foreign Policy at Midterm," in C. Campbell and B. Rockman, eds., *The Clinton Presidency: First Appraisals* (Chatham, N.J.: Chatham House, 1996), p. 291.

201. For an overview of the design and implementation of the enlargement metapolicy, see Brinkley, "Democratic Enlargement," pp. 111–127.

202. For a profile of Gergen, see M. Kelley, "David Gergen: The Master of the Game," *New York Times Magazine*, October 31, 1993.

203. Elliott et al., "Damned Yankees," p. 24.

204. See, e.g., T. Friedman, "Clinton's Foreign Policy: Top Adviser Speaks Up," *New York Times*, October 31, 1993, and De Parle, "The Man Inside Clinton's Foreign Policy."

205. Woodward, *The Agenda*, p. 320.

206. E. Sciolino, "State Department Awaits Gergen with Trepidation," *New York Times*, June 29, 1994, p. A8.

207. Drew, *On the Edge*, p. 423. See also G. Church, "Taking His Show on the Road: Clinton's New Success in Juggling Foreign Policy Problems Is More Than Good Luck," *Time*, October 31, 1994 (retrieved from Pathfinder database).

208. Renshon ("A Preliminary Assessment," p. 389) suggests that a combination of Clinton's domineering personality and his tendency to pick his staff on the basis of "chemistry" may make the Clinton team susceptible to "concurrence seeking." However, other factors seemed to mitigate this alleged danger during the early part of the administration. First, Clinton by most accounts did not adopt a domineering leadership style in foreign-policymaking. Second, Clinton is commonly described as a good listener who enjoys and encourages debate. These factors would seem to make conformity based on directive leadership less likely.

209. Friedman, "Clinton's Foreign Policy."

210. Powell, *An American Journey*, pp. 583–588.

211. J. Hirsch and R. B. Oakely, *Somalia and Operation Restore Hope* (Washington D.C.: The United States Institute of Peace Press, 1995).

212. Brinkley, "Democratic Enlargement," p. 119.

213. Clinton and Powell apparently developed a good working relationship relatively quickly, and, as a result, Powell became a far more influential player than might have been expected in light of his association with the previous two administrations (E. Schmitt and T. Friedman, "Clinton and Powell Discover That They Need Each Other," *New York Times*, June 4, 1993, pp. Al, A15. See also Powell, *An American Journey*, pp. 578–588.

214. Perry became Clinton's choice after his initial nominee, Admiral Bobby Ray Inman, withdrew his candidacy under heavy media pressure. For an interesting psychological analysis of the Inman incident, see M. Feinberg and J. Tarrrant, *Why Smart People Do Dumb Things* (New York: Simon & Schuster, 1995), pp. 101–108.

215. The most spectacular of these incidents was the stranding of a North Korean submarine in South Korean territory in September 1996. For an account of the repercussions of this incident, see S. Myers, "U.S. Reports Foes in

Korea Willing to Discuss Peace," *New York Times,* December 31, 1996, p. 1. For an overview, see S. Harrison, "Promoting a Soft Landing in Korea," *Foreign Policy* 106 (Spring 1997), pp. 57–75.

216. Clinton's change of heart on this issue may have been facilitated by an experience he had as governor of Arkansas. According to Moore (*Clinton,* pp. 60–63), one of the causes of his defeat in the election of 1980 was antirefugee sentiment aroused by the placement of Cuban detainees from the Mariel boat lift in Arkansas, a sentiment aggravated by the detainees' rioting and escapes from the camps and by federal government announcements of further placements in Arkansas in the months before the election. Brinkley ("Democratic Enlargement," p. 120) emphasizes the role of domestic constituencies such as the Cuban-Americans in Florida and the congressional Black Caucus in pressing for a resolution to the Haiti problem.

217. De Parle, "The Man Inside Bill Clinton's Foreign Policy," p. 37.

218. Ibid.

219. For accounts of Gore's role, see Drew, *On the Edge,* pp. 28, 68, and D. Broder, "Gore Sets a New Standard for the Vice Presidency," *International Herald Tribune,* August 27, 1996, pp. 1, 6.

220. P. Tyler, "Beijing Steps Up Military Pressure," *New York Times,* March 7, 1996, p. 1, and T. Friedman, "Foreign Affairs; Help Wanted: Deal Makers," *New York Times,* March 24, 1996, p. 15. See also T. Christensen, "Chinese Realpolitik," *Foreign Affairs* (September-October 1996), pp. 45–52.

221. For profiles of Albright, see, e.g., J. McGreary, "Mix and Match: In Search of Good Chemistry, Clinton Picks a Team for Personalities Rather Than Policies," *Time,* December 16, 1996, pp. 29–31; N. Gibbs, "The Many Lives of Madeleine Albright," *Time,* February 17, 1997, pp. 31–37; and "Albright: A Strong Foreign Policy Voice," *CQ,* December 7, 1996, p. 3346.

222. "Cohen: Mainstream Republican for Defense," *CQ,* December 7, 1996, p. 3345. See also McGreary, "Mix and Match," p. 30.

223. Elaine Scioliano, "Nominee for Top CIA Post Braces for Senate Showdown," *New York Times,* March 8, 1997, p. 8.

224. See E. Stern, "Probing the Plausibility of Newgroup Syndrome," in E. Stern and B. Sundelius, eds., *Beyond Groupthink* (Ann Arbor: University of Michigan Press, 1997), pp. 153–189.

225. Johnson, *Managing the White House,* chapter 8; reproduced with minor changes and additions in *The Stanford Business School Alumni Bulletin,* Fall 1973.

226. Johnson, *Managing the White House,* pp. 237–239.

227. Important refinements in the description of each president's preferred executive work style are introduced by David K. Hall, "Evaluating the Feasibility of Multiple Advocacy Theory for National Security Decisionmaking," Ph.D. diss., Stanford University, 1980.

228. For a discussion of these three procedures, see chapters 9, 10, and 11 in A. L. George, *Presidential Decisionmaking in Foreign Policy: The Effective Use of Information and Advice* (Boulder: Westview Press, 1980).

Index